IN THE KEY OF BE

for Steve,
like-minded UU friend.
with love,

IN THE KEY OF BE

A Memoir

LENA HUBIN

CHATNOIR PRESS
Prescott, Arizona

Library of Congress Control Number: 2018901784

ISBN 978-1-73-201270-7

Book design by Longworth Creative, LLC
Text set in Alegreya

First Edition
Printed in the United States of America

Chatnoir Press
127 Garden St.
Prescott, AZ 86305

For Tim and Holly

A Note About the Title

For piano players, a piece written in the key of B, with its five sharps, is no walk in the park—just as, for me, to "be" takes practice.

I can still get caught up in things I should be doing, instead of simply being. I intend never to stop practicing.

Contents

PART II

Preface

I used to do pretty much what people told me to. Peel potatoes for supper before you get home? Don't worry, Mom. Practice piano a half hour every day? I promise, Mrs. Bjugstad. Drop this LSD? Whatever you say, Mick.

When friends told me to write a book, I booted up my Mac to recount my years abroad. But like our dog when pulled off-track by a provocative scent, I veered from the path, chasing earlier memories. Brought up short at my addled youth, I cracked off three rough chapters about my time in the psych ward during the '60's.

Then my son, acting out in his alcoholism, yanked me by the writing leash in a new direction. I covered page after page with descriptions of his real-time behavior. Soon I was overlapping vignettes of his young-adult life with those of my own—four decades earlier but speeding forward in bundles of years—until my past caught up with both of our presents, and The End emerged.

"When I write, the truth falls out," I heard someone say. And so it's been for me. People and events in this book are the truth of my experience, though I've changed names of all but immediate family. For several chapters I use my given first name, "Eileen," because that's who I was until I arrived in Africa and took on the nickname "Lena."

Though Bombay was renamed Mumbai during our time there, I call it by its former name. "Bombay" sounds punchier, befitting my time there. Likewise, despite its decline in favor, I cling to the term "Third World" to describe countries in which I lived, because that's how I knew and loved them back in the day.

In keeping with its Eleventh Tradition, which requires "anonymity at the level of press, radio, films, and TV," I often call a worldwide Twelve-Step support organization for families and friends of alcoholics simply the "Program."

Special thanks to my husband, Russ Erickson, whose patient first-responder reading of each chapter has been eminently helpful and affirming. Deep, still-water daughter Holly Misa, your even keel always buoys me up. And son Tim, sweet Bunty, you and I are One in this. I hope the book lives up to your expectations.

Merci mille fois to my savvy, professional little writing group: Gretchen Brinck, for weeding out unneeded adverbs and phrases—always totally helpful—and for gentle urging toward reflectiveness. Maggie McConnell, for cutting me to the chase time after time, and for freely offering up apt analogies as if they were those great gluten-free cookies. You two have made me a better writer.

Warm thanks to Cheryl Berry, Shauna Bowcutt-Anderson, Kate Bradley, Janer Eldridge, Kim Holland, Mary Erickson, and Barb Neuser for insightful help and encouragement. To Elaine Jordan, deep appreciation for final polishing and editing—and apologies for my persistence in creative punctuation.

All of your kind tugs on my leash have kept me on the trail and helped me bring this book home.

Prelude

The entry to the Wisconsin farmhouse of my 1950's childhood was small and windowless. My dad's barn overalls and our coats and jackets hung from wall hooks to the right and left. A door on the right opened into the kitchen. An assortment of boots lined the floorboards, where the edges of the linoleum were ragged: When Mom let Cookie, our black cocker spaniel, in during thunderstorms, the poor dog gnawed at the floor like a nail biter chews to the quick.

But anybody flapping through the screen door from outside couldn't miss the huge map of the world on the wall straight ahead. My mother tacked the thing there, above a trunk—she, whose 1940 "normal school" yearbook proclaimed her goal to teach in Alaska; who, despite three kids and meager means, would earn a masters degree in education; who forever warbled "Those far-away places with the strange-sounding names/ are calling, calling me" as she cooked and washed and gardened.

Mom never went to Alaska. Instead, she settled down with my dad on a small dairy farm and raised three daughters. Rarely venturing far from home, she taught in public schools nearby for forty years. The traveling was left to me. Today, our home office space is plastered with maps of the countries where my husband and I have lived.

My parents did well by their three daughters, providing us with pets, piano lessons, the opportunity to go to college, and the example of a steadfast relationship. The benefits have accompanied me through the years.

But less favorable elements of my Midwest upbringing have also traveled with me. My folks' need to beat back the Depression with hard work and little play; Mom's efforts to control and perfect everything, especially me, her first-born—and thus my fear that I never could do well enough. These became burdens I hauled along like unwieldy bags whose contents, when unpacked, attacked me as anxiety. My guts churned; my teeth clenched; my shoulders sat high and tight. Hypochondria plagued me. My fear of flying worsened with each flight.

I spent a decade self-medicating with alcohol, drugs, and sex before jumping off the continent. Eventually, in Africa, I met the man with whom I would enter a lasting relationship. We lived and worked together in exotic foreign places; we adopted a son from India, then a daughter from Madagascar.

Through it all my angst persisted. After twenty years abroad, settled with my husband and kids in Arizona, I still longed for release from some vague perennial distress I could not name.

For ten years more I squelched disquietude, until in 2009, a crisis threatened my sanity. Someone suggested a path, and in desperation, I took it.

PART I

1

Not Himself Yet

"CHRISTMAS IS USELESS." Our twenty-two-year-old son Tim rips at Santa paper and tosses aside a gift of wool socks.

Unlike in past years, Tim has no presents for me, his dad, or his twenty-year-old sister Holly. He yanks a Harkins movie gift card from its wrapping—a present from Holly—and smirks. Holly rolls her eyes at me across the littered coffee table. *"It's o-kay,"* I mouth at her.

It's the evening of December 23rd, 2009—our eleventh Christmas back in the U.S. Before moving here, Russ and I spent twenty-five years working in schools overseas. Our children attended some of those schools, then went through middle and high school here in pine-and-boulder-strewn northern Arizona. I've just retired from full-time teaching; Russ will soon follow. Tonight, the four of us are strung around our living room eating sweets and opening gifts, having family Christmas early so Tim can go off to a cabin with friends—his fortyish work supervisor Libby and her family—tomorrow.

Tim has recently moved back home, and he isn't himself yet. Christmas festivities probably make things worse. They do for me. Each year I hang tinsel and lights and my mom's old glass Christmas bulbs and my little African angels. I make dozens of sugar-sprinkled cookies, Russian teacakes, Grandma Welch's date-filled oatmeal cookies. My sisters send artfully-wrapped gifts, and my Santa-husband brings me what I ask for. As Tim said, it's useless. I think I'm a victim of SAD, Seasonal Affective Disorder. Maybe my son is too.

He rises from the couch and steps over my legs. "I'm going to bed."

Russ reaches for another piece of my sister Carol's homemade fudge—as if he needs more fudge. "What's up with Tim?" he asks. "It's early."

"It's gotta be hard, moving back home." I brush crumbs from the coffee table into my hand.

The next week Tim is back from his friends' cabin. On a Sunday, supper finished, he sits slumped in his chair at the kitchen table. As I clear dishes, he flicks a corner of the tablecloth up and down. "What's up, Tim? You seem gloomy." Lame words from a mom—but I must keep it light. I want this month-long downswing in my son's spirits to be nothing.

Head hanging, he rolls his soupspoon into the tablecloth corner. When I reach for the spoon, he nudges it toward me. "I think I'm depressed."

"What do you mean, *depressed*?" I put down a handful of silverware. "How do you know?"

He stares out the big window at the leafless Russian sage. "There's no point to life."

My heart flops like a caught fish. "Oh, God. I'm so sorry. I know that feeling."

He knows I've battled this monster, depression. I've told him about my own hospitalization when I was his age, how I said they might as well send me to the state mental hospital for the rest of my life because I was a lump of nothing.

I stack the bowls with their pea-soup residue into each other, pretending what he's telling me is nothing. Hoping. "How long have you been feeling like this?"

"I dunno." He fiddles with a seam on his black Opeth T-shirt, fingers always moving. "Prob'ly three years. Since high school."

Since high school? But he came through that dismal time just fine! And for the past couple of years he's done well....

I take his hand and muster my calm teacher-voice. "I feel for you, Timmy. But this'll go away, you know. Like it did for me. You will get over it." I stroke the warm brown hand. "It might take time. You may have some things to work through, but— "

He twists his hand away. "I drink."

Of course he drinks. What young adult doesn't? He'd showed us photos on his phone of his twenty-first birthday last year, barhopping on Whiskey Row with his buddies, shit-faced happy in his Lamb-of-God band hat. "What do you mean, you drink?"

"Tequila."

"But not a lot, right?"

"More than before."

"More than before *when*? How much, exactly?"

He leans back and drums his nail-bitten fingertips on the table. "I'm kinda surprised when I see how much is gone. Maybe a bottle in a couple days."

This kid barely weighs a hundred pounds. He's ethnic Dravidian, adopted from the south of India. That much alcohol could kill him. "Do you drink it straight?"

He shakes his head. "With O.J."

Hence the constant orders on the grocery list for more orange juice. I thought it was a healthy thing. He doesn't eat anything green, never has; orange might be his new green.

Cold consternation grips me as I picture him upstairs pouring O.J. into a big glass of tequila, guzzling it down. "A bottle in *two days*? You've got to stop."

"I'm not gonna." He slaps his hands on the table. "What's the point?" He bolts from his chair and bounds upstairs to his room.

I sit back as a memory flares of Russ years ago pulling out one of our liquor bottles, finding it almost empty. "Tim, "he'd said to me. We rarely drank the stuff ourselves. Russ drew the other two bottles from the shelf over the fridge: Virgin Islands rum and cheap whiskey—both way down. But we deemed it a teenage prank, told him to stop. Now he's buying his own liquor.

Outside the window a Mexican jay with a load in its beak lands on a nearby pine branch. These pesky birds abound in mid-winter, scrabbling for food. They swoop in and make off with chunks of our greyhound's chow from the porch. Like my son is now stealing my peace of mind.

Tim did well on his own for two years. He had a full-time job at Panchito's Baja-Mexican Restaurant, paid his own bills. He seemed content living with his long-time friend Ryan in the upstairs apartment with the leafy tree outside his bedroom window. His life was full with work, guitar, computer games, TV. We'd have him out for weekend suppers. Russ went to a movie with him sometimes, and grocery shopping. Things were fine. But this past November he asked to come home. Ryan was selling drugs out of the apartment, and Tim wanted no part of it.

Home from college for Thanksgiving, Holly said, "He's matured." Russ and I agreed. We admired Tim for wanting to leave a bad situation, and were glad to have him with us for a while; we'd have fun helping him find a new place. In exchange for his old room back, Tim agreed to pay rent and do chores. He moved in Thanksgiving weekend.

♫

On the first Monday of the new year, Tim agrees to see Dr. Massey, our primary care physician—the only place I know to start. I go with him and give my two-cents' worth to the doc right away: "He's drinking alcohol because he feels depressed. *Too much* alcohol, if you ask me." The doc hadn't. But he asks Tim a couple of questions, then leaves us in the exam room as Tim completes a short computer questionnaire. He reads a question aloud: "How hopeful are you about your future? 1. *Very,* 2. *Somewhat,* 3. *Very little,* 4. *Not at all.*" He doesn't say the answer. I don't ask.

The doc returns and does the calculations to diagnose "moderate to severe depression." He puts Tim on Zoloft. On the way home Tim agrees to see a counselor. I'm relieved. He'll be fine!

But that night I jerk awake at some ghastly hour: *A bottle in two days?* Leaving Russ asleep, I pad upstairs to Tim's room. He's riveted to his computer screen, where snipers appear from behind tall buildings and blow people into flaming bursts of blood. "Why are you awake?"

He clicks at the keys. "I can't sleep."

"Have you been drinking?"

"No."

"Tim, I can smell it."

"Leave me alone!"

"Motherfucker!" yells the sniper on the screen. A big-boobed woman in a revealing dress explodes into gory halves.

I put my hands on my son's shoulders. "Want something to eat? I'll make you some scrambled eggs. Be good for you."

"No thanks."

"How about a back rub? Maybe help you relax, so you can sleep...."

"No!" He shrugs me off.

"Did you take your Zoloft?"

His head jerks *Yes*, fingers flying on the keys.

As I leave him fear has a strangle-hold on me, stifling my breath. Lying next to Russ, I cry tears into my pillow and plead soundlessly, *Please God, just make him stop drinking....*

On Tuesday Tim's off work. He doesn't come down from his room, and I realize by mid-afternoon that he hasn't taken out the trash. I discover him asleep on his bed covers and shake him lightly. As he drags himself to semi-consciousness, I rail: "You need to put the garbage out, Tim. *Now.* And you've got to stop this drinking!"

"I'm not drinking anything. Stop *hounding* me!" He flops back down.

"Come *on*, Tim. I can smell it."

"I'm *fine.*" He gathers himself up. Within the hour he's collected the trash, and I hear the bin rumble down the long gravel drive.

Roller-coaster days pass. The more I nag and plead to squelch my son's drinking, the more irrepressible the drinking—and my anxiety—become. The odor of liquor infuses his room; it hits me every time I spy on him. When he's at work or out with friends I go up and search for liquor bottles under the bed, in the closet, behind the computer. I find only empty O.J. cartons—but there's that appalling smell.

♫

One night I creep up and put on the hall light, peer into Tim's room and catch him asleep; his arm is draped over his black cat, Metro, who blinks up at me. As I gaze at my son, the taut noose of my anxiety loosens.

Tim's a survivor. Flown to us in Chicago from his birth home in Cochin, India, he was a year old and sick, weighing less than twelve pounds. But as the escort from the adoption agency held him ready for my arms, he reached for me as if to say, *I'm home now, everything's fine*. When I held him, the tiny body of my sweet new son melted into me.

We took him straight to the doctor, then to the hospital the next day. Diagnosed with pneumonia and malnutrition, he had an IV in his small head for four days.

But we kept faith, and when he was well we took him back with us to our jobs at the American School of Kinshasa in Zaire, Africa. During his first year with us there he babbled cheerily in his crib. He was soon crawling, and his cheeks and thighs grew plump. He got healthy on mashed bananas and formula mixed by Albertine, our strong Zairian nanny; with the back of a little fist he'd wipe the excess from the corners of his mouth.

Next stop, Madagascar, our second French-speaking country, where in the *Zoma* market I bought Tim a tiny dark-green polo shirt like Russ's. When Tim had it on he said with pride, *"Comme Dadi!"*—"Like Daddy."

In preschool he played the drum for "12 drummers drumming" in a Christmas show, and upon receiving kudos, proclaimed, "They don't call me Tim for nothin'!" A first grade teacher, amused by his kinetic body language, called him a "doll."

Through his young years Tim sparkled like a bright star in our lives, the embodiment of the nickname he'd borne from India, which we'd made his middle name: "Bunty," Hindi for *gift*.

Fast-forward through years and schools and countries,

through his skirmish-riddled high school time in Arizona to an Outward Bound expedition in Alaska at age nineteen: On the two-week hike of the Kenai peninsula he braved freezing cold with seventy pounds of gear on his small back. He was my height, 5'6", but weighed little more than 100 pounds. The Outward Bound people had turned him down at first because of his size, but on the phone I vouched for him. "That's how they're built in the south of India. He's strong. He can do this." He trained for weeks with a heavy weight of kitty litter on his back. After the trek, he flew home triumphant. "It's ninety percent mind, ten percent matter," he said.

Watching him sleep now, I wonder what goes on in that same mind that propelled him through so many challenges and hardships—but I know he can get through this. He'll be just fine.

I pet the cat and tiptoe out.

The next day I find an empty Jose Cuervo bottle under his bed.

Tim on Alaska hike

2

Bud's Bar and Grill

Mrs. Hawthorne leaned her ample bosom over the table, engulfing me in flowery perfume. She tucked a wayward strand back into her orange beehive as her gray eyes studied me. "Why do you want to work here?"

"Well…." Across from her, I wiggled my mini-skirted bottom in the formica chair. "I saw your ad on the college board…."

By that afternoon in June of 1968, I'd been off our tiny Wisconsin farm and at college in the big town of Eau Claire for three years—but this was the first time I'd set foot in a bar. My rural Methodist Sunday school lessons had forbidden drinking. Even Coca Cola was suspect. One summer the two spinster sisters who ran Vacation Bible School plopped someone's baby tooth in a glass of Coke so we could watch it rot. My parents were teetotalers, and I'd not known alcohol in any form until I got to college. In the three years since leaving home, my total intake of liquor had been two glasses of wine at an ecumenical church party—and I'd felt pangs of guilt. Why *did* I want this job?

The ad had drawn me like a bee to honey. The past semester, having exchanged my butterfly-frame glasses for contact lenses and had my dark hair cut short and sleek like Twiggy's, I'd begun to feel attractive. And I'd liked the effect of that white wine….

I looked the proprietor in the eye. "I'm a hard worker. I think I'd be a good waitress."

A phone rang, and Mrs. Hawthorne rose to take the call behind the bar. Keeping my smile on, I looked around from where I sat near the back at one of the square tables that ran down the center of the place. Red vinyl-cushioned booths hugged the wall to my right, and on the opposite side, bottles glinted in the light from above the long shiny bar. A few customers sat with glasses that sparkled in hazy lamplight. The place smelled exotic—like cigarette smoke, fried food, and what must have been liquor.

A dish clattered from the high counter that separated my table from the small kitchen. A woman in a hairnet reached up, plucked something green from an opaque plastic container atop the counter, and with a thumb and forefinger, placed the leafy bit on a plate of food. She smiled at me and turned back to the sizzling stove.

As Mrs. Hawthorne returned, I chirped, "This place seems nice."

She sat down and cleared her throat. "The ad said you must be of age. I assume you are."

"I turned twenty-one almost three months ago. The end of March."

A man in a dark suit waved at Mrs. Hawthorne and slid into a booth to my right. She nodded at him, then peered at me. "So you've never been in Bud's before."

"No.... No, but I've had jobs. Full-time, in a factory at a turkey plant one summer in my home town." I didn't tell her I got so sick of stapling together boxes for dead, naked, smelly turkeys that I quit before the summer's end. "And I did work-study during the school year—played piano in the music department. They trusted me to keep track of my own hours."

Her red-tipped fingers fondled the pearly necklace at her throat. "You'd have to get a bartender's license down at the county office.... Not that you'd need to mix drinks often, mind you. But you'd be the only one tending bar during breakfast. In case someone wanted something." She cleared her throat. "It's not difficult to get a license. Everyone who serves here has one."

"Would someone teach me to make drinks?" The variety of bottles over the bar was daunting.

"Of course. My three bartenders alternate lunch shifts. They'll help you. So will Kathy."

She nodded toward a middle-aged waitress with teased blonde hair, delivering a glass of amber-colored liquid from a tray to the suited man nearby. She stood chatting by his table, her tray balanced on her hip; then she and the man erupted in a shared laugh.

Mrs. Hawthorne glanced at them. "That gentleman is a manager at Sears. We have many regular customers from nearby businesses." She raised an eyebrow at me. "You know, this place is quite established. I've grown the business since my husband Bud died four years ago. College students come in at night now. We're quite close to the campus. I'm surprised you've never been here."

"I've just never spent any time around bars...." I adjusted myself in my chair and brightened. "But I'd like working here." I was dead sure. Damn the tiny tug of what—fear? guilt?—that made my hands grip each other beneath the table. I longed to know this alluring world.

"Your hair is nice and short, so you wouldn't need a hairnet. Just a black dress and apron, like Kathy's." My potential boss nodded over her shoulder at the blonde waitress, who now stood with her tray at the bar, talking to a good-looking young bartender. "There's a uniform store just down the street; you could buy one there. I'd need you to start next Monday morning at 7:00."

I had just finished the last final of my junior year. Monday would give me a few days to move from the dorm into the shared apartment I'd found; my boyfriend Andy would help me. I'd get the bartender's license and the uniform today. "Yes—that's perfect. Thank you, Mrs. Hawthorne!" I pulled my purse from my lap.

"Everyone calls me Irene." She smiled.

I floated out of the dimness and squinted into the bright afternoon sun of South Barstow Street. I could hardly wait to start down my new path.

During my first week at Bud's, Jack, the manager from Sears, taught me to make a Bloody Mary the way he liked it, with an overpour. "Stick in a stalk of celery and call it breakfast." He winked.

Jack came in each day before work for a Bloody Mary, then returned for lunch and a whiskey soda or two. Once while setting a full bowl of steaming soup in front of him, I spilled some in his lap. He snapped to his feet. "*Sorry!*" I yelped as he slapped at his dark pants with a cloth napkin.

"No problem, darlin'." He grinned and took a sip of his drink before sitting back down.

Other regulars were as congenial as Jack. The guys from A-One Carpets next door—Rudy, with the German accent, and Paul, his young, handsome employee—always came in for lunch at the bar, where over sandwiches they'd make off-color jokes about misshapen carpet remnants and deliveries to nearby towns.

Phil, the balding guy from Hank's Service Center, always had a cigarette between his lips. One day I picked up his pack of Winstons from the bar for a closer look.

"Want one?" He tapped the pack at a tilt so a few came out just right, then pointed them at me over the bar. I drew the closest tan filter tip out with my thumb and index finger. I held it at my lips between two fingers and, feeling worldly, bent toward him to meet the match flame sheltered in the hollow of his hands. "Quick, breathe in and suck it down your throat."

I spluttered and choked till my eyes watered. Chuckling, Phil held his water glass in front of me. "Here, take a drink."

"*God,*" I coughed out. "I'm not sure if I can—"

"You'll learn."

Soon I was smoking every day, buying Kents in their classy white package from the machine. When I served a table I left a cigarette burning in an ashtray on the bar, then returned for a drag. After work I relaxed in a booth over a drink, a cigarette between my lips, smoke curling around me—chic, like Audrey Hepburn in *Breakfast at Tiffany's*. Bartender Mick Chase even taught me to blow smoke rings.

Once as I was pouring a glass of milk for a customer, beefy, red-haired Mick Chase murmured, "Mother's milk is better, and it comes in cuter packages." I flushed with self-consciousness—and with pleasure at the attention. My constant closeness to friendly bartenders like Mick, and to male customers, as I slipped among tables and behind the bar, tantalized me, but scared me a little.

I saw less and less of Andy, my safe, loyal, French-horn-playing boyfriend of three years. He didn't come into Bud's, didn't fit the scene where I was spending more and more time.

One night, without telling Andy, I went bowling with Julian, a warm-eyed bartender. He kissed me at my door, then drew back. "I can't do this. I'm getting married in August."

I was relieved he'd pulled away: His kiss had provoked a startling desire. My mother had instilled in me that sex before marriage was wrong. It was bad enough I'd given in to it with Andy and enjoyed it—but sex with someone outside that steady relationship was unthinkable.

Back at Bud's, Julian and I reverted to skirting each other at a distance. Then I developed a major crush on Paul, the guy from A-One Carpets. We laughed and flirted every day at lunch, but he never asked me out. A few years later he would make a three-hour trip to visit me in Madison and tell me he was gay.

♫

On a muggy afternoon in late June, a tall, dark man came in and sank into a back booth in my section. He fixed smiling eyes on me as I approached. "What can I get you?" I asked. He gazed at me as if I mystified him. "Well?"

Then he beamed. "Bring me a nice big frosty beer."

As I waited at the bar for his tap beer, I watched the guy gather up his gangly body in his bluejeans and faded chambray shirt and stride to the juke box. His neat beard and the fringe of hair that brushed his collar were almost black. He stroked his beard as he studied the selections, then punched in some music and ambled to his booth. "Bonnie and Clyde" began to play as I walked over with his drink. Still smiling, he tapped the table to the beat as I set down his beer. "Thanks a million," he said, like I had made his day.

My shift was ending. I filled salts and peppers and sugars, doused sprigs of parsley in the container of water for reuse, and glanced at my lingering lunch customers for last needs. The tall guy, still sprawled against the booth's red plastic cushions, grinned at me. When his glass was empty, I went over.

"Anything else you'd like?"

He leaned forward, his hazel eyes arrestingly clear, his expression infused with that smile. "Join me for a drink when you get off?"

Sitting with my own beer in the cozy booth beside him, I learned Roger Ainsworth was five years older than I, and he'd been around. He'd attended the demonstration at the Lincoln Memorial in Washington the previous October. "It was far out. Thousands of people. A lot of us went to the Pentagon afterwards to protest, and that's where this cop beat me with a club." He leaned the left side of his forehead toward me and touched a reddish scar.

He said he'd fled to Montreal to avoid Vietnam when his draft number came up; he'd just come back across the border. "So here I am in the Midwest, a fugitive from injustice." His large hands splayed open on the table beside me. "I s'pose I'd be in trouble if the Feds found out." I wanted to grasp those rugged hands and offer him safe haven.

My roommate gone for the summer, I invited Roger to my upstairs apartment in a big old house. The owners, an older couple who lived downstairs, had hung a huge Stars-and-Stripes across the porch for the 4th of July. "Welcome to my country." I held the flag aside, Vanna White-like, for Roger.

We sat on the couch eating boiled hot dogs, drinking beers, and smoking cigarettes. He told me more about his anti-war activities: the Human Be-In in San Francisco in January of '67, and a protest following the My Lai massacre in March, around my birthday. "Far out," I said. I'd joined one puny candlelight march right there in my college town with my United Campus Ministry group. "You're so *brave*."

"It was just something I had to do."

When he told me he was a Quaker, I said, "I have Mennonite

heritage on my dad's side."

"So we're fellow peaceniks because of our religion."

"Maybe...." I drew on my cigarette and expelled the smoke through pursed lips. "But I'm not Mennonite myself. That was only my great-grandparents. I was raised strict Methodist. My parents never drank or smoked or even swore. But in college I've been with UCM—United Campus Ministry. They're pretty liberal. They're against the war. I guess they've loosened me up. I even had my first drink with them, at a party." I stopped myself. "Sorry for babbling."

"No, I like it." He gazed at me. "You're unspoiled. Don't lose that innocence."

Did he fancy me some virtuous dairy maid because I'd had the dubious fortune of growing up on a small farm with some Jersey cows? Because I'd lived for years without indoor plumbing or TV, sleeping in a bed with my younger sister till I left for college? Roger was a few years older than I, and he never made physical advances; was he being a gentleman? His attention beguiled me and I longed for more—but was too shy to make a pass myself.

Though Andy had ushered me into pleasant, titillating-enough sex, and we'd made love when we could find a place, I did not miss it—nor him. Something bigger was astir with Roger.

After our 4th of July hot dogs, we lay together on my single bed, chain-smoked one shared cigarette at a time, and talked of passions. George Harrison was our favorite Beatle. Roger quoted some line about knowing the ways of heaven from a song called "The Inner Light."

"Far out. I never heard of that one."

He knew them all. He knew that "In-A-Gadda-Da-Vida" by Iron Butterfly was a take-off on "In the Garden of Eden." I was impressed. He said, "We're Adam and Eve, you know. We can make our own Eden if we want." Maybe he knew the way.

Though we were both fans of literature, he knew books better than I. He loved Charles Dickens. "I'm like Pip in *Great Expectations*," he said. "Lower-class. I learned to act genteel to fit into the world I want to inhabit." He looked at me as if he'd had a revelation. "You could be Estella. She studied abroad. She loved Pip, you know, but couldn't let herself show it...."

I'd read that book in high school, but only remembered the crotchety old spinster Miss Havisham, who died.

As the summer progressed, my fascination with Roger Ainsworth displaced the comfortable bond I had with short, grounded Andy. Roger enveloped me in dreams of exotic, made-up worlds. Simply walking and talking with him proved more exhilarating than the tame parties, the opera, even the sex I'd had with Andy. Despite the lack of physical intimacy, I had been drawn into Roger's far-out orbit.

What was he doing in Eau Claire, Wisconsin, anyway? How did he support himself? What were his plans? I don't remember knowing. I had no clue where my relationship with him was headed—never thought about it, didn't care.

All summer he came into Bud's and sat nursing beers, smoking and reading until I finished work. Then we'd walk the leafy streets to his spartan apartment or my cozy one and drink beer and smoke and talk till late at night. Sometimes we'd forget to eat.

"We're like Bonnie and Clyde," Roger said once while we huddled on the peeling linoleum floor at his place. "The Merle Haggard version, where Bonnie's a small-time waitress and Clyde takes her away. I'd like to take you away. We could do and be anything we want, you and I."

I only knew Bonnie and Clyde lived a lot together and then died. That was the Bud's Bar and Grill version.

By August I was so wrapped in Roger's world, so beguiled by his tall, calm presence beside me that I cared about no one else. I waited on Roger, and I waited with him, for *something*. Never mind my lack of knowing who he really was; he was all I wanted—perhaps in part because I didn't really have him.

Like the good girl I was, I returned to school for my senior year at Wisconsin State. But hurtling from Roger's orbit back into college, I crashed on reentry.

3

The Loony Bin

"...I SAW THE WORDS just crawl up off the page like they were alive!"

I sat in Dr. Rubin's small office on the fourth floor of Luther Hospital, reliving for him the incident in my apartment two nights earlier, when I hadn't been able to wrestle meaning from a sociology text paragraph. The little black words had rebelled, marching into the air like a trail of ants. I shuddered. "I've just started the school year, and I think I'm going insane!"

"What else happened?" the doctor asked.

"What do you mean, 'what else'? Isn't that *enough*? I saw the words parade off the page in front of me. I'm *seeing* things. There's something wrong with my mind!"

This hospital psychiatrist was my last hope. Back in school, I'd begun sinking like a leaky rowboat. No one could bale me out of my sudden madness: not my old boyfriend Andy; not John, the campus minister with UCM; not Dr. White, the college shrink. I'd panicked.

But Dr. Rubin wasn't helping. He sat like a bent scarecrow, studying the papers scattered over his desk. "Your admittance info mentions another incident." His small eyes squinted at me through wire-rimmed glasses.

"Well, if it's there, why do I have to tell it again? I've already explained all this to two people here."

"I'd like you to describe it for me personally, if you don't mind." The doc opened a desk drawer and took out a pipe.

His equanimity set me on edge. "Please, can't you just read it in the report?"

His bony old hand shook as he struck a match and lit the pipe. "Tell me what else happened, Eileen." He leaned back with a lop-sided smile and puffed. "Take your time."

"Too much time's already been taken! You must have the results of all those tests I took. What else do you need?" I'd waded through the Minnesota Multiphasic Personality Inventory, the Thematic Apperception Test, some muddy Rorschachs where I saw Jesus throwing stones. Shouldn't this top-of-the-line shrink know what to do with me by now? I was frantic.

But I was trapped, nowhere to turn. As smoke from his pipe swirled, I droned out the rest: "Yesterday at the end of conducting lab, Dr. Byrne put on a record of this Mozart music and made us stand and direct it. The jumpy beat scared me. I wanted to cover my ears and run away." My voice quavered. "And the others were taking it so damn *seriously*, everybody holding up the stupid little sticks in their hands like puppets, and I felt so *out of it*, I could hardly hold the stick up. It *scared* me."

"And then?" The doddering doctor's head leaned back, his lips pursed around the pipe stem.

"Dr Byrne came up behind me and took hold of my elbow and said, 'It's simple 4/4 time,' like I was some idiot, and he started pushing my arm back and forth...." Anxiety rose in my stomach. "Him touching my arm like that, it made me feel *nauseous*, like I was gonna pass out. I sat back and hung my head down so I wouldn't faint."

More puffs on the pipe. "And you didn't faint."

"No..., the bell rang, and I went out to the hallway and found Andy—that's my old boyfriend. He felt my forehead and said, 'You're prob'ly coming down with something.' Then he just picked up his French horn and went into his practice room."

"But you continued to feel anxious." His eyes followed the

smoke drifting upward. I was sick of his pipe, of the smell. I was also dying for a cigarette, but having been told smoking was only allowed in the day room, I'd left my pack in my room.

"I couldn't *stand* it any more. I knew something was wrong. I rushed over to see John, that's the UCM minister, and told him what was happening to my mind. And about Roger, this strange guy I spent the summer with—then he asked me if Roger could've slipped me a *drug*, but I know he didn't; we just drank beer. Then John got me an appointment with Dr. White, this campus shrink, and—"

"I know Dr. White. He's a good psychologist." Puff, puff on the pipe.

"Well, he didn't help me. He just gave me tissues and told me to cry it out."

"So you were frustrated."

"And then he said maybe I was overtired. He told me to go home and sleep as long as I could, and I slept sixteen hours straight—but it didn't help. *Nothing* helps!"

"But you went back to Dr. White...." Dr. Rubin peered at a paper in front of him, his pipe poised in a quaking hand.

"Yeah, yesterday afternoon. There was nothing else to do! He said if I felt that bad, I could come here. So I went home and packed my suitcase and took a taxi, and here I am." I drew in a sharp breath. "I *committed* myself!" I sagged into the back of my chair.

"And here you are." His voice was dead-calm. "How do you feel right now?"

"I'm just *sick* of all this. I want it to go *away!*" I wrestled back tears.

"*What* are you sick of, exactly? *What* do you want to go away?" He still sucked at the pipe.

I sat up straight and leveled it at him: "All those other people out there, *normal* people, I feel like they're in a different world, and I'm set apart—I can't connect. It's like I'm trapped in some kind of bubble, looking at everything from the inside out, stuck in here like one of those paperweight bugs in acrylic. Nothing outside makes sense!" I leaned back, and my voice pitch rose with a finale: "I had a 3.94 grade point last semester, for Godsake, and now I can't even read! I can't play piano. I can't do *anything!* I'm just floating inside this damned, eerie bubble and I *can't get out!*"

Tears stung my eyes. I began to sniffle; then I was gasping out faltering breaths. I let my head fall into my arms on Dr. Rubin's desk and dissolved into racking sobs.

When I felt the doctor's light touch on the back of my shoulder, I stopped crying. "You will get through this, Eileen. It will take some time and effort, but we'll help you, and you'll get well."

I could have been a little kid with her parent telling her the monsters weren't real. The doctor's pipe bowl rapped against the glass ashtray. I opened my bleary eyes to see him shaking where he stood, bent like a question mark, beside his desk. He smiled gently at me and beckoned with his pipe stem toward the open door.

Dr. Rubin lied. I'd been in the fourth-floor loony bin for over a week and was not getting better. In fact, I felt worse: anxious, bored, and useless, incapable of any normal thought or action. My mother came to visit. "We're worried. We don't really understand why you're here." I didn't either; I couldn't explain. I didn't want to talk to her. Her teachers' insurance was footing the bill, but I just wanted her to go away.

"Do you ever think of killing yourself?" Dr. Goldberg asked one day. He was the psychologist of my "team," the team of him and Dr. Rubin.

"Why should I? I'm dead already."

"You are clinically depressed," he said. "Your test results are clear. And these are not unusual feelings for depression. Try to be patient. With some weeks of therapy and medication you'll feel much better."

"Some *weeks!* I can't stand this for *weeks*. Send me to Mendota if you want. I might as well sit there in the state asylum in a rocking chair for the rest of my life."

Dr. Goldberg jotted something on his clipboard. Then he smiled at me. "Let's meet again in a couple of days, shall we? It must be almost time for dinner."

Days on the fourth floor comprised a tedious litany. At 7 a.m. a breakfast cart rattled in, jarring me awake. I pulled myself up in bed and downed the orange juice, sloppy oatmeal, and limp toast. I pulled on clothes and sidled into the dayroom for a smoke, avoiding the eyes of a couple of loonies in there already playing cards. I trudged down the hall to a padded bench by the wall in a cavernous waiting area with a nurses' station as the hub. I sat there fidgeting, hoping for a shrink to summon me for a session; meetings with the docs were haphazard, as far as I could tell. When I finally did get called I felt as if I'd won the lottery. I popped off the bench, salivating for the boredom displacement that was in store, an hour of attention focused on the hapless blob that was *me*.

Mostly I sat idle, staring at the dull green walls, at patients and nurses and doctors and orderlies who drifted through and chatted with folks for a spell and then moved on.

Back in my room at noon for lunch, alone by my request, I'd maw down whatever amorphous vegetables, starch, meat, and pudding or jello they served up, then dread the arrival of the prim, gray-haired lady at the door with her perky voice: "Coming to OT today?" Under doctors' orders to take part in Occupational Therapy, I'd drag myself off my bed and trail her to a room with other patients at a long table, where I strung hundreds of beads, length after length, into necklaces no one would ever wear.

Group therapy met after OT, but I begged off. "I don't want to talk with other crazy people," I told Dr. Goldberg. "What's the point? The problem's in my *head*." He didn't make me go. Except to smoke, I avoided the dayroom, too, where the TV blared soap operas and people sat around playing gin rummy. Instead, I lay on my bed and stared at nothing for as long as I could stand it. Then I returned to the nurses' station, and like a dog anticipating its master's return, awaited a doctor's call which rarely came.

In my room again at 5:00, I ate the entire crappy supper; feeding my face was something to do. Then I shuffled back to the waiting room.

The tedium-drenched days were as leaden as the skies outside my window, which threatened to drop their heavy load of winter any day. But after supper, as dusk fell into darkness, I perked up. In this best part of my day, I could revel in the anticipation of escape into hours of sweet, dead unconsciousness: *sleep*, my bosom buddy, the only prolonged relief from the anxious, aching dullness of my waking days.

One afternoon the orderlies herded squirmy patients across a road to a gaping public gymnasium, where they lined us up in teams on the slick wood floor. I stood where they planted me. A large rubber ball was suddenly in motion, people racing around me in pursuit. An orderly had barked out an explanation of the game—but I couldn't concentrate enough to *get* it, and this filled me with terror. I kicked at the ball when it came near me—but I just wanted to vanish. A blur of patients scuffled past and shoved at me; sides changed up and an orderly snapped, "*Eileen!* Other side!" I winced, loped past where he was pointing, slunk down by a wall, and sat there in a shriveled heap until the game was over and I could shamble back to safety in the psych ward.

The next day when the nurse came with my meds in the little white paper cup, I whined, "The afternoons are killing me. I just lie around waiting for dinner. It's pointless. Can't you give me something after lunch to let me sleep?"

Besides the Thorazine and whatever other pills they dished out to me three times a day, Dr. Rubin prescribed an afternoon sleeping pill. I sank into blissful nothingness, dead again, for a few more hours each day.

4

Shocked

One morning during my second week, I was sitting in my usual spot on the bench when a normal-looking guy in a tailored shirt and pants approached the nurses' station. The nurse told him to have a seat; he sat down next to me and said hello.

I nodded, then turned and sidled my bluejeaned butt a ways away. I gathered my knees up under my chin, my slippered feet on the bench.

"How do you like this place?"

He wasn't going to leave me alone—but his voice was kind. "I hate it. But there's nowhere else to be, nothing else to do." I'd let the truth fall out of me.

"Gosh. I was that depressed, at first." He cleared his throat. "I spent a week here myself, about a year ago."

I glanced sideways at him and let my feet down to the floor. "Just a week?"

"Yeah. I was fortunate to feel better pretty quick." He flicked a bit of lint from the crease in his pants. "After they diagnosed me with depression, they gave me shock treatments. It helped right away. I've been coming in every month since for a treatment. It keeps the depression away."

He asked me about myself, and I muttered something

about college. He blathered on, said he was an accountant, had some kids—but his talk about shock treatments had captivated me. Maybe they could cure my depression, too. I grilled him for information.

"You don't even know it's happening," he said. "It's painless. You're kind of wiped out for a few hours afterwards. Then you just feel better. At least I do."

It sounded like a miracle cure. I had to have it! The next day when Dr. Goldberg called me in for a session, I told him about the man I'd met. "Couldn't shock treatments help me?"

The doc fingered his clipboard. "You're young, Eileen. Your prognosis for recovery is good." His eyebrows drew to the middle. "We try to avoid—"

"But I'm *not* recovering! This guy is *cured!* He said it happened right away!"

"Ray's case is different."

"But he was depressed, like me, and now he's fine. *"Please!"*

"Sometimes patients ask for electro-convulsive therapy as a punishment. They feel guilty, and they—"

"Well maybe I *deserve*—"

"You see?"

I'd caught myself, but too late. Dr. Goldberg accused me of a Freudian slip. Guilt had rolled from the tip of my tongue, proof I was shot through with it.

Well, I had reason to feel guilty. I'd been behaving badly since elementary school. That time my mother found the note in my jeans pocket that said "shit," I thought I was doomed. I barely escaped again when she caught my little sister and a friend naked in bed playing doctor, me beside them; I pled innocence on grounds that I was just the doctor, so she yelled at them, not me. And what about that C in 5th grade social studies? Mom was right—I could've gotten an *A*.

Now there was the shit-load of guilt I'd built up since leaving home: drinking liquor, having sex, forsaking my good old-time religion.... Maybe I *deserved* that spanking my mother often threatened but never delivered. It was about time.

"We'll try a series of three," said Dr. Rubin. "Each one will send an electric current into your brain through cables. It will momentarily convulse your body."

I looked forward to ECT. It sounded potent, a jolt that would cure a person of anything.

Before each of my three treatments, they fed me just dry toast for breakfast. Later I lay in a hospital gown on a white-sheeted cot. They rubbed something cool on my temples and put a stiff rubber thing like a dog bone between my teeth.

I felt the thing in my mouth; then I was asleep, and then awake again. Dr. Rubin's face floated over me. "How are you?"

"Fine." He helped me up, and I looked around. "I feel like there's nothing in my head." Amazing! My brain was wiped clean of its confusion.

That day, adrift in a pleasant haze, I allowed hope to flood into the freshly-vacant spaces in my mind. I smiled weakly at the lunch lady, who patted my arm. "Well, congratulations, honey. That smile's a first!" After lunch I strung my OT beads in a color order—purple, red, green; purple, red, green.

But then, without my afternoon sleeping pill, I felt anxiety creep back in, and by suppertime my neurotic gloom was back. That evening Dr. Goldberg asked how I felt.

"Like nothing. Everything's the same as yesterday. It didn't work."

They administered the two remaining shock treatments in the series with the same result. ECT was not my magic cure. And taken off my afternoon sleeping pill for good, I was back to frittering away more endless hours in the loony bin.

Decades later, I wonder at the doctors' acquiescence to my frenzied young requests, especially for electro-convulsive therapy. Dr. Goldman had said some people liked to punish themselves with ECT; did he think I might benefit from knowing I had cleansed myself with this high-tech brand of self-flagellation? Or did the doctors think it might actually make a change in my nerve circuitry, be the magic bullet that would blast me out of my depression, as I'd hoped? ECT seems to have done me no lasting harm, but when I read *One Flew Over the Cuckoo's Nest* a few years later, I thought it might have, or still could.

I know now that healthy doses of faith, hope, and patience would have served me better at the time than any medical instrument or drug. But those were inaccessible to me, locked away in the storage closet of the future.

♫

Toward the end of September, Dr. Rubin handed me a blank piece of paper and a pencil. "Please, draw a person for me."

"What for? What kind of person?"

"Any kind of person you like. Feel free."

This seemed stupid, but I began to sketch a girl, starting at the head: blank oval face, strands of long dark hair. Dr. Rubin looked on and lit his pipe. I drew arms held out loosely at the girl's sides, a simple top tapering to the waist, flared skirt. Then slim legs, tennis-type shoes. I sat back and studied her, then drew a gash turned upward for a mouth, shortened her skirt, and added big, shreddy pompoms at her hands, going up her forearms. She had turned into a cheerleader.

Dr. Rubin tilted his head to look at her. "Okay. Let's suppose this is you. What kind of person is she?"

"It's *not* me. I'm nothing like this person. I never was a cheerleader, never would be. I put pompoms in because I can't draw hands."

"Just for the sake of discussion, let's pretend she could be you. What is this person like?" His tobacco smoke smelled like something sweet—what was it?

"She's a show-off, then, I guess. Uninhibited. She wants other people to see her."

"What does she want others to see when they look at her?"

"Maybe that she's not just a little kid, not a stupid brat. That she can *do* things, that she *knows* some things."

After two long puffs on the pipe, the doc said, "Do you believe anyone thinks you're a stupid brat?"

"My mother, for one. I can never do things right for her. She's always telling me what to do different."

"Your mother visited yesterday, didn't she?" Dr. Rubin's left hand, holding the pipe, had the usual tremor. I'd heard an orderly say that he had Parkinson's.

"Yeah. She comes on Sundays." Dr. Rubin had met my mother the first time she came, soon after I was admitted. She would often drive the sixty-five miles to see me without Dad, who was virtually deaf.

"She's a smart woman, and she cares for you. But you're smart, too, and old enough to live your own life. You are not a stupid brat, are you? You're on the dean's list."

"I know, but somehow she always ends up making me feel stupid."

"Can you give me an example?"

I watched a climbing whorl of smoke and told the doc about an earlier visit, when Mom had asked me about therapy. "Well, sex is a big thing we talk about," I'd told her. "The docs think I shouldn't feel guilty about having sex with Andy, but I still do."

Mom had fingered the arms of her chair and said quietly, "Maybe you could try praying for forgiveness."

And on her next visit, she'd said, "Dad thinks you and Andy having sex are 'behaving like animals'...."

The smoke whorl dissipated near the ceiling, and I cringed, recalling my parents' poor opinion of me.

"Do you think they believe that sex is bad?" said Dr. Rubin.

"If you're not married anyway, yeah. When I was in 5th grade my mom told me my best friend's sister Tracy Ann was going to hell because she got pregnant when she wasn't married—unless she asked for forgiveness...." I drew in a breath. "My mom's so damn—I don't know—*religious,* and I don't think I even believe in God any more! And Jesus, turning water to wine and raising people from the dead? *Stupid!*" I blinked back tears.

Dr. Rubin set his pipe in the glass ashtray, then leaned back in his chair and narrowed his birdlike eyes. "Eileen, you're twenty-one. Do you think you are mature enough to have your own beliefs?"

"Maybe....but I feel so *guilty!*"

"You know the three parts inside you—Parent, Adult, Child. Can you tell your Child to stop knuckling under to your Parent's beliefs about things? Tell that little girl inside that *you*, the Adult, will decide for yourself that it's *okay* to have sex if you want. That it's *okay* to have different ideas about religion than your parents."

I brushed away a tear.

Both doctors had been working on this three-part therapy thing with me. Dr. Goldberg had showed me a chart with circles. "It's called Transactional Analysis," he said. "*T.A.* The three parts of you—Parent, Adult, Child—are like Freud's old superego, ego and id. Think of them as different people inside you that affect each other."

I'd fidgeted in my chair. "That sounds weird. I'm twenty-one. Doesn't that make me an adult?"

He said of course, but that healthy people have all three parts. And if the Child or Parent takes over it can cause confusion. "In your case, your inner Parent may be wrestling with the Child too much, and your Adult is lost. Do you feel that's possible?"

"I don't know."

"You can learn to figure out which one is acting, and put your Adult in charge when you want to, with practice."

One day Dr. Rubin handed me *Games People Play*. "This book explains Transactional Analysis. I did research for it. Maybe it will help you understand." I wouldn't read it till years later. But the docs helped me practice, and the paradigm began to make some sense.

Now Dr. Rubin picked up his pipe, and with quivering hands, relit it and took a puff. "I think you may be allowing your real-life parents to influence the Child in you with *their* beliefs about right and wrong."

He paused for another puff on the pipe—*cherry*, that's what it was—then looked at me. "Is it time to start being okay with your own ideas and feelings, Eileen? Maybe not tell your mother everything you talk about in therapy?"

"But she asks, and I owe her. She's my mom! She comes so far...." And her insurance was covering my hospital expenses.

"What we talk about is *our* business, yours and mine and Dr. Goldberg's. It's confidential. Your mother doesn't need to know the details. Can you still care about her without telling her everything?"

The next day at our session, Dr. Goldberg put an empty chair in front of me. "Pretend your mom is sitting here. Can you tell her that you are finding your own beliefs about sex and religion?"

I wiggled in my chair. "I feel like a fake." But at the doc's urging I jumped in. "I'm an Adult," I told my invisible mom. "I need to figure out my own life." And I wasn't acting.

Learning that I could be okay with my *self*, different and separate from my mother, was a start. But when I left the psych ward, this knowledge would slip from my mind like facts crammed for a college final—and I'd default to the Parent and Child battling inside me.

It would take my son's struggle forty years later to free me from my own quagmire; to lead me to accept and love my own imperfect *self*—and thus my troubled son, and my mother as she was. By the time I got this, Mom was gone.

But in the psych ward, the doctors' T.A. sessions threw a switch that put me on the right track. I stopped telling my mother details of my therapy, and I released my Adult more often—the Adult who, after three weeks in this place, was beginning to feel better.

♫

One night a disheveled, bloody-skirted woman came onto the ward, orderlies gripping her arms as she flailed forward and back. Her hands clutched each other and she wailed, "For-*give* them! Take this burden from me!" Her eyes rolled upward and she flopped from side to side. I stifled hysterical giggles.

From the nurses' station we soon heard the woman thrashing water in a bath, uttering wild prayers, orderlies still trying to calm her. Someone said they'd found her, Miriam, barricaded in her attic for days without eating. She'd had her period and believed she'd given birth to Jesus Christ. My eyes watered as I squelched laughter.

My mirth sprang from a heady blend of pity and relief. Miriam was living proof that religion could mess you up. Thinking she was the mother of Christ? *Crazy*! Thank God I was letting go of that old-time religion and the guilt it caused me. Thank God I wasn't in her moccasins.

Another whoop came from the bath. I laughed out loud.

In the '90's I would learn a joke: *Did you hear about the guy who walks into a psychiatrist's office dressed in Saran wrap? The shrink looks him up and down and says, "Well, I can clearly see you're nuts...."*

Poor Miriam was clearly nuts. So was obese, dirty-blonde Jackie Phillips, a short-time hospital roommate of mine, who had scars up and down the insides of her thick arms from cutting herself. And Roy Bauer, the burly young buck who yelled in people's faces and was strait-jacketed and put in solitary confinement.

Just plain nuts, all of them. Unlike me, who looked and acted perfectly normal—had even begun to *feel* that way. What was I doing in this place with all these crackpots?

In October at the doctors' urging, I returned to college. The end of my first week back in classes, walking into Schofield Hall, I spied a tall, familiar figure, and my heart plunged: Roger Ainsworth was ambling my direction, carrying books—he'd enrolled in college! I slunk toward the opposite wall, but he moved toward me and blocked my escape. "I heard about your illness."

I nodded, unable to speak; my eyes flicked past him.

I'd swept Roger from my mind. But his appearance in that hallway shot me back to weeks before, to summer and those murky days spent floating in his illusionary world—the Bonnie-and-Clyde narrative, the two of us oblivious to others.... *He* had caused my headlong crash into the loony bin. When I'd started school in August and he'd dropped from my life, I was stranded in that weird bubble, couldn't act normal, couldn't *read*—because of *him!* My heart raced.

"You look good. How're you doing?" His voice oozed concern.

"Fine." I forced a smile, then pulled my books into my chest, sidled off and merged into the flow of students down the hall.

The psych ward's elevator door closed behind me as I faced my doctors in the fourth-floor hall. "I'm *sorry,*" I blubbered. "I just couldn't do it!"

Dr. Goldberg nodded. "It's okay, Eileen. We gave it the good old college try, didn't we." He patted my shoulder.

"Seeing Roger brought it all back. I was trapped in my bubble again!" I brushed at tears.

"You weren't ready." Dr. Rubin smiled and laid a shaky hand on my arm. "We haven't got you well yet. We need more time."

We: the three of us, then. I was on their team. My doctors shared responsibility with me for my relapse and my dense guilt over failing to get normal, for my slinking back like a wimp to my loony-bin womb. I shuddered with relief.

My two savior-docs held me, one on either side, and walked me down the hallway. They consoled me perfectly, welcoming me back to my hospital home where I would settle in again, full-time, for two more entire months. They would teach me a relaxing breathing technique; their therapy would sink further in; and as they'd promised, I would get well.

But the holidays came first.

That year my parents dragged me, like a cat to the vet, from the psych ward to the traditional Thanksgiving meal with relatives in Eau Claire. My mother took pictures with her Brownie camera.

I'm wearing a turquoise mohair sweater pulled neatly over a wool skirt. My dark earlobe-length hair is brushed and gleaming. In one photo I stand bright and expectant beside my cousins' dining table, clutching an empty plate. No one would guess I lived in a loony bin.

A photo from after dinner is more telling: I lie across two vinyl chairs under the table, hair strewn across a cheek, brows furrowed; a turquoise arm fends off the German shepherd trying to lick my face. Harder to ward off than the dog was my weariness over the holiday affair.

More photos capture cousin Viv smiling in her frilly apron, her dry-alcoholic husband Joe carving the turkey as usual, grinning as he lofts the knife over the plump bird. Sitting on the floor, my sisters and young cousins laugh over a card game.

Back in the hospital, looking at the photos my mother sent made me wistful. That Thanksgiving was normal, but bogged down by my illness, I was not.

Though I'd always loved Christmas, that year's holiday, like Thanksgiving, was depressing. Perhaps the humbug about the virgin birthing of a Savior who was Christ the Lord ruffled my fledgling gospel-sloughing feathers; likely the religiousness, as I sat in church next to my God-fearing parents, stifled any Peace on Earth in my embattled soul.

Me and Mom

5

A Family Disease

On a Sunday morning four decades later, I stand with my long-time friend Jack O'Brien in the fellowship hall of the Unitarian Universalist Congregation in Prescott, Arizona. We're nursing cups of coffee after a morning service for which I've played piano. "I'm a Loony Bird," Jack says. His gray eyes flit across the room. "We meet early mornings, right here. A hundred people sometimes."

Wispy-haired and long-bearded, Jack wears wild political buttons and teaches chemistry at Embry Riddle Aeronautical University. Having remembered he's done substance abuse counseling of some sort, I've poured out my worries about my son Tim's drinking. Turns out the Loony Birds are just one of four weekly meetings for alcoholics Jack attends. He hasn't had a drink in twenty-five years. Who knew?

Jack takes Tim under his wing, getting him to meetings every day. The heavy weight of worry leaves my chest—until four days later, when Tim shuts Jack out, and fear oppresses me again. I talk to Jack.

"Alcoholism is a family disease." His gaze pierces me. "Tim is on *his* journey. You need to concentrate on *yours*. You need meetings of your own."

What? Who says Tim's problem is *alcoholism*? I've settled on *depression* and alcohol *abuse*. No one else in our families—mine or Russ's—drinks too much. I have no reason ever to have thought about this problem, don't want to now. It's *not* a family disease, not in *my* family!

But I'm desperate, and I trust Jack. I attend a meeting in a church basement, and when the circle comes to me I sob out Tim's problem. A woman pats my shoulder, and a couple of people say, "Keep coming back."

I go to two more meetings at two more churches. I hear the 3 C's of the Program for the first time: "I know I didn't *cause*, I can't *cure*, and I can't *control* my husband's drinking," an attractive woman says. "That helps me detach from his problem." I learn that I'm like everyone else in these rooms, powerless over someone else's drinking or drugging. I accept that I must take care of myself first, that I should live and let live. I feel hope flow in like holy water.

I attach the word *angel* to Jack—for taking Tim under his wing, and for getting me to my own meetings, which have begun creating breathing spaces in my life.

But back home, Tim's room incubates death: the sickly aroma and trashed bottles, his soggy listlessness—I can't bear it. Forget the freaking Program's Higher Power—who will save my son, if not me?

I take Tim to an addiction psychologist; Russ drags him to meetings for alcoholics, which use the same steps as our Program. Our son will suffer neither. We don't stop nagging.

We're still groping for solutions during Martin Luther King weekend when friends from our teaching days in Africa, Marty and Jerome, visit from L.A. As Jerome prepares a stir fry in our kitchen, Russ and I tell about Tim. Jerome turns from the pan he's stirring. "I went to those meetings for a few weeks, a couple years ago. I was drinking too much."

I grab his arm. "Could you share that with Tim?"

"I'll see what I can do."

Tim breezes in from his cooking job at Panchito's and halts at the kitchen to greet us. He's known Marty and Jerome since Africa. "You're welcome to eat with us, Tim," I say.

"Naw, thanks." He's half-way up the stairs.

After dinner the four of us are drinking coffee in the living room when Tim comes down, slumps on the couch and hangs his head. "I lost my job."

"What?" My wounded yelp jerks Tim's head up; his eyes flicker in my direction. *"Why?"*

"I. Have. No. Idea." He wags his head, like he's already been slugging down tequila again. It hits me—of course he has!

"Aww. That's too bad, Tim." Russ's voice is thick with disappointment.

I flop back against the couch. Things have been better this last week! Yes, Tim's drinking, but with help from Program meetings we've come to tolerate it better. He's been working, paying rent....

Now he has no job.

We sip cold coffee in silence. Jerome says, "That's a bummer, Tim."

"Fuck," I mutter, then grab the coffee pot and flee to the kitchen, where Tim's black cat Metro lies curled on a chair. I pick her up and sit down, burying my face in her fur. I stroke her as she purrs in my lap. Tears of despair well up.

"What happened, Tim? What did they say?" I hear Russ ask.

"Just it was my last day."

Marty murmurs, "Oh, I'm so sorry."

"That's really too bad." Russ's voice reeks of sympathy. "I guess you'll just have to find another job."

Christ, that won't help now, I think. *How's he supposed to find another job?* I pull the cat closer and glare at Russ from where I sit in the kitchen. He doesn't see me.

Tim pops off the couch, stumbles over Jerome's legs and goes upstairs. The cat leaps from my lap.

As Russ and our two friends gather cups and saucers, I skirt past them and enter our bedroom—Marty and Jerome's room during their visit. I shut the door, flop across the comforter on our bed and lie staring through blurred eyes at Marty's big suitcase, splayed open, clothes tumbling out onto the floor.

The bell on the back door jingles as the other three go outside to the patio. I rise from the bed like a marionette drawn by strings and plod upstairs to Tim's room.

He's lying beside the empty bottle on the dull carpet, front down, left leg and arm moving slowly, fish-like. A low, garbled sound comes from him; I think he's on the phone, but then he turns his head, eyes half-mast, and laughs—and the sound is not Tim. It's grotesque—low and slurred and *ugly*. "....Just chop off her mother-fuckin' tits. Jesus fuckin'-ass *Christ*.... *Kill* the cock-suckin' bastard." More derisive, unfamiliar laughter. Like a horror movie.

He hasn't noticed me. I flee through the family room and make it to the stairs before letting out stifled cries: "*Oh-my-God, oh-my-God!*" I sob my way to the bottom, rush panting for the kitchen phone book. I zero blindly in on West Yavapai Guidance Clinic, the only place with a drug treatment center I know of in our little Arizona town; I'm acquainted with someone who works there.

I punch in the number, then hurry out to the front porch where I sit crying on the swing in the encroaching dark. The phone rings and rings on the other end until a woman's calm voice says, "Hello, this is the crisis line. Can I help you?"

"My *son* needs help," I blurt through sobs. "He's drunk upstairs; he drank a whole bottle of tequila and he only weighs a hundred pounds! He could *die!*"

"Ma'am, I'm—"

"He's not himself. I don't even recognize his voice. There's something *wrong* with him—he's schizophrenic or something!"

"Oh dear. I'm so sorry."

I stare out at the yard, where the globe willow lifts its arc of bare branches in supplication to the sky. "What can I do? Take him to the emergency room? *Commit* him somewhere?"

"How old is your son, ma'am?"

"He's twenty-two."

"He's an adult. So there's really nothing you can do. Unless he wants to get help himself. Or if he is a danger to himself or others. Then you can call the police."

Christ. Where have I heard that before? *A danger to himself or others....* Maybe on some dumb TV show. "Well, isn't he a danger to *himself*? He could *die!*"

"That doesn't really sound like the case right now. Of course, if he is in your home, you can decide if he stays...."

"So, there's nothing else? *Nothing* we can do?"

"I'm sorry."

Still whimpering, I hang up the phone. But the call, the woman's reassuring voice, like heavy silk, her words, "*...not the case right now...*," have eased my desperation. I push myself on the porch swing as cold and darkness deepen. Then I go into the living room and see through the glass pane of the door that Russ and our visitors are still on the back patio. They have jackets on; they huddle over wine glasses at the picnic table. Escaping.

I must see Tim, must still do *something*.... I begin to mount the stairs—but half-way up I change my mind, fly downstairs, pour a hefty glass of wine and take a long drink; then I carry the glass out through the front door to Tim's black Honda by the gate. I can see his license plate in the moonlight, easily make out the purple fairyland silhouette of Arizona cactus and mountains, the fading sun behind, the blue letters and numbers in foreground relief. Between gulps of wine I chant: "Oh-six-four, L-D-Z; oh-six-four, L-D-Z...." It's cold without a jacket, but I memorize the license. Because if I ever again suspect that Tim is driving drunk, I'll call the police.

Inside, I write the license stats on a hot-pink sticky note, file it in my purse, and slug down the dregs of my wine. I stick my head out to the patio to say goodnight. Then I drop into bed in my absent daughter's old upstairs room and lie staring at the dark wall. On the other side of it, my beloved son lies drunk.

♫

The next morning the four of us are to go to the Grand Canyon for an overnight. It's just a two-hour drive and we have reservations at Bright Angel Lodge. But I'm afraid to leave Tim. He's so bummed over losing his job; what if he drinks himself to death—or commits suicide some other way? Or gets drunk and drives? Then he *will* be a danger to himself or others, and I won't be here to call the cops....

But it's morning, Tim is sober, and Russ says, "Don't worry.

He'll be okay. Even if he drinks." My Program is in my head enough to know I don't have to sacrifice my own life for the alcoholic, and I want this escape. I wonder if Tim will feed the cat and dog as we've requested—but they won't die in the few hours we're gone. I just hope *he* doesn't either.

The Canyon is frosted with a fresh skin of snow. Knife-like icicles drip from the low roof of Bright Angel, where we settle into our rustic, light-filled rooms. We hike along the South Rim and take photos. The snow on red and purple rock is dazzling in the sun. A bird of prey soars over white-crusted Battleship Rock, and my spirits lighten.

In late afternoon we stop at El Tovar Lodge, and sitting over drinks in the dim bar, I tell the others about the previous night. "Tim's so messed-up, and it *is* my fault, I don't care what they say at those meetings. He's always been high-maintenance, and I never maintained him for *shit!*" I slurp wine and become weepy. "I can't see how he'll ever get over this. How can he? He's gonna *die!*"

Marty grips my arm. "No, he's not. He's always been a good, smart kid. He just needs to grow up."

"You don't know him. We should've paid more attention to him, *always*. I neglected him! I left him to the overseas nannies when he should've had more attention from his *mom*."

Still clutching my arm, Marty looks me in the eye through smart, teal-colored glasses frames. "No. It doesn't matter, Lena. You've been good parents, both of you."

I remember that she lost a son to an overdose in Amsterdam, and I think, *What does* she *know? How can she be so well-adjusted to her own kid's tragedy? What's wrong with her?* But grateful for her encouragement, I hug her.

"You need a plan of action," Jerome says. Russ agrees.

I pull my little notebook from my purse. As we talk, I write down conditions for Tim:

1. *Apply for jobs, 4(+) / week.*
2. *Go to alcoholics' meetings, 4(+) / week.*
3. *Allowance: $20/week for gas, etc., from education fund.*
4. *Show all receipts.*
5. *No drinking!*

We have a plan. I feel better.

After dinner back at Bright Angel we play *Balderdash* and have some laughs. I sleep better that night than I have in a long time.

♫

Before our friends leave for L.A. Monday morning, I hear Jerome with Tim in the kitchen. "Alcohol can be a real bitch. Those meetings can help." His words sound light and honest.

"That 'Higher Power' thing...," Tim mumbles. "*Stupid.*"

"You can get past that. There's a lot more to it. It helped me."

As I hug our friends goodbye, I say I'm sorry to see them go. It seems a miracle they've come just now.

Tim's at his computer that afternoon when Russ and I deliver our typed plan. "We think this will help you if you want to stay here," Russ says. "Us too."

Tim stops playing his game to grab the paper from Russ's hand. He skims it, grunts, slaps it onto his dresser and turns back to the computer.

We escape into our teaching jobs the rest of the week, fancying that we are "detaching with love," as our meetings exhort. Tim job-hunts and goes to meetings—or says he does. I'm relieved each time he bounds down the stairs for something to eat.

We give him the agreed-on twenty bucks a week for gas. But when I look in at his messy room one day, I spy a crumpled receipt he hasn't shown us—for two bottles of Jose Cuervo. I go ballistic.

♫

Despite the meetings for families of alcoholics that I've been attending for a month, my life is still 'unmanageable.' I have taken that first step of the Program, *admitted* my life is totally screwed. I even have hope that a 'Power greater than myself can restore me to sanity,' as promised by Step 2; that Power is my meetings, three a week—though they don't hold me through the intervening hours.

Like Tim, I balk at the third step. I'm a Unitarian Universalist; I feel free *not* to follow the commandment in Step 3, which requires me to 'turn my will and my life over to the care of God *as I understand Him.*' I chafe at the word '*Him.*' No god of mine could be a man—a woman either, for that matter; God has no gender. Anyway, the word *god* itself feels abrupt, with its hard consonants on both ends. *Allah* rolls better off my tongue, but I can't in good faith say that, either, much less turn everything over to it. I can't get past the words. I'm stuck at the bottom of Step 3.

Unitarian Universalism—"UU-ism"—came as a breath of fresh air when I was in my forties, long after I had dropped the Methodist beliefs of my mother and left off seeing God as a man in a gray suit, like my dad on Sundays. Who knew there was a 'lite' religion that could fill my Sunday-morning void without espousing dogma? I became a UU soon after discovering it; my husband Russ did too.

But UU principles do say we are 'committed to a free and responsible search for truth and meaning.' Maybe it's time to step up that search and come to terms with this 'God' business. I want to get with the Program.

Understanding slowly comes. "I can't 'let go and let *God*,'" I tell Carla, my Program sponsor, "but I think I can 'let go.'" I tell her what happened the night before, when I'd gone berserk over Tim's tequila receipt: "I couldn't sleep; I kept obsessing about it. Then I started taking deep breaths. When I exhaled I imagined molecules of worry rolling from my head off my shoulders into the Universe, where they evaporated. Pretty soon I was asleep."

"You're getting it," Carla says.

When I try, I *can* let a Power outside me restore my sanity. I start calling on the Universe, when I remember.

♫

"Stop hounding me!" Tim stands midway up the stairs where I've trapped him with my latest rant from down below.

So much for sanity. The latest tequila receipt has turned me into the Liquor Police again, haranguing Tim for his every move—what is it this time? Did he reek of alcohol as we crossed paths?

"It's *your* fault I drink!"

His words crush me. He's never blamed me for his problem. I'm not supposed to believe I caused his drinking—but I do now: With his accusation, I am broken.

That same day brings a miracle. Frantic and forlorn, I call West Yavapai Guidance Clinic—not the crisis line this time—and beg them to interview Tim for detox. Then I wield the whip over my son: "Go to detox, or we'll lock you out of this house." Beaten, he acquiesces, and though he doesn't fit all their clinical criteria, a pair of capable, caring angels take him in.

When we drive him to Windhaven for admittance, Tim is drunk. I watch him stride bold and confident across the parking lot, and I wish to God that he could be that way without the booze.

In those dreary, waning days of February, Russ and I visit a zombie. Tim's on withdrawal drugs and who-knows-what, his black sweatshirt hood pulled over his shaved head. He seems absent from his body as we hug him goodbye.

With help from the therapist Tim saw a couple of times, we enroll him in Chandler Valley Hope, a rehab place near Phoenix. The shrink says they'll take his Blue Cross insurance.

Since my twenties I've thought of *angels*—like *God*—as flimsy notions dreamed up by weak humans with a pitiful need for help. But I've been naming angels: Tim's therapist. Jack O'Brien, Marty and Jerome, the West Yavapai Guidance people. All flew gently in at the right time and pointed the way.

I'd like to keep them coming. And if I can let them into my life, why not a God "of my understanding," as suggested by Step Three?

I reread some Program info about the step, which says God can be anything I decide: an object, some part of nature, a spirit. Well, there it is! My God can be *angels*. Maybe I *can* turn 'my will and my life over to the care of 'God' as I understand 'Him.'"

If I can latch onto angels—or the Universe—and give my stuff to either or both or all or *anything*, I can get Step Three. It's only *words*, for Godsake.

6

The Sheer Beneficence of Love

"EACH PATIENT PAINTED one. A black ribbon on the handle means the person died from his addiction. Yellow means still sober."

Tim's new counselor, Jane, is pointing at cups that hang on the meeting room walls of Chandler Valley Hope. Lined up in two rows like church votive candles, the cups are splashed with colors and names and slogans. Yellow handle ribbons overwhelm black ones by a landslide.

Tucked into a neighborhood of modest houses, this rehab facility reminds me of hotels we knew in Africa and India: plaza-style, worn around the edges, plain but comfortable. Russ and Tim and I follow Jane outside through a plant-lined courtyard.

The sunny little chapel has a Buddha statue, a Muslim prayer rug, an altar with a cross—all beliefs welcome. "There's a short service here each morning," Jane says. "We encourage patients to attend, but it's not mandatory."

Our last stop is the cozy dining room, where we're treated to a rich lunch of fried chicken, mashed potatoes, corn, salad, and peach pie. We sit at round tables with patients, people who welcome and chat with us as if we are new neighbors.

During Tim's first week we drive the two hours down to Chandler to join his counseling session with Jane, who elicits my respect; she is about my age, well-dressed and professional, her tasteful office lined with books and plants. Russ and I sit across the glass coffee table from Tim and Jane. "Alcoholism is hereditary," she tells our son. "Someone in your birth family in India must have suffered from it." I've heard that alcoholism may be genetic, but this is the first time the words have come from a clinician's God-like lips; it must be true. "It's a deadly disease, and there's no cure. Only *you* can control it."

Her words cause me a pang of fear. She turns to me and Russ. "All the counselors here are experienced with addiction, our own or a loved one's. We know first-hand how tough it is."

As I release pent-up tears, Jane says, "What's making you cry, Mom?" She pushes the tissues toward me and I take one.

"He could *die!*"

"Yes, he could. If that's his journey, he could die from alcoholism. What would that mean to you?"

I can hardly talk for blubbering. "It... would be... *unbearable!*"

"I don't want to *lose* him." Russ is sobbing too.

Jane turns to Tim. "I see that you are crying." Sure enough, he's wiping at the corner of an eye. Have we ever seen him cry since he was little? "Why?" she asks.

"Because they are." He nods toward me and Russ.

"Why does seeing them cry make you cry?"

"I'm making them sad."

"You don't have the power to make them sad. Their sadness is their own. You love them very much, don't you, Tim?"

"Yeah."

I dab at my nose with the tissue. "Maybe deep-down he's angry at us, though. For neglecting him. Maybe he has adoption abandonment issues." A scene from his first days with us comes to mind: On maternity leave as Russ went back to work in Africa, I spent most of two weeks alone with Tim in Illinois. Still weak after his hospital stay, he clung to me; when I wasn't holding him, he cried. I swept the floor and washed dishes with him on my back. I read and did paperwork as he sat on my lap. One afternoon as I used the toilet he sat fretting on the floor in front of me. When I finished, I swooped him up in frustration and almost dropped him on his head. "I was too impatient...."

Both Tim and Jane shake their heads. Jane says, "We've talked about this. Do you resent your parents for anything, Tim?"

He shakes his head again and casts untroubled eyes at me.

"It's obvious how much Tim loves you, and you clearly love him," Jane says.

Suddenly I get it—the sheer beneficence of *love*, the comfort of it. I draw a deep breath and let it go. Hope floods in. I love Tim to death—his or mine. His dying first would be terrible. But I know my Twelve-Step Program would help me. I would live, and continue on my journey. Like Marty, our L.A. friend, after her son's death in Amsterdam. I get that now.

I walk out with my arm around Tim's shoulders, and I think he *won't* die....but if he did, I'd live. I have my hopes up, for my son, and for myself.

We're home in Prescott for two weeks—relaxing into our lives knowing Tim is safe in rehab—when he calls from a patient phone at CV Hope. "I'm leaving here at the end of this week."

"Wait—are you allowed to do that?"

"They said insurance won't pay past three weeks. That'll save money. I'm ready to get *out* of here."

"Are you sure it's long enough? What does Jane say?"

"It's up to me. One guy only stayed two weeks."

"Remember, you can't live at home...." I hate the warning in my voice. But he's supposed to be looking for a sober house in Prescott; Jane said she'd help.

When I arrive to pick him up from rehab, Tim has his hand out. "Where's my phone?"

I'm clambering from the car after my two-hour drive from Prescott. "Don't you still have to go to the speaker meeting? Say goodbye?"

"I don't care. I am so *over* this place." His fingers motion for the phone. I fumble it from my purse and pass it to him.

During the meeting a distinguished-looking speaker in his 50's falls to his knees on-stage, hands behind him as if bound by chains, to show the hold alcohol had on him, how he's surrendered and gotten help from his Higher Power. Tim would never give himself up like this, I think. He's paying no attention, anyway. He texts wildly under the table and snickers at responses on his phone.

After the meeting Tim endures the long line of CV Hope goodbye-sayers. A middle-aged guy shakes his hand and says, "Good luck, man. You'll need it. We all do."

I open the car trunk and Tim throws in his duffel bag and guitar; the guitar twangs. "I'll drive." His hand demands the keys. "I can get there faster."

"Wait—no, sorry, *I'm* driving." I get behind the wheel. He flops into the back seat. "Where are you staying tonight?"

"I dunno. Maybe Libby's." She's his former boss's daughter, a friend and some-time work supervisor, in her forties. He hasn't made plans for a sober house, then. "I can stay home and play my new video game till you kick me out at 5:00, right?"

Kick him out? What kind of bitch-mother *am* I?

I gaze at him in the rearview mirror: iPod in his ears, black hood up, eyes closed, he's shutting out the world so completely that he doesn't notice I've turned the wrong way leaving CV Hope. Neither do I, for a long time. I've been driving deep in thought: He's agitated. He wants to play his game so badly. Jane told him he needed to rein in his gaming.... He is addicted to *gaming*, too! I get this now.

By the time I realize I'm going the wrong way and turn around, I'm back in my Program mode, got my boundary set: He *won't* play games for six hours at my house.

By Fain Road, close to home, his hood is off; he's brightened. "It's a new game. Joe'll be playing with me on-line and I'll beat his—"

"Sorry, Tim. I'm going to limit it to 2:00 today. Three hours is enough. Jane said you need to control your gaming, remember?"

"But it's a new game! I haven't played for three weeks. When I beat it, it's done. I won't be playing all the time."

"Sorry. It's my house. Three hours is long enough."

"Whatever." The hood goes back up.

Hibernating in his room, Tim plays his game straight till 2:00, then bounds down the stairs toward the door.

"Where are you going?"

"I dunno."

"If you find a place and need your stuff, Dad and I won't be here tomorrow; we're both teaching. You can stop by after 3:00 when we're home."

"Okay."

"We'll pay for a sober house, whatever it takes. Just let us know...."

"O-*kay*." He lets out an exasperated breath.

"We have your old house key, right?"

"Yep." He sticks his hands in his pockets, pulls out nothing. "You took it away after detox."

"Okay, Tim." I grab his rigid body in a quick hug. "Love you."

He pulls away and leaves with no belongings.

Next day after sub-teaching, I stop by Jolly Krishna's Coffee House, Tim's sometime supervisor Libby's new business in a historic house downtown. She's wrapping homemade oatmeal cookies behind the counter. "Yeah, he was with us last night," she says—meaning with her and her two girls. "He wanted to play video games but I wouldn't let him. We were watching a movie." She arranges the cookies on a plate. "You know Tim's addicted to video games."

"I've been getting that." I look at my watch; it's 3:10. "Do you know what he's up to now?"

"No idea. I kicked him out when I left for work at 7:00."

"I told him he couldn't come back home. We took his key away."

Libby raises an eyebrow. "Sure your doors are all locked?"

We hadn't always locked the house, but we've begun—to keep Tim out. *Wait*—the upstairs sliding door: He was up there in his room yesterday. "Dammit. I'm gonna call him."

I step outside. When he answers brightly I'm relieved. "What're you doing?"

"Drivin' around."

"Hope you're finding somewhere to live...."

"I'm checking out some places." He sounds impatient. I wish him good luck and say goodbye.

"He's out looking for a sober house," I tell Libby.

She glares at me. "I'll bet he's in your house right now, gaming. You're gonna have to change your locks."

I drive home, check the upstairs sliding door, and sure enough, it's unlocked. Tim's probably played games all day. I lock the door.

I call Tim the next day. "Where'd you stay last night?"

"Libby's. But I'm moving into First Step today. I need to come back home and get my computer and some clothes."

"So they're letting you have your computer? You can play games there?"

"Yeah, but they limit it."

The little sober house called "First Step," on a corner street near a creek, packs in eight recovering guys. We meet the resident managers, all recovering addicts themselves. Tall, tattooed Mike Rodriguez is affable and convincing. "These guys need a little time to relax. We make 'em go to Program meetings and house meetings." He flashes a fat, impressive-looking study book, which I flip through, unseeing. "But there's plenty of down time. We don't force 'em to look for work right away."

Not very structured. And very expensive. Within a few years, with new city regulations, First Step will close, along with several other disreputable sober houses in our little town.

Tim tolerates the house managers and likes some of the clients. One day he comes home to pick up his big flat-screen TV. With him is Jay, a bright, gay, recovering heroin addict with what look like diamonds on his belt buckle. He admires the African tapestries on our walls. "I'd like to live in Japan someday," he says.

A week later Tim says, "Jay was jealous I have you guys for parents." And then, off-handedly, "He shot up heroin and got kicked out of First Step yesterday."

Jay is one of many relapsers during Tim's sojourn at First Step. But despite his abiding dislike of the 12-step meetings and reluctance to get a sponsor as urged by Mike Rodriguez, he stays sober.

Three weeks into his stay, a miracle: He lands a job at a popular down-town eatery, "thirty hours a week. Salad and dessert prep." He's not crazy about being back in the food industry, but it's a job. "I go for training tomorrow."

So now he's dying to move out of First Step and run his own life. "Can you loan me the deposit on an apartment?"

Russ and I feel he's not ready. When we say no to his request, his always-clean-and-sober buddy Joe fronts him the money.

Tim is alone in his new place, a front-window studio in a classy-looking old three-story building, across from Libby's coffee house and down the alley from his new job. "I won't have to spend much on gas," he says. We help him move in a single bed, his dresser, his huge TV.

He bolts across the street to Jolly Krishna each day until Libby gets sick of it. "He says he needs to use the bathroom and has no toilet paper. Why can't he get his own TP? He's got a job!"

I know it's because he's lonely, at loose ends, poor guy. Maybe trying to evade the pull of his computer or TV. Or alcohol.

One weekend when Holly's back from college, she and Russ and I meet Tim in downtown Prescott, on his turf. It's a balmy spring day. The four of us saunter through an old brick-lined alley after lunch, the breeze blowing dust and leaves, and I love it: We're this closed family unit again, alone and strong together, like when we lived in Bolivia and St. John and India.

As we visit back at Libby's over coffee, Tim seems jittery. He jabbers constantly, complaining about Libby's attitude, people in general, the world. I don't interrupt and contradict as I would have in pre-Program days; I watch from a distance, detaching with love. But my son's burden of joylessness makes me sad.

For two weeks he labors alone in his corner of the restaurant kitchen, preparing endless salads and desserts. He says it's boring. I imagine him going home to his little apartment, watching TV, playing video games and falling into bed.

One night after work he drives to Fry's and buys a bottle of Jose Cuervo.

7

Acting Normal

I WAS SITTING in my usual place by the psych ward nurse's station one evening when a guy with dark, Marine-cut hair parked himself beside me on the padded bench, wagged his head my direction and said, "You look normal." He was maybe ten years older than my nearly twenty-two, and he looked more normal than I felt. "What're you in here for?"

I hesitated. I knew looks could be deceiving. A ratty-haired man in a bathrobe sat across from us staring into space; occasionally he'd shake his head. Nothing deceiving about *his* looks—he was obviously nuts. This guy talking to me now, who knew?

It was early January of '69. For three months I'd been sitting on this bench, avoiding people with ratty hair and odd mannerisms, connecting with no one but the doctors. "Depression," I blurted. "I feel okay in the hospital, but I don't like going out. It's weird out there."

"You just gotta act normal." The Marine guy looked around. "I'm nervous as hell myself. I almost cut my throat shaving once when my little boy showed up in the bathroom." His eyes darted back to me. "I'm a basket case—that's why I'm here. Two weeks now. Spent Christmas here."

Why had I never seen him?

He scanned the room again. "Gotta leave soon and get back to drivin' my truck. Family needs the money."

This guy, Rex Bailey, listened to my story: How I'd been scared by my own fear—the hallucinations, the loss of concentration. How I'd committed myself, just like him. How I had started to trust the doctors. How I was maybe *better*—but not well enough.

Rex shook his head. "You need to get out on your own, like me. I walk to burn off stress. They'll let you out, won't they?"

"I don't feel like going out."

"*Make* yourself. Get some fresh air."

"It's freezing out there." It was winter in Wisconsin, for Godsake. The sky hung bleak and gray outside my window. The sidewalks were flanked with dirty snow.

"It doesn't matter." He leaned closer and spoke in an urgent whisper. "You gotta make yourself do some things. Make yourself *act* normal. That's how you get to *be* normal."

I inched away. This guy Rex was intense. I had no faith in what he said. Still, he was paying attention to me, and I felt safe with him. I tilted my head in his direction.

"Come *on*." He jabbed me with his elbow. "Take a walk. Tomorrow. I'll go with you."

The next day, Rex in his split-hood parka and I in my wool college coat walked the cold streets for what seemed like forever. Afterward, though exhausted, I felt my spirits lifted. Maybe Rex was right: If I *acted* normal, I could *be* normal.

When he left the hospital for good, I went out walking on my own.

Roger Ainsworth had been the catalyst for my depression in September, and Rex Bailey catapulted me out of it in January. In both instances the timing was right. I was ready to risk actions which would prove to be life-changing.

Decades later, I might label these guys angels.

On a walk one day I spied a sign over a deli counter and was stabbed with fear: A four-foot hot dog, tan and wet, lay poised on relish in a bun. "It looked like a giant penis!" I told Dr. Goldberg. Was I hallucinating again?

Dr. Goldberg chuckled. "Well, they *do* resemble penises." He reminded me that I'd been casting out my inner Parent's useless guilt over sex. And Dr. Rubin had just prescribed The Pill. "Sex is on your mind. That's normal."

But was sex too much on my mind?

I'd let most of the '60's bleed away like colors from a tie-dyed shirt. But when I left the psych ward early in '69, I grasped the decade's tail end with both hands: tuned in, turned on, and embraced Sex, Drugs, and Rock-and-Roll—and the greatest of these was Sex.

Any attractive guy who looked my way was a candidate. First, that tawny German hunk who appeared at Bud's, where I was working again; what was his name?—the son of Rudy from A-One Carpets. His warm smile and his touch on my arm across the bar made me lead him down the path to the river, where on a blanket we joined bodies, banishing the light spring chill. In town visiting his dad that week, he never showed up again, except in fantasies.

Then pony-tailed Jed Halpert came down from his apartment over Bud's for a beer. We locked knowing eyes, and I was in his bed upstairs that afternoon for the first of many frequent, lusty interludes. As I worked lunch shifts in the restaurant below, flitting between tables and dousing left-over parsley in the container for reuse, I'd imagine making love with Jed. After work I'd sneak up to his place.

While wrestling with a music-class treatise on Gregorian chant one afternoon, I reached across my tall, blond fellow student and project partner Jon Carlson for a text from a shelf above his bed, and my breast brushed his arm. I clutched him close, ostensibly steadying myself, and we fell onto the bed, our papers with their ancient staves and squiggly ciphers floating to the floor.

I'd walked myself back into normal life on Eau Claire's winter streets. Then, like Forrest Gump, I just kept walking. Usually alone, sometimes breaking into a run. Around the campus, down Water Street, across the Chippewa River bridge. As full of fresh, pulsating life as the Wisconsin spring around me, I skipped into mild days filled with puffy-clouded skies and erupting green. I was Windy from the Association song, tripping down the streets of Eau Claire in my clicky-heeled boots, smiling at everybody I met.

Sex was a manifestation of the same exuberance—I was doing what came naturally. At one of my twice-weekly therapy appointments, hearing details of my new-found pleasures, Dr. Goldberg said, "It's great that you're enjoying yourself. But understand, you've just come out of a depression. You're in a manic phase. This euphoria won't last...."

The hell it wouldn't. I was living happily ever after.

♫

Big, fiery bartender Mick Chase began sashaying close to me at Bud's, reaching around me to pour tap beer or plunk a dirty glass in water. Sometimes his arm would brush me and I'd smell his musky after-shave. One day at the end of my shift, as I loosened my hair from its short ponytail, he untied my apron with a deft tug. "Want to come home with me and take the cats for a drag?"

Though he sometimes took the two reluctant Siamese out on skinny red leashes, we didn't walk them that day. Mick shoved them from the bed, and with an adroitness I could not have imagined, furnished me with intense multiple orgasms.

Smart and charismatic, Mick beguiled all the girls in town. But his attentions soon fastened on me, and I meant to keep them there. I dropped other guys from my radar and spent my free time laughing and talking and making love with Mick, who seemed to adore me. After night shifts at Bud's, he would take me to Jimmy Woo's for Chinese. Then we'd have sex back at his place. Or we'd go down to Water Street to friends' apartments and smoke pot—Mick had introduced me to it. I laughed and laughed. Everything was fun, and sex with Mick was the most fun of all.

Months cruised blissfully into hot, humid summer. Mick

breezed in one day as I was taking off my apron and said, "Let's go!"

"Where?" He'd turned me on to vodka gimlets with those compact filbert nuts I liked to roll on my tongue; I was looking forward to a gimlet after work.

But his hand was on my back. "You'll see."

He whisked me to a blue Corvette convertible parked out front.

"Whose is this?"

"Mine." He opened the passenger door.

"I thought you didn't have a car." I slid into the smooth bucket seat.

"I told my ex-wife she could have it."

"Wait—your *ex-wife*?" We'd been together months now; why didn't I know?

"I hated hurting Rhonda, so I let her have the car. I just borrow it now and then." He gunned the motor and we were off, his wild red hair and my dark tresses whipping at our faces.

Within six months, Rhonda and Mick's baby boy was born. "I still care for Rhonda, but she's not *you*." He took my hand as I wiped my tears. "I'm sorry. I just need to be there for her—be a good father."

I accepted his need to spend time with Rhonda and little Bradley. When he came back to me the stars aligned again.

One night I found an earring beside Mick's bed. "Rachael came over and took off all her clothes," he said. "She stood there naked, just offering herself. What could I do?"

I knew Rachael. She was pathetic with her straggly hair and pudgy body. I knew Mick had no feelings for her. I pitied her.

Then Mick informed me of a tryst with an older woman. "She was lonely. Thirty-four and just divorced. I felt sorry for her. She's nothing like you."

These were the ones Mick told me of. Julian, the now-married bartender I'd once gone out with, said confidentially, "Mick sleeps with other women all the time. Everybody knows."

Hurt and confused, I went down to Water Street, whose hippie types I now preferred to Bud's' frat boys. Long-haired, laid-back Bill Riley showed up at the Blue Front. We talked and drank; then I went home with him till almost dawn.

Mick shook me awake in my own bed at 9:00 a.m. His livid face loomed over me. "Where were you last night? I came by at 3:00 and you weren't here."

Untwisting my long, clingy nightgown, I drew myself up. "I went down to the Blue Front after work."

"Not till 3:00…."

"O-*kay*. I slept with Bill Riley."

He lunged for me. I shrank back, but he grabbed me by the shoulders and shook me. "What's *wrong* with you? I guess he didn't tell you he had gonorrhea. Everybody at the Blue Front knows." He slapped me hard, and I fell back on the bed.

I cupped my burning cheek. "I didn't know…."

Mick insisted we get tested for venereal disease. The results were negative. "Maybe you learned a lesson," he said.

From then on I kept my sexual encounters with other guys hidden from Mick—as he had surely hidden dozens of affairs from me.

The drama flowed like the swollen Chippewa River.

By January of 1971, Mick and I had graduated. I followed him to Madison, which he called "the Mecca of the Midwest" for its progressive state capitol and the sprawling, liberal University of Wisconsin; both were on an isthmus lined with huge trees and grand old houses, between Lakes Monona and Mendota. I came to love the town.

I admired Mick's dedication to his writing, his studies, and his enigmatic anti-war activities. Blindly believing in him, I worked days at Sears, nights and weekends at Nino's Steak Round-up, to support us both. Soon stressed by the overload of work and from not knowing Mick's whereabouts, I moved to an apartment of my own, on the opposite end of Mifflin Street from Mick's. I still slept with him often, at his place or mine—and I slept secretly with others, as I knew he was doing.

One of these others for me was Rusty Wilson. Blonde, square-jawed and muscly, Rusty drove a forklift at the Sears warehouse just outside the little office from which I fielded calls about fencing supplies. We began calling each other after-hours to arrange warm, congenial sex. One night his phone voice was mellow: "I'm tripping on acid. Come on over." We smoked some grass, and listening to *Abbey Road*, we came together perfectly in bed.

Once, when he was between places, Rusty slept on the couch in my East Mifflin Street apartment. We played it so cool that Mick, in bed with me behind the closed bedroom door, never suspected my connection with Rusty, beyond work.

On weekends Mick and I tripped on LSD and angel dust. He'd hand me a crinkly paper with a dab of color on it. "This is great stuff." I'd lick it and be off for roller-coaster hours, watching undulating designs on an Indian bedspread; on sidewalks and tree trunks; and once, on Mick's grotesque, unfamiliar face. Sometimes I had an awful fear of dying. I'd drink liquor, eat, perhaps throw up, then find solace in Mick's body.

When he was out womanizing or politicizing, I drank beer, listened to jukebox rock, and met sexual partners at the 602 Club on East Johnson: Anthropology grad student Rick Simmons, with a cock so small I couldn't tell if he was in me; Smitty Albert, backwoods fishing aficionado, whose penis resembled the giant deli hot dog I'd seen while in the psych ward—too big for comfort; Glenn Watson, who, when I revealed distress over Mick, said in his British accent, "You need a cup of tea, love." After a cozy night in bed he sautéed mushrooms for my breakfast.

"Why don't we get married?" Mick said one Sunday night when we were stoned.

"Nah. We don't know what we're doing—we're so young!" I didn't want to hurt him, but our relationship was so messed-up; how could he even think of marriage?

Like shooting heroin, marrying Mick Chase would have been the death of me. I drew the line at both.

Mick had introduced me to cocktails at Bud's Bar and Grill, marijuana and psilocybin mushrooms on Water Street, varieties of LSD and PCP in Madison. One Sunday when I was hung-over and due to work at Nino's Steak Round-Up, he cradled a little white pill in his palm. "Speed. It'll keep you going."

I'd never felt so buoyant as I did that day, strutting in my leather mini-skirt and cowboy boots, serving cocktails, steaks and salads—and the tips were great. But after work I crashed hard, depressed, and with a headache no amount of Bufferin could cure. As I lay on Mick's bed he handed me a glass of whiskey. "This will help it go away."

Then it hit me: I wanted *him* to go away; *he* caused all my misery. I waved away the whiskey, went home to my apartment on East Mifflin, and never did amphetamines again.

But Mick did plenty. Stoned on pot from morning till night, he popped speed as well. "It enhances my creativity." He drank whiskey and stayed up late, alone in his West Mifflin basement, tapping out articles for underground journals on a Royal typewriter: "The Sterling Hall bombing was justified. Sometimes violence is the only way to peace." I lay upstairs waiting, uneasy in his bed.

One morning I stumbled from the tangle of Mick's sheets into the dim living room to find four disheveled, passed-out people strung across the floor and couch. I picked my way through them and found Mick in the kitchen. Closing the fridge, he leveled angry eyes at me. "We're out of milk." He pushed me against a cabinet, causing a clatter.

Someone coughed in the living room, and I stepped quickly to the door. "Who are these people?"

"They're here from Cincinnati for an SDS meeting. And I'm out of fucking *milk*. How could you use it up and not get more?"

I fled to my own end of the street.

Later Mick came over meek and apologetic, and I took him to bed—but things were changing. Drugs and alcohol seemed to rule him now. I never stayed with him at his place on West Mifflin again.

In January of '72, bent on filling the hollow in my life, I quit my job at Sears and started grad school at Madison's U of W. I had a music minor; I'd been good at music. I would earn a masters in it. I began studying in earnest.

In February, Will Prince, a strong-bodied, introverted

construction worker, sauntered into the 602 Club. "I'm not all educated like you," he said, "but I like my job. Work's outside, and the pay is good." The skin crinkled in the corners of his warm, brown-eyed smile.

At some friend's farm outside Madison, Will and I tramped hand-in-hand in sparkling snow. Back in the house we had hot cocoa and finished a joint by the fire. Then we stripped off our clothes, and under patchwork quilts on the living room couch, fell together to Led Zeppelin's throbbing "Whole Lotta Love," not stopping till we were both wrung out.

The tangled relationship with Mick behind me, I longed for a saner, safer love. Will Prince may have been perfect, but the timing was off. Still smarting from Mick and wary of entrapment, I let Will slip away.

Then I spotted Tom Kelly at the 602. We'd been classmates in Eau Claire. He was visiting in Madison, up from Rockford, Illinois, where he lived now. We became reacquainted, and I soon pegged Tom as my Ideal Man. He was John Lennon with those round, wire-rim glasses, but with very dark long hair and beard. Like me, he had a degree in psychology from WSU-Eau Claire. A conscientious objector, he'd done voluntary service with patients in a mental institution in lieu of Vietnam. A player of guitar, wanderer in the woods, and scrambler of perfect eggs, he'd been raised in Shell Lake in northern Wisconsin, where my dad's family came from. The sex was good. Best of all, he lived on a farm with some musician roommates and some dogs and cats. Sprung from a farm myself, I romanticized them as idyllic—safe and isolated—and I loved pets and music. Tom was my first real keeper.

When he went back to Illinois, I wrote letters inviting him up to Madison, inviting myself to his farm. "Any time," I wrote, willing to let work and studies go.

Finally he replied. "I'm really busy right now with some tough new patients." He was an orderly at the hospital where he'd worked as a conscientious objector. Now he was conscientiously objecting to me.

The dreary winter semester wore on. My music theory and

Romantic Era courses became drudgery. A masters in music? What was the point? But though Nino's Steak Roundup's sleazy manager had a crush on me, I held him off; there was no future in a boring restaurant job—and my psych degree wasn't worth much....

Then Mick showed up on my doorstep with his meek, alluring grin. "I thought it was time to butter you up." He pulled a handful of bright yellow flowers from behind him, and within the hour we were in bed. Afterwards I told myself it was that age-old attraction between two blazing Aries. What could I do? I'd been feeling blue; he chased my blues away. What was wrong with that?

But he came back and back, until I felt smothered by the too-easy sex, on guard for the disaster that lurked around the corner.

To release Mick's hold on me, I decided to leave Madison—where my options were running out, anyway. On a cold March morning, my life savings of $125 in my pocket and my mother's words, "You can always find a job," in mind, I boarded a Greyhound bus bound for Chicago. As I waited on the chilly seat for departure, Mick materialized at the open door. Frizzy red hair fanning over the fleece collar of his denim jacket, he charged down the aisle. "Why didn't you tell me?" he barked. "I don't want you to go!"

I had never seen him cry. I teared up myself and put my gloved hand on his. "I have to go...."

He grasped my forearms. "Please! *Stay!* Let's talk about this!" Nearby passengers gawked.

The driver's voice commanded, "All aboard!" The engine fired up.

"I'm *sorry.*" I gave Mick a quick hug and a little push.

He hurried off the bus, and I breathed a faltering sigh. Through the blurred window I watched him watch me. Then his intense, blue-gray eyes, his big mesomorph body and wild hair were gone.

8

Good in the Water

"Why'd you buy that bottle?" Russ is calm, but curious.

"I saw it on the shelf. My hand just went for it." Tim's words are leaden. He stares through half-mast eyes at the kitchen table. "I'm good for nothing."

I cup the back of his vulnerable shaved head like he's still my baby. "Not true. I'm just sorry this had to happen." My sixty-three-year-old heart is broken again, but I'm holding it together this time, because I know I must accept the things I cannot change.

Tim had informed us by email of his relapse, and Russ asked him to drive out and talk with us. He arrived drunk. I could always tell. "Not *very* drunk...," he mumbled. It's a warm May afternoon in northern Arizona, but he wears his black sweatshirt zipped up.

Before Tim arrived I reviewed my Program's Step 7, which says to humbly ask for help from the 'God of my understanding.' I closed my eyes, breathed deep, and asked the Universe to ward off worry. It was hovering again, this damnable anxiety that would creep back and back and grip my lungs and claw at my guts and compress my heart, if I allowed it—but I've prayed, and for now, the Universe has my back; I'm maintaining serenity.

Tim exhales a vocal trail of breath. "I blew everything again. *So fast*. I'm worthless."

After just two weeks his hard-won job and apartment are gone. I stroke his head. "You know the ropes now, don't you. It's rehab or the highway."

"I don't know if I can do rehab again...." He wags his head.

Russ is sympathetic. "It's your choice. There's nothing we can do except encourage you to go."

Like me, Russ keeps attending Program meetings, where we've learned to regard 'enabling' as anathema: We will not contribute to our son's wallowing in his illness—we're united on this.

"I know," Tim mumbles.

West Yavapai Guidance Clinic directs us to Hillside Recovery Center in our little town of Prescott. Tim's car is almost out of gas, so I pick him up at his place and drive him to the appointment. We enter one of the gray-green buildings and meet in a shabby office with the interviewing counselor, a friendly, long-haired, thirty-something woman who sits before a boxy old computer. "Are you drinking now?" she asks Tim.

"No." This is the truth. He's been sober the two days since he relapsed.

"Are you on AHCCCS?"

Thank God he qualified, and I've signed him up for this low-income Arizona health insurance, which pays all rehab expenses at Hillside. The kind counselor clicks into the computer the info needed to admit him. "I'm afraid you'll have to wait for a bed," she says. "It might be a couple of weeks."

As we leave I throw an arm around my son's shoulders. "Good work, Tim. You're back in business." He shrugs, but his admittance to Hillside has flooded me with hope for his recovery.

Driving Tim back to his place, I ponder my own recovery. Alcoholism is a 'family disease,' my Program says; it affects everyone in the family, so I must get better too—get over decades of "defects" I've identified in Step 4 of the Program: perfectionism, needing to control, anxiety, judgementalism, cynicism, superiority, inferiority—a long list of traits. I try to replace them with ones kinder to myself, and thus to others. I'm often *Aware* when one of my demon mind-habits pops up, and I can *Accept* it. I sometimes even *Act* to change my attitude. I'm mastering these three *A*'s; they're often automatic. I'm dealing with Tim's relapse calmly and with hope. I've grown since his first descent into Jose Cuervo hell.

But when I drop Tim at his studio apartment, which he must leave by Thursday, I am limp with sadness. I hug him goodbye and murmur, "Love you," then drive away crying. He'll get drunk now; how could he not? He's back at the scene of his relapse—it'll trigger him. How can he stay sober for two weeks waiting for a bed, hopeless as he is?

I stop by good friends Rob and Melinda's, hoping for solace. They aren't home, so I sit in their yard and gaze at their giant cottonwoods and fiery, dark-eyed California poppies. I close my eyes and breathe in, breathe out. Looking into the treetops I pray, "Please guide Tim on his journey."

On Thursday Tim comes to stay with us as he waits for a place at Hillside. Bored and at loose ends, he smokes cigarettes on the porch, but he does not drink. He is polite and cordial. Russ and I go about our business; we're at ease with Tim's presence. We pay him to clean up the yard and paint the porch. I tell friends proudly, "He detoxed himself this time."

It takes three weeks for a place to open up at Hillside. Tim moves in.

♫

"We'll be miles away in the Midwest when he gets out of rehab. How will we arrange for another sober house?" I'm stashing socks and running shoes in the bottom of the carry-on roller bag for our road trip. "He won't have any money!"

"He'll figure it out," Russ says. "He's almost twenty-three."

But we're not allowed to communicate with Tim before we leave on our long summer drive. My stomach knots with worry. At a Program meeting I say, "We'll be two thousand miles away before he's even allowed to make calls! What if he needs something?"

After the meeting, Roxanne, a tall and classy Program vet, is adamant. "This is meant to be. The perfect opportunity to let go and let God. Leave Tim to his journey."

"But how will we—"

She shakes her head. "Time to detach with love again, Mom. Go. Take your own journey. Have fun."

We sail through fifteen states in twenty-one days, visiting family and friends, museums and parks. I text and email daughter Holly, who is house-sitting for us back home.

"We're in Little Rock. I went to a good Program meeting last night. Visited Little Rock Central High today. Attaching a photo. How's Rumble?" Our thirteen-year-old greyhound has melanoma but is still going strong. We've opted for him to live out his life without surgery. "Thx for walking him." I hope she does, but anyway I'm sure he'll be fine when we get home. "Love you."

I manage not to fret about Tim until Michigan. We're in Mackinaw City, where we'll spend the night, having ferried that day to picturesque—but tourist-ridden—Mackinaw Island and back. On a carriage ride, it occurs to me that Tim has only one more week of rehab. Over fried fish that night at a local café I ask Russ, "Think we should check in with Tim's counselor? She said we could call her. We still don't know where he'll go when he gets out...."

"Go ahead, if you want." I envy Russ his nonchalance.

I consent to having dessert if we can share a piece of apple pie. Then as Russ waits for the check, I go outside and leave Kim a message. "Just wondering how things are going with Tim. Want to make sure you know we'll pay for a sober house when he gets out of Hillside. You can call us...."

Light shines through a silvery sky the next morning as we drive over the five-mile span of Mackinac Bridge—which I'd been over once before, as a kid, when it was new. Dad was driving, looking off into the blue so much I was afraid he'd steer us into the drink. No such fear this time.

In Escanaba, an old industrial town on the tip of Michigan's Upper Peninsula, we climb the stairs of a historic lighthouse. We spend the night in a cheap motel in town, and the next day we are in Wisconsin, my homeland. We drive west across the lake-laden top of the state to my sister Chrissie's home in the woods near the little tourist town of Hayward. Chrissie and Craig feed us barbecued chicken, and we settle in. The next day Russ and I attend a Program meeting in town.

These meetings for families and friends of alcoholics are everywhere—upwards of 30,000 weekly meetings world-wide. Wisconsin is prime territory, with its bleak winters and bars and all those famous beers. I drank more than my share of Pabst and Schlitz and Leinenkugels back in the day—just lucky I don't have the gene or penchant for alcoholism.

The morning meeting we attend in Hayward has its own building they call a "club"; as we meet, alcoholics and addicts convene down the hall in another room. The eight of us family-and-friends are cozy in cushioned chairs around the perimeter of the little book-lined space. The leader welcomes us out-of-town visitors. Then she reads a selection from the literature about "letting go and letting God"—just what Roxanne counseled before we left—and about how focusing on a pleasant concrete image could help one do that.

When her turn comes a young woman with a baby on her lap says, "Jeff drank his way though deer-hunting season last year, then never stopped. This week he lost his job." Her eyes are sad as she joggles the baby. "I don't know what we'll do. But I can picture all three of us wrapped in our fleece camouflage blanket, all warm and protected by my Higher Power, and I feel safe—for now." She wipes spit-up from her baby's mouth with a tissue. "And we've still got big hunks of deer meat in the freezer."

By the time the circle gets to me I've come up with an image of Tim and me and Russ and Holly snorkeling in the warm, buoyant waters off the island of St. John, as we did when we lived there. I share the picture, then add, "Tim's always been good in the water; he knows how to stay afloat. Why should I worry?"

Water, air, the ground we walk, it's all of a piece. I can let the Universe take care of Tim and everything else. Driving away from the meeting, I feel washed free of fear.

Back at Chrissie's I get a call from Kim. "Tim's doing really well. He's looking at some sober houses in town."

"We'll pay the rent, if there's a way."

"It'll work out."

The next day we head west, crossing the Mississippi where it's just a trickle making its way through lush greenery in northern Minnesota. We stop to take photos.

Then as I'm riding, worry seizes me in the chest again: I still don't know how we'll get Tim the money to pay for a place. "What if he has nowhere to go? He'll drink!"

Russ says, "No use worrying."

I take deep breaths, pray, and imagine Tim swimming in the warm sea. I'm okay.

A few more days down the road we arrive at my sister Carol's house in Colorado, and I find a message in Kim's clear voice. "All's well here. Tim's settled in at Providence House."

Not a word about paying. Apparently no problem. Kim has sprouted angel wings. I settle into serenity for the rest of the trip.

"Hillside was way better than Chandler Valley Hope," Tim says.

We're standing on the sidewalk in front of Providence House the day after we get home. A patch of scraggly grass covers the front yard. The house is old, smallish and two-story, with a steep gabled roof. It's on the low-rent end of Mount Vernon Street, but from the front it looks much like its rich historical-register cousins a few blocks away. "So how was Hillside better?" I ask as Tim leads us up the sidewalk to the front porch.

"The counselors were really honest. There was more discipline, I guess."

I'd seen the daily schedule, thick with mandatory exercise and meetings and counseling sessions. No communal lounge, no visits from outsiders, no calls. So that's what he needs: more structure, more rules. I should have been a stricter, more attentive parent back in the day.... But there's no changing the past. Now I see it's better that Tim was out of touch with us for his entire month of treatment.

He opens the door to a small, plain hallway. "I probably shouldn't have you in here, but nobody else is home. Damien won't care." We follow him into a room at the right which he shares with another guy; it has two single beds and a window. "There's our bathroom." He points to the small room off the corner. I can see his electric shaver lying on a corner shelf, its cord dangling.

It registers with me that Tim has changed. He seems more relaxed, more self-possessed. He looks me in the eye. I think he may be taller. His new presence warms my heart. "I like your place." I give him a sideways hug. "No computer?"

"Not allowed."

Different from Step One, his first post-rehab place. There's a strict curfew at Providence, too. Tim has to prove he goes to meetings, which he seems to appreciate now; he even has a sponsor. He must have approved reasons for wherever else he goes, can't be out for long, has to look for work. And blessedly, the place is much less expensive than Step One.

Providence house recommends three months' stay as a minimum. Tim spent the full twenty-eight days at Hillside; maybe he'll stick it out at the sober house, too—but there's nothing I can do to assure that.

Of course I want my kids to be well and happy, but how they run their young adult lives is not my business. I'm finally catching on. Tim is recovering from this disease, which warrants attention, like any illness. But with this one—so "cunning and baffling," as someone at a meeting said—the attention must be to my own *dis-ease* of fretting and controlling. The only way to help Tim is to help myself, and let him deal with his disease. Though Russ and I live just ten miles away from Providence House and are in town often, we see little of Tim and don't communicate with him much while he's there. We pay the rent from his dwindling education fund and mostly let him be, unless he calls.

In September, he's been at Providence for two months when he drives out for a visit. He sits at the kitchen table—not in his usual place at the back, but closer to me, where I stand chopping carrots at the counter. "I'm not single any more," he says.

"Oh?" I glance at him, then return to chopping.

Turns out he met this girl named Haley on a dating site—he's allowed to use computers at the library—and she lives two hours north in Flagstaff. Though Providence House rules don't allow consorting with the opposite sex, he's met Haley on weekends at a midpoint near Sedona. "I told Damien I was visiting you guys," he says, sheepish.

"So what's that mean, you're 'not single'?" I chop the last carrot.

"We're boyfriend-girlfriend."

So they've had sex.

Introverted as Tim has always been, he's not a virgin; he let Russ know that long ago. And by now, daughter Holly's probably had sex with her long-time boyfriend Rick. My kids' volume of sexual experiences put together can't hold a candle to that of mine at their ages. In this realm I'm not their model, thank God.

I gather the carrots in the center of the cutting board. "What about the no-relationship rule at Providence?"

"Haley supports my program, so yeah, we're gonna cool it for awhile."

I slide the carrots into my pan of Caribbean chicken on the stove.

Over dinner we learn Haley is seven years older than Tim and has a ten-year-old daughter. Haley teaches full-time at Northern Arizona University. She's a vegetarian and has seven cats.

"Interesting," Russ says.

Tim calls a couple of weeks later, in October. "I'm in Flagstaff. I'm moving in with Haley." He sounds breathless, excited. "I'll call you guys in a while. Just wanted to let you know."

So he spent almost the recommended three months in Providence House, and now he's moving to Flagstaff.

"Wow," I say.

9

A Bigger Happiness

In the spring of '72, two weeks into my new Chicago life, a letter came from Madison. Mick Chase wrote, "Can we be friends?"

After days spent on my own, hunting down an apartment and a job, I was lonely and exhausted. Then I turned a quarter-century old in my bare new place, bereft of friends or festivity. Mick's spare handwriting evoked a longing for him. Living three hours apart, maybe we could salvage a safe, soothing friendship from the wreckage of our three-year affair. "I'm free next weekend," I wrote back.

He arrived on a bright Friday afternoon in April, and that night we made love with abandon, rekindling the best of our past.

Through my courtyard window, an overcast Saturday arrived. We dragged ourselves from bed, pulled on shirts and jeans and headed out for a walk. As we ambled along the shore of Lake Michigan, Mick launched into the sort of witty discourse that had dazzled me in the past: "So, Eileen, you heard the one about the three generals in Vietnam, right? One day this marine was...." But his words morphed into background noise, and all I heard was his anxiety; he must have sensed my detachment. Struck by sympathy, I chuckled and nodded now and then, prolonging his compulsive ramblings.

Arm-in-arm on the way back, we stopped at my mailbox. I fished out an envelope and couldn't stifle a murmur of pleasure at the return address: Tom Kelly, in Rockford. Mick saw it too. He let go of my arm.

Upstairs I laid the letter aside and turned on my little AM/FM radio to Elton John singing "Rocket Man." I opened a couple of beers, and we ate tuna salad sandwiches. When Mick went to the bathroom, I sliced into Tom's letter and pored over his words.

As Mick returned I shoved the letter back into its envelope—but he jerked it from my hand and threw it. "What the fuck do you want with *him?*" He grabbed me by the shoulders. The back of my head hit the multi-paned French doors of my closet, splattering glass.

Mick stooped to pick up shards of the broken pane. Then, like an afterthought, he glanced up. "You okay?"

"Yeah." I touched my head. No blood, no pain. Just shattered hopes.

On the radio Carole King sang "It's Too Late." I gathered our plates and empty beer bottles and called from the kitchen: "This isn't working, Mick."

He hitched back to Madison that afternoon.

♫

Tom's letter was an invitation to visit him—finally!

We walked in the woods on his farm and talked and took photos of each other in our surprisingly similar leather-fringed jackets. We played with Buck, his big tan mutt, and listened to Arlo Guthrie and John Prine. We had sex and cuddled in his old four-poster bed as breeze wafted through gauzy curtains. For breakfast he made his signature soft-scrambled eggs.

On the Greyhound back to Chicago I stared at flat, endless plowed fields.

Tom never wrote. Within months I learned through my old college grapevine that he'd married some ordinary, boring girl back in Eau Claire. My romance-filled dreams floated up and away and dissolved into gray skies.

But my studio apartment above a grassy, brick-lined courtyard in New Town was often filled with light. Half-way down West Buckingham, my place was close to Lincoln Park, with its bike path along the lake. On days off from my nurse's aide job at Traemour Sheltered Care Home, I rode my bike, baked bread, and walked to Broadway to wash clothes in the bright, steamy Laundromat. One Saturday Nate Collins' eyes caught mine as I extricated bras and panties from the washer. Aiming a one-sided smile at me, he slowly separated wet blue jeans and threw them into a dryer. Adult and kid-size jeans, I noticed, but he wore no wedding band. He saw me looking.

We sat together and watched clothes spin. "I do all the laundry," he told me. "For me and my son—my sister and her daughter, too." There was that languorous smile again. I smiled back. "We live just down here on West Buckingham." A block from me, it turned out. As we folded clothes, he drawled, "I never wear underwear. Cuts down on laundry." His laugh clinked pleasingly, like bamboo wind chimes.

I was soon enjoying sex with this laid-back guy, and hanging out with him and his three-year-old boy Liam. Sometimes Nate's sister Sarah and her daughter Megan joined us. We played dominos; we tossed a Frisbee in the park; we bought ice cream cones. But the more at home I felt, the more I sensed the exclusive nature of Nate's clan. When I'd drop by, he'd say he was busy—or Sarah would.

Within a month, without a word, Nate and Liam left Chicago. "He's headed west. I'm not sure where he'll end up," Sarah said. A few days later she and Megan were gone, too.

Neither the company of my two cats nor my radio at full-blast could dispel the loneliness that hung over my place.

I spent a couple of nights with some pony-tailed guy I met bike-riding in the park. But when Jim Katsaros smiled at me in the Cloverleaf bar on Halstead, Pony Tail was history.

Fine-featured, lanky and sociable, "Jimmy the Greek" seemed at home in his own skin and everywhere outside it. We spent a few easy weeks together, playing pool, listening to music, having sex. He let me drive his big old car. At a Johnny Cash concert, we drank Wild Turkey and danced in the aisle.

When Jimmy invited me to make love with him and his buddy Dale at the same time, we broke up. With his outlandish proposition, Jimmy had crossed the line.

I was alone again, on the prowl for the next man.

Shibboleths of the '60's sexual revolution might explain my promiscuity: "Make love, not war," and "love the one you're with." As an Arizona woman-friend of my vintage says, "Everybody was doing it." And Dr. Goldberg had exhorted me to "have fun, as long as you don't hurt anybody."

But it wasn't all fun. I was anxious—in the grip of an unquenchable longing. Was I a love addict? I fit twenty-first century descriptions: attracted to emotionally-unavailable, avoidant partners; replacing real intimacy with melodrama and roller-coaster passions; driven by the fantastic hope that my drug of choice, *men*, could complete me....

It would take me years to realize that until I embraced my own entire, flawed, lovable self, no man could love me enough, nor I him.

"Want to go west?"

Beth Adler called in August of '72, a few months after Mick Chase's disastrous visit. I hadn't heard from her in months. A friend from my college days, she had earned a degree in biology, as useless as my psych degree. "Paul and Keith live in Arizona now, you know. We could go see them. I'll drive."

Paul, my handsome friend from Bud's Bar and Grill in Eau Claire, had visited me in Madison the year before to tell me he was gay. We'd exchanged a letter or two since, but I didn't know he'd left Wisconsin. It would be good to see him again.

My Chicago workdays as a nurse's aide were long and hard for little pay, my nights and weekends lonely despite occasional trysts. Still a country girl, I'd never come to tolerate the hard, earth-to-sky concrete nature of the big city, nor its constant thunder-rush of traffic. Summer was slipping away, and I feared spending winter there.

Beth and I camped our way west, and by October we were settled with two cats, hers and mine, in a cheap little adobe house on Roosevelt Street in Phoenix. We found jobs, she testing things in Petri dishes for bacteria, I as an administrative secretary for a daycare center. We also found sexy, pot-smoking Mexican boyfriends who lived in a big yellow house across the street. Alejandro proudly showed me a picture of himself holding his cherubic baby; he and the baby's young mother weren't together. I'd never been on a waterbed before, and the rhythmic sloshing during our lovemaking lulled me like ocean waves.

One weekend Beth and I drove to Tucson, where we met a couple of young hippie guys in a bar; we went home to bed with them. When they visited Phoenix, our straight-laced neighbors, apparently disapproving of our long-haired guests, called the cops on us.

We let the two policemen in that night without a warrant. They hand-cuffed us in the living room, me to Beth, the two guys to each other. Then they pulled out drawers and ransacked cupboards and containers. One cop strode in from the back porch with a small, shriveled plant. "I think we got 'em, Gary," he said to his partner, who lounged in our recliner. Beth and I smirked: Not-Gary held a dried-up tomato plant. But he found the lid of grass Beth had tried to hide in the bathroom. Then Gary pried open my gold pillbox with the enameled rose on top, an heirloom from my godmother, Aunt Bertha. The little box held marijuana roaches.

They drove the four of us off in two police cars for finger-printing, mug shots and jail. On the way into the gray block building, Beth and I gazed at the sky, not sure when we'd see it again. We called in sick with our one-phone-calls and spent the night in a bleak room with rough-talking women in bunk beds. One eyed my embroidered bell bottoms. "You don' look like you belong here, honey." Later that night she was administered a methadone shot by a nurse.

The next morning a female warden called our names. "You're

free to go."

We were back at work the following day. No lasting consequences, though I never got my little pillbox back.

Old boyfriends visited from Wisconsin, and I had a fling with a handsome, Apache-looking Mexican who dropped his kids at the mission daycare where I worked. He taught me Spanish: *Yo te quiero*—I love you—but like all the rest, this relationship didn't stick. Miguel was married.

My mother rarely called, so when I heard her voice on the phone in December I knew it was important. "Grandma died yesterday." She meant her mother, Grandma Welch, my favorite. "Her neighbor Mort found her sitting in front of the TV with her hands folded." Announced like some flat, ordinary fact; it hardly registered. "You don't need to come home for the funeral. You're working. It's too much time and money."

She asked about my life in Phoenix, and I fed her details of my job, the weather, my travels. Silence. Then Mom's voice, tentative: "Are you happy?"

I felt blind-sided. "Yeah, of course I'm happy, sometimes. I'm not ecstatic every minute, if that's what you mean." Not happy enough to please her, it seemed.

After Mom's call I went to my closet for the '40's-style, floor-length, white seersucker lounging dress I often wore around the house. It had been Grandma Welch's. Bordered with pink roses and green leaves, flared and snug-waisted, it fit me perfectly. I slipped it on, then sank onto my bed and gathered the hem of the soft skirt to my eyes to absorb the tears.

Two days later a Christmas card arrived from Grandma with some dollar bills tucked inside. I stared through blurred eyes at her cheerful words.

Grandma Welch was gone. Her African violets, her hot porridge made just for me for breakfast, the distant sound of trains through her spare bedroom window, all vanished. I had only her lounging dress, and it was becoming threadbare.

My mother's question had piqued me: There *was* a bigger happiness out there, the kind I knew she sensed I didn't have, damn her—the kind I longed for.

But the sky was always blue in Phoenix, the air clean and crisp. My sinuses cleared of their perennial stuffiness. And December in Phoenix felt like May in Wisconsin. My parents sent an eight-track tape player for Christmas, and Stevie Wonder's "You Are the Sunshine of my Life" became the theme song of my days. Never mind the lack of an actual "you"; the sunshine was for real.

Beth and I became vegetarians and baked whole-grain bread. We visited Wisconsin friends Paul and Keith, who lived past the rocky hills of Papago Park in Tempe, the nearby college town. We explored our corner of Arizona in Beth's blue VW bug, and I learned to love subtle colors in beige landscapes.

I rode my bike across the 7th Avenue Bridge to my pleasant daycare center job. Sometimes I'd stop on the way home and play the piano in the sanctuary of a tall-spired church whose door was never locked.

Beth was not as fond of her job as I was of mine. When the weather heated up in June, Paul and Keith moved to California, and Beth soon followed them, leaving me behind. I went back to my folks' house in Wisconsin to figure out my future.

Within a week, a letter arrived. "San Diego is the Garden of Eden," Beth wrote. "You'd love it here."

In Grandma Welch's dress

Phoenix, AZ - 1971

10

Getting a Life

By the time I got to San Diego, Beth had a one-bedroom apartment high on Laurel Street overlooking the bay, and a job making macramé belts and plant hangers. I stayed with her for a few days until I found a job and my own place.

San Diego's balmy, sub-tropical climate was mood-lifting. Lush lantana and hibiscus spilled onto sidewalks. Beth and I walked and biked and saw each other often. We partied with our old Wisconsin friends most weekends.

But my weekday minimum-wage job at Casa Blanca Nursing Home was tough— comprised of spoon-feeding and changing diapers on profoundly-retarded adults. I would ride the bus home to my dark, tie-dye-curtained apartment in an alley off 34th Street, pop open a beer, and howl with Linda Rondstadt's "When Will I Be Loved." Like my upstairs back-porch view criss-crossed by a tangle of power lines, my life was in disarray.

"I know you got a big...black...snake up there...."

Three loud thumps sounded through the floor.

Bob sat up in bed beside me. "What the fuck?"

"It's Frank. He's just drunk. Pounding with a broom or something."

More slurred, hellish words rumbled from the apartment below mine: "You like that big black snake, don't'cha?…." *Thump, thump, thump.*

"Jesus Christ." Bob stood up naked and stomped on the floor. "Shut your crazy ass up!" *Stomp, stomp, stomp.*

The devil's raging petered out for the time being, and Bob and I went back to sleep.

Bob Wilson, a tall high school counselor with two masters degrees and a bulldog, was my first San Diego boyfriend and my first black lover. I'd met him in Balboa Park soon after my move to 34th Street. I lay in cut-offs, reading on the grass; he reined in his bulldog and smiled. "Nice legs." That night at his sparse apartment he locked the dog in a spare room. "Can't have Max botherin' me when I'm takin' care of business." Business was quick and hard and soon over for us both. After that first time, he'd call late and pop over for sex, spend a short night, and get up and out early for work.

I knew I wouldn't stay with Bob. We never went out. All we did was drink beer and joke around and have sex. Once, as he bore on beneath me during the act, he groaned, "Tell me I'm your man." No way was I saying that; it wasn't true. I held my hand over his mouth and carried on.

Like the Bufferin that banished my occasional headaches, Bob took away the acute pain of loneliness. But a chronic ache persisted.

To cheer things up I planted flowers in the little strip of dirt near the bottom of my stairs. The flowers grew scraggly and died. I painted my kitchen robin's-egg blue—a shade too dark, it turned out. The apartment was gloomier than ever, and Frank's drunken night-time tirades became more disquieting. I decided to move.

My new place was perched on a hill on sunny Georgia Street. The downstairs of a little house, it had lace curtains and a picture window for plants. Balboa Park was a five-minute walk away. I found myself a better-paying, easier job with the March of Dimes. I adopted Sadie, a black cat, and cracked a window open for her to come and go. I began baking bread again and spending fewer nights with Bob.

Bob had told me up-front that he had an ex-wife, two kids, and a vasectomy. "Sometimes they grow back," he'd warned, but I went off the pill, thinking it would do my body good.

When I learned I was pregnant I holed up in my new house and didn't tell Bob. I would never marry him, and I wasn't about to raise a baby on my own. "We can set you up for an abortion," my kind gynecologist, Dr. Klein, said. "A *D & C*—dilation and curettage. It's very safe. You'll be fine in a couple of days." MediCal would pay.

The procedure was set for a Friday. As I boarded the bus to work that week, my hand went lightly to my abdomen. I was less than two months pregnant, but my jeans felt tight. Walking down the aisle, I sensed other passengers must know, from some glow I was emitting. I'd heard of this effect: I felt special, Madonna-like....

But I had no choice. Giving birth, then putting a baby up for adoption, was unthinkable. I couldn't hide away somewhere; I had to work. My stomach would grow huge; people would know, and the truth would come out: I had no partner, wasn't married, was going to give the baby away. *Shame!*

On Friday a hospital nurse pointed me to a bed. As she turned to go she muttered, "There ought to be a law...." I cried silently as I waited in my flimsy gown. But soon I was sedated, then awake and home in my own bed under the gold brocade bedspread Mom had given me when I moved to San Diego.

On Saturday I dragged myself up, put on Grandma's lounging dress and ate some yogurt. Then, tears clouding my eyes, I walked slowly down the block toward tall eucalyptus trees, cradling Sadie in my arms.

♫

With Ian things were different. Again pregnancy came as a shock—a rubber had slipped, we figured—but now I knew the ropes. Ian agreed that we couldn't have a baby. "I'll be here for you, Baby-cakes."

Dr. Klein said, "We haven't taken good enough care of you." Did he think he and I both should have had a better plan for birth control? His words allayed the guilt I'd heaped up with this second offense. He set me up for another D & C.

Afterwards, Ian made poached eggs on milk toast for me in my kitchen. He kept his arm around me as I ate.

By the time I'd met Ian Burns I was a full-time student at San Diego State, studying for a teaching degree while working part-time at the March of Dimes. Ian was taking horticulture classes at the community college and collecting unemployment. A sensuous Scorpio to my fiery Aries, both of us wiry and energetic, we meshed in and out of bed. He was gentle and appreciative. He complimented my cooking, my body, the way I lived my life. Like me, he was interested in music and books and plants. I loved that he called me Baby-cakes.

After the abortion we gave up our apartments and moved into a little house in Hillcrest. We'd known each other for three months. I called my mother. "I think I'm going to marry this guy."

"Are you sure? This seems pretty sudden."

What did she know? We would live together first. That would be the test, and I knew we'd pass.

We stationed Ian's wooden rocker in the living room and bought a second-hand couch. We varnished one end of an electrical cable spool for a headboard on our bed, then threw on the gold brocade bedspread from Mom. Ian put Sadie's cat food beside cans of beans and tomato sauce in the kitchen cupboard.

During our second week together, we painted the living room walls. Ian put on my favorite album, by Three Dog Night; I filled our coffee cups and set them nearby. A half-hour into the job, my foot hit the paint pan and a dab of the off-white paint spilled onto the beige carpet. "Oops."

"You idiot!" Ian's face contorted.

I gasped, reached for my coffee cup and clutched it to my chest.

"Watch what you're doing!" Ian pushed my shoulder.

Propelled by reflex, I threw my coffee at him. We backed apart. Three Dog Night sang "Mama Told Me Not to Come."

Ian wiped the dab of cold coffee from his face with a sleeve. "I'm sorry." As I grappled to fathom my own reaction, he returned to his gentle self. "I shouldn't've yelled." He ran water on a rag and began scrubbing the carpet as Three Dog Night blared on.

The following week I made a big pot of chili. We were eating it with slabs of my homemade bread when Ian told me he wasn't going to horticulture classes any more. "They're useless. I know more than the teachers do."

After supper he turned from washing dishes and scowled at me. "You put poison in my chili, didn't you?"

Now he reminded me of my disturbed psych-ward mates of years before. Something was wrong. Were issues from his past causing paranoia or something? He'd lost touch with his adoptive parents, both doctors.... "He's acting weird," I told Beth.

"They're all weird." Beth was involved with a Mexican from Tijuana. "I have no clue what Jose is up to half the time. But the sex is great." She would eventually marry Jose and have his child. When he became abusive she would divorce him.

I began tiptoeing around Ian. To avoid him, I stayed out later after school or work, studying or visiting with friends.

One afternoon I walked into the darkened living room to find him in his rocker, his head in a cloud of marijuana, listening to Steely Dan. I felt his eyes on me as I tossed my books onto the table, opened the fridge and drew out a beer. As I sat on the couch his look bored into me. "You're having an affair with that guy in the antiques place, aren't you?"

I set my beer down. "What? Both those guys are gay."

"And Beth. You sleep with her, too, don't you?"

I left Ian brooding in his rocker and called a crisis line.

The next morning we sat with a counselor in his office in a big old house. Like a burst dam, I spilled out details of Ian's paranoid episodes as my recently-beloved boyfriend stared at the wall.

The counselor peered over his reading specs and spoke gently to Ian. "You can talk to someone here, if you want."

Ian shrugged.

I told the counselor Ian scared me. "He keeps accusing me of things."

"What can you do about your fear?"

I glanced at Ian, who looked away. "I think I have to break

up with him." I pulled a tissue from the nearby box and wiped my eyes.

On the way out Ian said, "You're having an affair with that guy, aren't you?"

When my friend Jill drove me in her truck that afternoon to help me move, we found my belongings strewn over the front lawn: boxes of clothes and books and dishes beneath sheets and my gold brocade bedspread, Sadie hiding under the porch. As Jill and I loaded the stuff, I saw Ian spying on us from behind a curtain. I coaxed Sadie to me from under the house, and we drove away.

♫

Despite my bungled love life, I completed the rigorous project requirements for a year-long experimental program for teacher training at San Diego State, and in June of '75, at the age of twenty-eight, I had my California teaching credential, good for life.

My first contract said "Teacher, Music and Resources, K through 8." On the phone my mother said, "Well, congratulations! Dad says you're really going to do it this time"—meaning *get a life,* I figured. "We're happy for you."

I had avoided following in my mother's teacher-footsteps the first time around, dropping out of stodgy education classes in Wisconsin to pursue a psych degree. Now I'd become a teacher after all, just like Mom—by default? I'd pursued the only avenue I saw to a profession with decent pay.

I bought my parents' old beige VW for the move two hours east of San Diego to the dusty, sunken cropland of California's Imperial Valley. I loaded my new car, plopped Sadie in the front seat and dragged my baggage to Calipatria, California—the "lowest-down city in the Western Hemisphere."

♫

If I were lucky, my professional life might soon fall into place. But in my late twenties, I was still a failure at relationships. Even if I pulled off this teacher thing, did I have a crack at a decent love life? I hadn't yet met a man I could abide with.

I knew some reasons. I had no brothers, and my father was a mystery man. Deaf, sensitive, and withdrawn, Dad seldom made his thoughts or feelings known. In those ways, minus the deafness, I was much like him; we rarely talked. Since he never ate eggs, I believed for years that men didn't eat eggs.

I'd wanted to be close to my father, but he eluded me. When he started giving my younger sisters shoulder rides around the living room, making them squeal and laugh, I begged for a ride, but he said I was too big. A scrawny 5th grader who wouldn't start filling out for years—how was I too big?

Once during a youth-group roller skating trip, Dad glided silently with me around the wooden floor, his strong arm bracing my back, my hand in his. Filled with self-conscious delight, I barely breathed.

When I was a kid, males of the species were as foreign and fascinating to me as the far-off countries on maps in my geography book. Longing for boys' attention but tongue-tied in their presence, I shied away. For years in high school I pined secretly for the Baptist minister's son, who was tall, brown-haired, and skinny, like my dad. I dreamed of kissing Robert—but I avoided him in the halls. I never had a date in high school.

I made up for lost time in my twenties, had plenty of "dates"—but to what end?

Perhaps teaching would improve my love life.

11

The Universe of the Tile Floor

Tim reaches for his guitar. Though not given to performing, he sits on the couch near his favorite aunt and picks out a delicate riff. Nancy's brother Russ, her partner Ken, and I, her sister-in-law, sit nearby.

Nancy's voice is soft. "Did you write that?"

"Yeah. It's based on a poem by Rilke," Tim says. "'Let everything happen to you.... No feeling is final.' Remember? You gave me the book."

"Ohh...." Nancy smiles and reaches a tremulous hand toward Tim.

Nancy plays flute and piano herself. A retired teacher, she travels, entertains, works for social justice, exercises, reads and writes. She is an insatiable learner. She's managed her Parkinson's amazingly well, become more active and engaged with life than ever.

As she listens to Tim she sits propped by pillows, feebly nibbling soda crackers.

Tim had driven down from Flagstaff and rode south with me and Russ to Nancy's home in Mesa. An hour into the drive we approached Sunset Point, the rest area between Prescott and Phoenix, where paths of native shrubs and cactus—and multilayered mountain views—make it a popular stop. I turned from the passenger seat to Tim in back. He extracted his ear buds and I quizzed him on his new life with Haley in Flagstaff. "It's good," he said. "I applied everywhere for a job, but it's hard to get one. I might go to school. Haley'll help. She's really supportive. She's got more experience than me but it doesn't feel like she's seven years older."

The flow of words evoked the sound of his babbling in his crib as he grew strong and healthy his first year with us in Africa: Lyrical and free of care, it fell easy on my ear.

"Right now I do a lot of housework. Wash dishes and floors, clean cat litter. The cats are cool, though. Caffrey's our favorite... I'm learning to cook vegetarian food. Some weeks I cook more than Haley does."

His voice meandered on, light-filled. I prompted him with questions to keep the lyrics coming as we sailed past Sunset Point and began the winding, Saguaro-lined descent into the Valley.

♫

Nancy was there twenty-two years before when Tim was handed to us off the plane, a scant, sick bundle of year-old flesh and bone from India. Russ and I spent that first night with our new son at Nancy's Chicago apartment, taking turns holding, feeding, cuddling him. She held his tiny body upright next to her birdcage and pointed. "This is Tweets. Tweets, meet Tim. Tweets likes you. See? He's singing for you." She slept on the couch that night as our fragile, fledgling family of three occupied her double bed.

The next week, when Russ took off to start work at our school in Africa and I still had maternity leave, Nancy was an angel. She came down to our Bloomington, Illinois, house and helped me care for Tim as he recovered from malnutrition and pneumonia.

We'd put in for a "healthy" child. The last photo we received from the orphanage showed a smiling baby with spindly arms and a full belly. They'd done their best. But we hadn't bargained for the immediate hospital stay, doctor visits and medicines. The physical needs made the intense task of caring for and bonding with our displaced, emotionally-bereft baby even more consuming.

I got some breaks that week as Nancy carried Tim, fed him, played with him. Together we pushed him in his stroller to the park, held him on the swing and slide, coaxed smiles, watched him strengthen. "What a fine baby you are," Nancy told him, and kissed him goodbye as she left.

Through the years, she wrote to Tim and talked to him one-on-one about philosophy, religion, music, life. She gave him money and presents, kept after him to perform on guitar despite his shyness. She believed in him, encouraged him to be his best self. He wore her friendship bracelet on his wrist until it fell apart.

Now in her living room, Tim continues strumming mellow tunes for his aunt. I lie on the rug and stroke eighteen-year-old Speedy, my favorite of Ken and Nancy's three cats. Despite his superabundance of years, Speedy is full of life; he splays himself upside down and purrs. Russ and Ken look on and listen, sipping drinks. Nancy sits, eyes closed, a faint smile on her lips. She nods to Tim's music until she dozes off into the pillows.

When we leave, Tim hugs her long and gently. I hear the "I love you's."

Settled in the back seat for the ride to Prescott, Tim looks up from his texting. "I won't see Nancy again, will I."

♫

Nancy weakens rapidly. She's lying in a hospital bed at home, and hospice comes. Our daughter Holly drives up from Tucson for Nancy's wedding—she and Ken had been planning to marry; it's now or never.

A hospice caregiver bathes Nancy and combs her hair. Her sister Mary and I dress the bride in Ken's white T-shirt, pulling her frail limbs through the sleeves like she's a flimsy-limbed doll. Nancy wears a white rose corsage; her blue hospital socks are "something blue"; Ken has bought rings. We arrange Nancy upright on her bed and swathe her loosely in a white sheet, waist to calves, going for a modicum of style and modesty without restricting the involuntary movement of her legs. Then, as Ken sits in a chair holding his bride's hand, I play the traditional Wedding March from *Lohengrin* on Nancy's spinet piano.

The minister asks Nancy to squeeze Ken's hand for "I do." Ken says later that she didn't; she was out of it at the moment. But the deed is done as Nancy would want, the hour filled with family, friends, music and food. "You're an old married lady now," I tell her, sitting close. She's sixty-seven; this is her first marriage. She graces me with a tiny smile of comprehension.

Tim hasn't come down for the impromptu wedding; he said goodbye during his visit the week before. Now it's Holly's turn. Before she returns to Tucson she sits tearful at Nancy's bedside, holding her hand. Nancy drifts in and out, can't speak, can barely listen. "She squeezed my hand sometimes, though," Holly says.

The celebration of life is held at Nancy's spiritual home, Chandler Valley UU Church. In a pew near the front of the tall white sanctuary, I have an arm around each of my kids. Russ is on the other side of Holly near his remaining siblings, Roy and Mary; all are wiping tears from their eyes. During the service I play "Come Thou Fount of Every Blessing," a piano piece I know Nancy liked, and a UU friend of hers sings "Somewhere Over the Rainbow." The congregation holds hands and sways as we sing Nancy's favorite hymn, "Blue Boat Home," sending music to the rafters.

During the public sharing, people tell fond memories of Nancy. I share a story of my own: "When I learned she hadn't washed her hair for weeks, I offered to do it. She propelled herself through the house and out to the patio, sometimes on hands and knees—she wanted to get there on her own. Then I helped her lie down on the table. I supported her head and took my time washing and massaging and rinsing; the water ran off into the gravel as she 'oohed' and 'ahed.' When I put the towel on, she said, 'You're good at this. Have you ever thought of working for hospice?' That's just how she was." People chuckled in agreement.

Afterwards Tim tells me, "I thought about saying something. I would've said, 'A bright star, burned out too soon.'"

"Nice. Sounds like lyrics to a song."

More than once after Nancy's autumn death and memorial service I think of what Tim said of his aunt—"A bright star, burned out too soon"—and I am grateful *his* bright star still burns.

He's coming down from Flagstaff for Thanksgiving with Haley and her daughter Abby. We will finally meet. I've placed gold cottonwood leaves with their three names as place cards on plates along one side of the table, Abby in the middle.

Russ and I are outside to greet them. Haley steps from Tim's car into the bright, crisp air wearing leggings and a large knitted shawl. She is soft and full and light-haired to my flat, dark skinniness. She looks me in the eye and gives me a warm hug. Tim was right—she's an Earth Mother type. I give her hand a little squeeze. From the back seat she takes a potted purple-heart plant and offers it to me. "I always like to bring a gift."

Ten-year-old Abby bounces blonde and spritely from the car, shakes our hands, then spies our black cat, Metro, whom she trails across the drive. Tim and Haley hand things to each other from the car to bring in: vegetarian stuffing, a salad, baba ganoush.

Inside, Haley draws a flat white box with a red grosgrain ribbon from a bag and hands it to me—another gift. "Here's the pie. Organic pumpkin." She gazes around the house. "I love your plants."

Eight of us sit down at the table: me, Russ, Russ's brother Roy and sister Mary, Holly up from Tucson, and the three from Flagstaff. Abby leans on Tim and smiles, seems to adore him. Tim grins.

Over drinks and relishes we go around saying what we're thankful for. Nancy is named, and there are tears. Everyone is glad for family, friends and health. When it's their turns, both Haley and her bright-spark daughter say they're thankful for each other and for Tim. "I'm also thankful for the strong body that contains me," Haley says. I might have said that, too.

We've done this before at Thanksgiving, named things we're grateful for, and this year's list is ordinary. But for me the gratitude sinks deeper now. I've been to hell and back with Tim this year.

He's a survivor, and he's made one of me. Continued practice of my Program has embedded its precepts in my soul. I'm growing into my life—it fits me better.

We pass the salads, potatoes, turkey, cranberries, stuffing, and "Nancy's memorial tabouli," which her twin brother Roy has made. We eat and eat; we talk and laugh. I'm pleased to learn that Haley teaches *Communication Between Genders*, among other college classes—no wonder she relates well with Tim. We do another round of food, refill sparkling cider. Later we sit around the living room drinking coffee and eating pumpkin pie. I am full of good food and serenity.

As of November, 2010, Thanksgiving is my favorite holiday.

Christmas comes lightly, like the snow in our little town. I don't feel pressured to send cards, decorate, or bake—though at my leisure I accomplish each. Russ brings in the stepladder and the century-plant tree from the garage. As we watched it over years, this sprawling, spiked-leaf Arizona plant in the backyard matured and shot its flowered, fifteen-foot stalk into the sky. We cut it down with ceremony, and now at Christmas the stalk's stiff, skinny arms with their dry flower pods hold ornaments. I climb the stepladder to hang Mom's old glass globes, the Caribbean fish, my stars from India, the little African angels. I appreciate each one's history, color and design as it dangles in open space against the light. When Holly comes home from college in Tucson she admires the tree. She helps me decorate sugar cookies.

Between Christmas and New Year's, Tim calls to tell us he has applied at Northern Arizona University, where Haley teaches. Russ, Holly and I drive up to Flagstaff for a holiday visit. We take Tim and his new family out for lunch. Afterward, as we walk around the old downtown, sun shines through plump gray clouds on glistening snow. Back at Tim and Haley's we loll around the fireplace playing gin rummy and petting cats. I take a photo of Holly holding the new kitten, Lulu. "Lulu pees in the grates," Tim says. "It reeks. I'm always cleaning it up." This is revolutionary.

He never cleaned up anything. He grins and leaves the couch to make, serve, and refill coffee whose flavor and richness is every bit as good as Russ's: like father, like son.

As of December, 2010, Christmas rivals Thanksgiving as my favorite holiday.

♫

On an evening in mid-January Russ and I are on our way out of town, driving to a steak dinner at a friend's, when my cell phone rings. It's Tim, his voice different—dull and low. "Haley threw me out. I'm in the yard."

"Oh, Tim. What happened?"

"She's pissed because I don't pay rent."

We'd figured he was working his way these past few months, being a house-husband of sorts, all that cooking, cleaning, pet and childcare. "*Why*, all of a sudden like this?"

I hear a sniffle. "I bought the computer today, and she says if I can afford that, why can't I pay rent." More sniffling.

When Tim said he was admitted to NAU, we told him to go ahead and buy the MacBook; we'd pay. "Did you tell her it comes out of your ed fund?"

"Yeah...but...it cost over $2,000.... She said that's a lot of rent."

"Wait. Tim. Why'd you get such an expensive one?"

"The guy in the bookstore talked me into it. Now they won't take it back...."

"Are you still out in the yard?" It's freezing in Prescott; Flagstaff's always colder.

"Yeah."

Russ turns onto our friend's street.

"Tim, can we call you back? We'll help you figure something out." I keep my voice gentle. "Can you go back in there?"

"I don't know." Now he sounds resentful, on the verge of anger.

"Do you want to go back in?"

"I...don'...know...." Then his deep, twenty-three-year-old man's voice collapses into uncontrolled sobs.

My core goes numb and caves in. His last year rushes through me and I'm awash in sympathy: the hopeless drunkenness, two harsh rounds of rehab and sober houses; then this fine new girlfriend, the move to Flag; the futile scramble to find work, followed by the relief of acceptance to college—success! Now, this. He's screwed up and blown it all. By giving in to a $2000 Mac. It's enough to drive a man to drink. "Tim, you can do it. You can go back in there. Maybe apologize for buying the computer?"

"Nyeah." His voice is quavery, but I think it's a yes.

"Go back in then. We'll call you back, Tim. After dinner. Tell her we'll help. I love you. You can work this out."

"Myeah...." He sounds like a wounded cat.

I hadn't planned to attend this dinner. I'm cutting down on meat consumption; steak doesn't appeal. Our friend Ron Glasser had offered it as a Unitarian fundraiser auction item that Russ bought months ago, and at Ron's invitation I tagged along with Russ. Now I'm glad for the distraction.

Ron serves huge slabs of New York steak with salad and corn on the cob at a long table covered with a red and white checked cloth. He pours red wine. I eat and drink slowly, enjoying the conversation of our Unitarian friends, including Don, the UU minister. He knows about Tim's alcoholism; I'd cried it out to him soon after I became aware, a year ago. Now he sits across from me and nods in sympathy as I tell him of Tim's present drama. "He'll work this out," he says.

I think so, too; he'll have to. But Tim's racking sobs resound.

More wine is poured, more tender steak devoured. I'm carried along by a swelling refrain of liberal political and philosophical banter. Mid-meal I retreat to the bathroom. I breathe deep, bow my head. "Guide Tim," I pray to the Universe of the tile floor. I close my eyes, take more deep breaths. "Please, just guide him."

I return and finish half my steak before the apple pie arrives.

12

More of Nowhere

My first week of teaching toppled onto me day by wearisome day like a ton of slow-release bricks, and by the fifth day I was crushed.

In my first music class Friday morning I heard a yelp. "I had it first!"

From across the room I saw Mario yank the tambourine from Wesley's grip.

"Did not!" Wesley elbowed Mario and wrested back the tambourine.

"Boys!" I dropped my basket of instruments and rushed toward them.

"Not fair!" Mario bawled.

I grasped his shoulder. "You get the tambourine next time."

Mario scowled. Wesley jangled the tambourine in Mario's face. I wanted to grab the wretched thing and beat their heads with it. Other students joined the fracas, banging at triangles, sticks, and drums. I spun to the front of the room and my hands shot up like a traffic cop's. "Stop!"

The cacophony faded to a single, incessant *ting, ting, ting* on a triangle; I couldn't spot its source. Some students giggled and pointed to a little dusty-haired girl, head down between her knees, dangling the triangle near the floor. "Hannah...," I warned.

"That's *Helen!*" someone shrieked. Peals of laughter followed, then *ting, ting, ting,* and random drum beats.

I glanced longingly at the clock: twenty-five excruciating minutes to go—in just this class; there were four more. Kids thrashed at drums and triangles and tambourines and maracas. I waded through the bedlam to my desk, fished two Bufferin from the bottle I'd bought in anticipation of headaches on this job, and gulped them down dry.

My teaching position in the Middle of Nowhere, California, had come with two shabby classrooms. This one, where I hosted music classes on Mondays, Wednesdays, and Fridays, held rows of brown metal folding chairs, shelves of antiquated music texts, two baskets of assorted instruments, and an old, ill-tempered piano. The other classroom, down a cracked sidewalk and across a corridor, was home to a jumble of donated games and books and toys in various states of disrepair, heaped on rickety shelves and tables; I was charged with assembling a "resource room" from the mess by mid-October. Building the Great Wall of China would have been easier—but I was duty-bound to spend prep periods and lunchtimes sorting and shelving the "resources."

That first dreary Friday dragged on till the last class ambled out and I could slump in tears over my ramshackle desk. Wrung out, I drove home to my tiny house on a deserted ranch in the low-down fields outside my little California town. I pulled a kitchen chair out the back door and opened a beer. Holding Sadie on my lap, I watched a giant sun smear the sky hot-pink and orange and sag behind the desert into more of nowhere.

Sunk in the Imperial Valley, the town of Calipatria, population 2,000, had a 184-foot flagpole whose stars and stripes topped out at sea level. A rusting yellow sign touted Calipat as the "lowest-down city in the western hemisphere." Now I was one of the hemisphere's lowest-down inhabitants.

Eight miles from Calipat and directly on the San Andreas Fault lies an anomaly called the Salton Sea. At its present thirty-five miles by fifteen, and some fifty feet deep, the "sea" is still the largest lake in California. This stinking expanse of water was formed in 1905 when the Colorado River flooded the sunken portion of the desert, then receded. The Salton Sea has been slowly dying from agricultural run-off with no outlet, leaving fish skeletons to bleach on its scorching shores. When the wind was right, the smell of rotting fish reached the playground of my school in Niland, an even-smaller town a few miles closer to the sea than Calipat.

By the end of my first week, two things were clear: This place was unfit for human habitation, and my teaching job was impossible. The prospect of one hundred seventy-six more school days until June weighed like a prison sentence.

♫

At a district meeting, strapping blond basketball coach Ron Jennings informed me that most teachers lived twelve miles south of Calipat in the bustling town of Brawley, population 20,000. Ron helped me haul my stuff to my new Brawley apartment, where we smoked a joint, pulled sheets onto my mattress on the floor, and had sex surrounded by a sea of marine-blue shag carpet. I fell hard and fast for this guy, but in a month, after I gifted him the new Eagles album, *One of These Nights*, he stopped returning my calls. "Take It To the Limit" was one of my favorite songs on the LP—I guessed we'd done that. I wished I'd kept that album for myself.

Thank God I had Doug, my lover a world away in San Diego....

But teaching became a wholesome diversion from men as my job turned manageable, even pleasant sometimes. By Halloween I'd whipped together a junior high chorus which the principal proclaimed "second to none." Proud singers' moms made red-print wrap-around skirts for the girls and shirts for the boys. We did shows in nearby towns, performed at the county fair and at school programs. I directed from the piano, banging out accompaniments to two-part songs with adolescent appeal, like "Sunshine, Lollipops and Rainbows" and "Breakin' Up Is Hard to Do."

One day in December as we practiced for the Christmas program, seventh-grade Sofia Zepeda caroled, "Five GOL-DEN Rings!" at the top of her voice—too soon. She had miscounted, passing up six geese a-laying. The earnest girl clamped her hand over her mouth, brown eyes flashing with embarrassment, and I smiled. "Good job, Sofie! You just sang yourself into a solo."

Thirty-some years later Sofia would tell me she had performed the National Anthem for an L.A. Dodgers game. "It was you who gave me the confidence to sing," she said, hands over her heart. My career, validated in an instant—a gift better than five golden rings.

In Brawley I made friends with district teachers. One taught me to ride horses. Another took me to her family's place in Laguna Beach. The 7th grade teacher and I carpooled on the eight-mile dust-and-bug-ridden drive to school in Niland; I also joined the weekly aerobics class she led. I took a stained-glass course and made some panels: a *fleur de lis* for my own window, Jonathan Livingston Seagull against a sunset for my bird-lover mom.

I was doing pretty well that year, considering. But summer loomed. With friends gone on vacation, and 110-degree temps added to the perennial pesticide, sea stench, and methane floating in that basin, July would be lethal. During the school year I'd fled over the mountains to San Diego as often as I could. I would escape there for the summer break—and Doug.

I'd fallen in love with Doug Lindley the previous spring, before I left the coast to teach. An ex-boyfriend of my friend Jan, he was a laid-back jazz musician who played at San Diego clubs, and repaired instruments on the side. We shared a passion for music. He took me to meet his mom, for whom I played piano. When I moved to the Valley and came back to San Diego on weekends, I stayed with Jan and visited Doug. We'd smoke grass, go out to eat, listen to music, have sex. For my birthday he took me to hear George Benson in an intimate bar. I felt easy with Doug, in bed and out. I couldn't wait to spend the summer with him.

In June Jan went to Massachusetts for two months, and I moved into her house to tend her plants. The day after my arrival, Jan's landlady caught sight of Sadie in the window. "She goes, or you both do," the old bat said, meaning me and Sadie.

Not about to give up my two-month refuge and my chance to be with Doug, I placed an ad in the *San Diego Tribune* which said, *I'll pay you $50 to board my sweet cat for the summer.*

Val Heinrich responded the first day. His phone voice had a cheery tenor lilt, his *L*'s a gargled twist. He sounded gay. "I have a class till 9:00 tonight, but you can come on over after," he crooned, and gave me his address. "You'll see the Christmas lights on my roof."

The multi-colored bulbs reflected off a black VW parked in front. A bumper sticker on the car said "Zero Population Growth." It made me smile. At twenty-nine I thought if, god-forbid, I ever wanted kids, I would adopt.

Val answered my knock flashing a broad smile. Dark-haired and olive-skinned, he reminded me of the soulful, oval-framed Jesus portrait hanging in our farm kitchen when I was a kid.

Val's tiny house was pungent with incense. He served me ginger tea and examined me like a visitor watching a rare panda at the zoo. I sat self-conscious on a straight-backed chair holding Sadie as Val introduced me to his menagerie: California king snakes, garters, boas, two ringnecks and a Baja coachwhip. Spellbound, I clutched Sadie close. "Where'd you get them all?"

"I caught some. With that." Val pointed at a two-pronged stick that stood in a corner to my left. He set down his cup, lifted Sadie gently from me and fed her near a table in the tiny kitchen, where I could watch. "I like snakes as pets, but I also study them," he said as he returned. He was working on a biology degree with an emphasis in herpetology. Hence the microscope near a pile of books on the little table to my right.

Lithe and long-waisted, Val moved as sinuously as his snakes. I let him drape his ten-foot boa, Sheila, around my neck; her heavy, slithering weight against my breasts and shoulders was oddly thrilling. He gently hefted the boa off me and laid her on his bed, which took up a major portion of the studio house. Then he sipped his tea and aimed a neon smile at me. "They're well-fed. Sadie will be safe here."

Val's light voice lulled me into trust, and I was fascinated by the snakes. A memory had come: my mother rescuing a garter snake with her bare hands from a deep hole on our farm. She held the striped, twisting thing out to us kids, and I touched it, surprised how cool and dry it was, not slimy at all.

My first summer days with Doug were heaven. I hung around his place as he worked on musical instruments. We listened to music and talked; I read, lying on his couch; I fixed him lunch. I went to music gigs with him at night. Afterwards we made love at his place or mine.

One afternoon he said, "You don't need to go to all my gigs, you know. They're boring. Just a job." He started distancing himself during the day, took a guitar into a different room, talked in a low voice on the phone. One day he called out to me, "You don't have to make lunch."

I went home and tried to lighten up. Bored and lonesome at Jan's house, I rented a piano, went to the library for more books, walked to Balboa Park, took a five-day solo drive up the coast—but every time Doug and I parted now I felt bereft, uncertain if I'd see him again.

One night when he was out playing music, I crept in through a window he left open for his cat, put on George Benson's "Breezin'," and crawled naked into bed.

"Whoa," Doug breathed when he discovered me. He lit a candle, slipped off his clothes, slid between the sheets and pulled me to him.

But the next morning he left without saying goodbye. I got dressed and drove away.

I left light, carefully-crafted phone messages: "Hey, I hear there's a new jazz band at Alfonso's. I'll buy you a drink if you'll go with me." He didn't call back.

A couple of weeks after Sadie was settled with him, Val Heinrich invited me to the beach. Propped on an elbow and leaning toward me on the sand, he let his intense gaze crawl along my body, giving me the shivers. "Lookin' good," he drawled, emitting that gravelly *L*-sound. I invited him to my place. That night his slim, strong body was insistent. I writhed beneath him, breathless. Afterwards he murmured, "That was great." I couldn't say the same. It wasn't bad; I'd come to orgasm—but I'd had to strive for it or there'd have been nothing. The sex left me perplexed.

Still, this new guy was different and intriguing. For the first time ever, I'd experienced a lack of chemistry in bed—but this was just a friendly fling to banish thoughts of Doug, who I still hoped would reappear.

Val and I matched well in other ways. Both energetic Aries, we fueled each other. He ran regularly, timing himself, striving to be faster, stronger; I soon started running—with him, and alone. We went to Balboa Park, where we sat on a blanket and ate nuts and berries. We frolicked like kids, standing on our heads and hands, pretending to be toreadors with the picnic blanket, taking photos of each other. I came to relish Val's slaughtered *L's*—"your speech impediment," I joked. I cooked up a practice line: "Little Lulu Likes Lemons." I loved to hear him say it.

I'd never known a scientist before, and I admired Val's dedication to his work. I also liked his commitment to running and to vegetarianism, his tending of his health; he set an example. I'd smoked cigarettes off and on for years, had taken it up again my first year of teaching in Niland. Now I quit for good.

Val seemed to appreciate me, too—my teaching profession, my devotion to Sadie, my piano talent. "I've never known anyone who plays like you do," he said. Never mind his own tin ear and irritating lack of rhythm; he professed to like my music.

We drove to Chula Vista, south of San Diego, to meet Val's Nana and old aunt, Dodo, who lived with plants and two cats in a small mobile home. We sipped tea with them from fine china cups; we laughed and chatted in their cozy place, telling stories of our pasts—Val's, theirs, and mine.

When we left, Dodo hugged us, and Nana took Val's face in both her hands and kissed him; then she did the same to me. I grew to love these two old ladies.

A few weeks into our accelerating relationship, Val and I sat on a park bench, cooling down after a run. A young woman passed by with a German shepherd on a leash. "He looks just like my old dog Jerry," Val said. "When I was thirteen and my mom left us,

Jerry was my comfort." He bent to rub his hamstrings. "I loved that dog so much I jacked him off once."

I drew away, repulsed.

Val leaned down further, massaging his calves. "When Jerry died I cut off his ear for a souvenir. I still miss him."

My breath caught. "That's all pretty weird."

Val smiled sheepishly. "I told you I was kind of a sociopath."

He'd diagnosed himself with the *S*-word to explain his several-day stints in jail—once for marijuana, once for harboring venomous snakes in San Diego County. "I don't care what anyone thinks," he said. "I live by my own rules."

Fine. I'd spent a night in jail myself. My residual '60's hippie self had applauded Val for being who he was. But this thing about his dog seemed depraved. I had to push it from my mind.

My first teaching home

13

Like Shedding Skin

VAL HEINRICH CONTINUED to reveal himself in layers, like shedding skin. One day he showed me an old photo of his birth-mom, dark and wiry like him. She'd left him and his dad and sister and run away to Oregon. "I see her every year or so," Val said. "I sometimes fantasize about having sex with her." He wiggled her picture back into his wallet.

More unpalatable personal information. He'd appalled me just days before when he said he'd once given his favorite professor a blow job. These sleazy tidbits following the unsavory dog business—it was almost too much.

My mind flip-flopped: Did his perverted thoughts and deeds mean Val really was a sociopath? He had symptoms I'd read about: narcissism, sexual deviancy, compulsiveness. Was he just plain nuts? Or simply acting on what was in his deepest, darkest heart—the sorts of things that might be in anyone's heart who plumbed as deep? Rationalizing, I chose the latter, tamping down my doubts and fears. Yes, the more Val divulged, the more proof there might be of his sociopathic nature—but his own description bespoke self-awareness, didn't it? And surely it exaggerated his worst side. From all outward appearances the guy was normal, healthy and happy. Squelching unease over Val's creepiness, I clung to him.

This required me to reconcile with other traits: Val wore only orange and black and yellow. He incessantly chanted a strange, rambling "Ananda Marga" meditation mantra. He nursed his "hypoglycemia," which I'd never heard of and doubted was real, but which caused him to eat only small amounts of nuts and fruit and veggies several times a day, instead of sitting down for meals. And despite his incarcerations, Val still caught venomous snakes and kept them—like the sidewinder rattler he caught in the desert the following year, which I would allow to live in a box in my Brawley apartment for weeks.

But then there'd be some rarefied, blessed instant like that night at Ocean Beach when we'd taken off at sunset in our swimsuits, barefoot, down the shore. We ran and ran in tandem, into the twilight and beyond it, then dropped panting on the firm wet sand. We lay quiet at the tide's edge watching stars appear. Then Val leaned over me and eased down my suit. I pulled off his trunks and we fell together moaning, lustful, heedless in the dark.

Val Heinrich disgusted and delighted, confounded and captivated me. Like the hapless snakes he trapped with his forked stick, I was caught.

♫

That summer in San Diego I searched hard for a teaching position somewhere near the coast—*anywhere*—but I was doomed to return to Brawley. I left Val to his university studies in San Diego, dragged myself to Lowest-Down and sank back into my teaching routine. On weekends the dullness lifted when I went to San Diego or Val came to the Valley. And I adopted a delightful young tabby with white feet to keep Sadie company. I named my new cat Boots and took him to a vet several miles away for neutering. When I went to pick him up the next day, Boots was gone; he had escaped—but four days later I heard his husky meow outside my door. Such devotion heartened me.

Val got his degree and was hired by a biological firm to milk deadly sea snakes for anti-venom in the Philippines. Relief mixed with my fear: I was better rid of Val and his obsession with snakes for a while—but what would I do without him?

He spent February and March with me in Brawley and flew to Asia in the spring. Before he left he said, "You could come to the Philippines when school's out."

My fear went into remission as I planned to flee the valley in June, joining Val for adventure in a distant, unknown land—but he was back by mid-May; the funding for his project had dried up.

During his last week in the Philippines Val had caught a cobra which spit in his face. "My eyes burned like hell," he said, mashing the *L*. "I washed them out with milk, and the next day I was fine."

I was aghast. "Why do you take such risks?"

Val had friends, a nematode expert and his artist wife, who had sent eighty letters to American and international schools in Central and South America and had been hired to teach in Honduras. As we chatted at a picnic in the desert, Val asked this friendly couple for addresses of the schools they'd written. Desperate to escape the Imperial Valley, I wrote to six. I was thrilled when the American School of Nicaragua in Managua called and hired me to teach music, starting in August. I made sure I could bring my boyfriend; the superintendent even said Val could substitute-teach, if he wanted.

"Boas in the wild," Val murmured, muddling the *L*.

A couple on a ranch outside Brawley took my intrepid cat Boots to ward off rattlesnakes. Val and I drove Sadie up to Oregon to live with his mom and step-dad and their peacocks on their farm bordering a national forest. We packed for our new, far-off life: clothes, books and folders, my sewing machine and eight-track tape player, an alarm clock.

Val sold his black VW, and we drove my newer beige beetle—its roof rack laden with trunks and bags—down through Mexico, Guatemala, and Honduras to Nicaragua. We stayed in cheap motels, and camped. One night Val pulled off the road near what looked like a waterless canal. "I'm exhausted. Let's sleep under that bridge."

In the gleam from the headlights I made out a cement bridge

over the canal. "I don't like it, Val. What if somebody comes—like thieves? Or it floods?"

Val was pulling the sleeping bags from the back seat. "It'll be fine." He tossed the bags under the bridge and loped down after them, peeling a banana. "Coming, Eileen?" His mangled *L*'s annoyed me.

The ground was hard. I slept little, fearful of every rustle in the nearby grass—and more so of my future with Val.

♫

In Managua, as I was busy starting school, Val got a grant from Banco Central to study snakes in the Masaya National Park. We found a lively little cat we named Cricket, and within months Val amassed a large snake collection. Most lived in boxes and cages in Val's study, in the back room of our house. But in the living room our coffee table, a glass-topped cage, held a tree branch and three sleek boas.

Our blue block house was in a middle-class Nicaraguan neighborhood. We had no hot water, but the climate was tropical; cold showers were fine. The house came with no stove; we cooked on a hot plate from the market. Steel bars embedded in cement protected our windows. At nightfall a whistle trilled again and again—a local guard or policeman patrolling the neighborhood, making us feel safe.

The American School was in a park-like setting on a hill. My music classroom had big windows that overlooked a tangle of tropical trees and plants. I made friends among the teachers, and with improved management skills, soon coped well with my elementary classes of wealthy kids, most from Nicaragua and the U.S. I studied Spanish and took a jazz ballet class taught by a talented young Nicaraguan woman; on Tuesday evenings I drove across town to her studio.

Val made connections with other scientists and traveled to herp sites, sometimes flying by helicopter into the jungle. One weekend I went with him. Gazing down from the helicopter's open door over the rainforest canopy, I was dazzled by a tall waterfall that appeared as we descended to a clearing.

I admired Val's work, but appreciated him most when he was gone, when I didn't have to deal with the growing tension between us. Val was restless in Managua. He didn't like running in the hot, humid streets; he couldn't exercise. He had difficulty finding foods that suited him. He was often crabby.

We were becoming a discordant fugue, our separate melodies out of sync. My self-esteem increased as my ease with teaching grew; was it this, coupled with Val's low spirits, that led to my intolerance for his quirks? I had no desire for him. He felt my withdrawal and pressed me for sex; this turned me off the more—but to keep the peace I would give in. Then as he lay sleeping, I filled with despair.

We got along best when we traveled, when our focus shifted to adventure. Over Thanksgiving we spent three days on the road exploring old Nicaraguan cities: Leon, Esteli, Matagalpa.

As we came home from the Thanksgiving trip and entered our house, something on the floor near the kitchen door startled me. Val approached it. "Feathers!"

Someone had opened all of our market-purchased pillows, dumped the downy feathers in a heap, filled the casings with our belongings and made off with them: clothing, jewelry, tape player, sewing machine, hot plate, alarm clock. The bent metal bars lay on the ground outside the window—they'd been pulled from the cement.

"You have to pay the guard who patrols with the whistle," my principal belatedly explained; she'd been in Nicaragua for years. "He probably directed the thieves to your house." She and most of the teachers lived up the hill on the other side of town in a cool, well-to-do area. It was Val's and my own problem that we'd chosen to "go local."

After the theft, our relationship felt as empty as our house. Val bent over his snake research day and night. He snacked on fruits and nuts around the clock—except when he suggested we go to the new, air-conditioned McDonald's, where he ate *hamburguesas*. "But you're vegetarian," I said. He hadn't eaten meat for years. How could he turn on himself like this? My shaky respect for some noble core in him slipped further.

I ate solo most evenings. Val never drank alcohol; I had an occasional beer on my own as I read and did schoolwork, and he studied, holed up in his room. I attended my ballet class, occasionally visited a friend or two, and went to bed first, alone on the mattress on the floor. Val crawled into the sheets late, waking me and wanting sex. If I pulled away, pleading school early the next morning, he pouted, then stayed distant and sullen the next day.

I seemed to be the only one Val couldn't charm. He was popular as a substitute teacher at the American School. He did his snake-feeding show to rave reviews from both elementary and high school kids. Staff and fellow scientists admired him and his work, and he basked in the attention. But with me, Val wanted everything his way; there was no compromising. "Why can't you sit down for supper with me?" I begged one night. "I made bean tortillas, no meat."

He clacked at his typewriter without looking up. "I need to send this off to that guy in Germany tomorrow." He zinged the carriage back.

In December we hired a wide-eyed, dusky maid to clean, and to stay in our place for protection when we were away. Val liked Esperanza, and I sensed an opportunity. "Why don't you sleep with her?"

Before long he did, on the little bed on the floor in his study. "Want to hear how it was?" he simpered, as if it would turn me on.

I should have awakened then and there: I did not belong with Val. I did not love him as a mate—never had, never would. But I suppressed the sordid episode, told no one, did nothing.

Over Christmas break Val took off for the jungle and I drove alone to Honduras, where I visited the teaching couple whose addresses I had used to get my job in Nicaragua. They were a happy, caring pair who, with their little girl and me, held hands and said thanks around the table before meals. We talked, played games, and traveled to the highlands and through banana plantations, past houses on stilts near the coast. These friends seemed the ideal family. I envied them.

Back home with Val, the shame of what we'd come to fell heavy on me. Our relationship was unwholesome and rancorous, not the way mates ought to be. But distracted by the pursuits of school and travel, I let things go on as they were. I'd thrown my lot in with this guy and bolted from the U.S. with him; there seemed no going back.

Though Val relished his work in Nicaragua, his dream had always been to study the snakes of Africa. In early spring of '78, he said, "If I got us teaching jobs in Africa, would you go?"

I weighed the options, just in case. I had decided I could spend another year with Val in Nicaragua: We'd move outside town to a hacienda; I'd get a piano. If my situation improved, so might our relationship.

But changing countries might be better yet. A move to Africa would deflect our problems, perhaps make them vanish—and the political climate in Managua was heating up. Burnings and shootings happened in the streets. Sometimes I drove to school and saw a sign that read, *"No hay clases"*—no school that day. One Tuesday night on my way home from ballet class, I was blocked by a big canvas-back truck on fire; people ran and shouted beside it, pushing it down the cobbled street. Soon the murder of Joaquin Chamorro, a well-known Nicaraguan anti-government newspaper reporter, made international news.

Still, I wasn't worried about being in Nicaragua. If we moved to the countryside we'd be away from the capital, beyond the troubles. And how likely was Val to come up with jobs in Africa on his own? He didn't even have a teaching credential.

14

Just a Piece of Paper

"JUST WHEN DO you plan to be married?"

The last line of the cable from Africa played over and over in my head like stuck lyrics on a record. We had jobs in Zaire—formerly the Belgian Congo, now the Democratic Republic of Congo—at the American School of Kinshasa, *if* we tied the knot.

In his March '78 letter of application, Val had called me his fiancée. The reply a month later invited him to teach high school biology; they liked his snake expertise and apparently overlooked his lack of teaching credentials. I would be hired as a classroom aide, guaranteed the next available teaching job.

I'd told Val I'd go—but *married?* Twisting in the clammy sheets next to his sleeping body, I wrestled with the frightful *M*-word that had crept onto the horizon of our relationship. Val had no problem with it—anything for the snakes of Africa. "It's just a piece of paper," he said.

A piece of paper that would bind us like Super Glue as husband and wife.

Yet what choice did I have? Val might go to Africa without me, and I was not brave enough to stay in Nicaragua on my own. I could press him to remain with me there another year, but if he deigned to stay, he would resent me forever. And going back to

Nowhere, California, would shrivel me to nothing, like the fish bones by the Salton Sea.

For our July wedding in San Diego, I made invitations bordered by little black snakes and red roses. A Nicaraguan seamstress fashioned my dress of black sailcloth, using Grandma Welch's disintegrating seersucker housedress as a pattern; I embroidered tiny red roses and snake-like squiggles at the edges. For Val I hand-sewed a plain, gauzy, long-sleeved red shirt embroidered with a black snake on the chest. He had forsaken orange for red at my request; I liked black with red: wild colors for the outrageous act we would commit while wearing them.

Friends on a cactus farm took our cat Cricket. We packed our few belongings into the VW, along with a heavy, docile boa named Zelda—one of the three of her species who had inhabited our glass-topped coffee table. Val had gotten written permission from the Nicaraguan government to take Zelda to the U.S. He fed her up for the trip and tied her in a flour sack that lay in the floor well behind the driver's seat. As we threaded our way through Central America, out one border, in the next, Val opened the sack for border inspections. Uniformed officials and bystanders at the borders of Nicaragua, El Salvador and Honduras in turn gathered round, laughed and exclaimed, pointed and poked. They peered at the official paper and sent us on our way.

When Val took the sack from the car at the border into Guatemala, he fumbled it. Recovering, he braced it with a hand and forearm across the bottom, eased it onto the ground, unknotted the top and gasped, "Oh, my God." Beaming, he held it open for me to see.

Dozens of miniature boas squirmed around Zelda. I caught my breath.

"One of her roommates was a lucky fellow," Val said, gurgling the *L*'s. "Must've been when I was away in November."

I obviously hadn't paid much attention to the coffee-table inhabitants myself; boas often mate for several days at a time. And because they're ovoviviparous, bearing live young, there were no eggs to alert us to the imminent births.

The mass of wiggly baby serpents was great entertainment for Guatemalan and Mexican border folks, who detained us gleefully for some time before letting us pass through.

Between the borders, our adventures northward were fraught with tension. On a wayside trip down a narrow dirt road to the Copan Ruins in Honduras, Val drove while wrestling with the map spread open on the steering wheel. "Watch the road," I warned, but he kept squinting at the map. The VW drifted toward a drop-off over the ditch. I tugged at the map, but Val held onto it. The steering wheel turned; the car lurched. In slow motion, dirt and grasses met me at the passenger-side window as we tipped off the road into the ditch.

Hondurans appeared from nowhere to watch us drag ourselves up and out the driver's door. Soon four wiry, willing hombres surrounded the car and made short work of hoisting it upright and onto the road. They stood grinning as we pressed centavos into their hands; then they waved us on our way.

Back on the road, Val said, "You shouldn't've grabbed the map."

"You were veering toward that cliff!"

"I was watching. There was no cliff."

Our headlights were weak, unable to pierce the thick darkness as we sped through desolate night countryside toward Guatemala City. Suddenly the smooth pavement ended and we sailed across a shallow ditch and jolted to a stop against the embankment on the other side. My body slammed forward and my head struck the windshield; trunks and suitcases flew off the roof rack and crashed onto the hood in front of me. I stared at the spray of spider-lines in the windshield, and my hand reached for my forehead as if directed by a mind of its own.

Behind the wheel, Val emerged from his daze. "Are you okay?"

I stared at my hand. "I guess so." No blood, no lump, no pain.

In stunned silence we got out. We pulled loose shards of safety glass from the windshield, gathered and reattached the baggage, and crawled into Guatemala City in our ailing little car.

Val had picked up two dead snakes from the road on our way.

In our cheap Guatemala City motel that night, he stayed up late dissecting them beneath the dangling bare bulb overhead. "The light's keeping me awake," I said. He was still up working at 4:30.

We didn't get the car in for windshield repair until almost noon, but that night we made it to Antigua, Guatemala, the colonial Spanish capital of Central America. We stayed two days there in the lovely old home of a teacher-friend from Managua. We walked the cobblestone streets and perused the colorful markets, using our improved Spanish with the friendly locals. But Volcan Fuego, erupting outside of town, was the star attraction for Val. We could see a glimmer of it from our street. The second night, he and I drove near enough to watch lava rolling down the side of the volcano like a red-orange waterfall.

Val wanted to go closer, so we left the car on the road and walked. When we'd hiked over an hour in the dark through tangled terrain, I'd had enough. "You can't stick your finger in the lava, Val. Let's go back."

"We'll never get a chance like this again."

"It's not safe—and we've gotta hike all the way back."

"It's *fine.* Just a little further...."

I turned around. Grudgingly, he followed. Back at our friend's we went to bed in stony silence.

We were continually at odds on the road. There'd be a stand-off, then hours of icy stillness—as when we drove on from Antigua into Mexico—then more bickering, then resignation. I told myself it was the strain of travel taking its toll, and not our strained relationship.

By Tapachula, Mexico, the car was overheating. Local mechanics fixed the muffler and cleaned the carburetor, and the VW hummed on easily for awhile. But with the unexpected car repairs, we were running out of money. I was afraid we'd have to break into the $500 cashier's check that traveled with us, drawn on my account with Banco Central in Managua—our entire worldly savings, hidden behind the VW's dashboard.

By the time we reached Monterey, Mexico, I was sick with cramps and diarrhea. But as we pulled into our hotel's garage, I checked on our money.

Before we'd left the U.S., Val had cut a piece of plywood to fit the space in the VW's dash where a radio might have been; I'd painted the little panel with vines and flowers. Friends in Managua had warned us not to carry big chunks of money on our bodies, or leave them in hotel rooms. So when we left Nicaragua, I tucked my $500 cashier's check, in an envelope, into the space behind the decorated panel. As we parked in the hotel garage in Monterey, I pried out the panel, reached in and felt the envelope—still safely there. We might need the money soon. I carefully replaced the plywood piece.

As we got into the car the next morning, the little wooden panel wasn't flush with the dash. The $500 check was gone. Though I had a guarantee and would contact the bank later, they would not respond.

Sickened, broke, and tired, we pressed on toward the U.S.

We said goodbye to the baby boas at a farm north of San Antonio, Texas, where Val sold all twenty-eight for $100. That afternoon in Austin, the VW overheated and threw a rod. Our little car's long, slow death march was over. We got $150 for it at a junkyard, condensed our belongings into Salvation Army suitcases, and the next day, Val hauling Zelda in her sack, we took Amtrak to San Diego.

Our wedding was a performance for which I was not well-prepared. At my friend Jill's house the night before, I barely slept—but I arose early the next day to arrange transport and directions to the wedding site for my family, who'd flown from Wisconsin and were camped in a hotel. I helped Val's nervous little step-sister practice her song, found a cloth for the pot-luck table in the park, and finalized my slapdash vows.

I had pulled on and fastened my black wedding dress and was brushing my long, wayward hair at a bathroom mirror when Jill looked in. "Eileen, where are the flowers?"

"Shit." I threw down my brush, sank onto the toilet seat and hung my head.

"You can't get married without flowers."

"Then maybe I can't get married!" Tears stung my eyes.

Jill drove to Mayfair grocery and came back with red carnations. I cut one to stick into my hair; the rest went into a vase for the center of the picnic table.

Val and I were married that afternoon, July 29th, 1978, on a La Jolla beach, as planned. We stood side-by-side in the center of the semi-circle of guests on folding chairs. Most of my family were in front on my side; sister Carol from Colorado stood beside me as my maid of honor. Not one of them blinked an eye at our strange colors or the impromptu nature of the event; they seemed just glad to be there. Val's dad and step-mom, his little sisters, and Nana and Dodo were with us, seated on his side. A sprinkling of friends sat behind family. A long-time, fifty-something friend of Val's, a chiropractor with a minister's license, stood gray-suited by Val and me to perform the ceremony.

At my request, the chiropractor-minister opened with an earthy saying: "Love is like manure. Spread it around." Guests chuckled. My voice strained as I blurted ad-lib words to Val, something about trying not to let things stagnate. Self-assured in public as always, Val read his message, enunciating the words, "I am yours, to experience and endure." The minister read what he had chosen: "Love does not consist of gazing at each other, but of looking together in the same direction."

As Val's twelve-year-old sister played guitar and sang Jim Croce's "Time in a Bottle," one line caught me and replayed in my head for days—a line about knowing I'd found the one I wanted to go through time with. I so wished it were true.

After the wedding we took my family to the apartment where Val's boa, Zelda, and other snakes were kept. Everyone but Dad was fascinated, holding and marveling at the snakes. But without a word, Dad fled. We soon found him striding back to us from far down the block. "I just needed some air," he said.

Soon we hugged goodbye, and Mom and Dad got in the car. When I saw the back door on Dad's side still open, I went around and discovered he was crying.

I'd seen my father cry once when I was a kid; it wrenched me now as it had then.

I knelt, laid my head in his lap and hugged his knees, tears welling in my own eyes. "Don't worry, Daddy. I'll be fine."

Showing sister Carol one of Val's Boas

San Diego, CA

15

It's a Jungle Out There

IN THAT AUGUST of '78 we arrived freshly-married at Kinshasa's N'djili Airport. Shuffling my carry-on from the plane onto the tarmac, I blinked through hazy morning sunlight at a sea of dozens, maybe hundreds, of black faces shining far above us on a balcony: Zairians awaiting passengers. Inside the building, one of them, a cordial Embassy expediter, did paperwork formalities as we tended our luggage and chatted with the American School superintendent, there to meet us.

An African driver sped us in a school van through the ramshackle city. Dazed from jet lag and the anxious rush which had led to the trip, I stared at the passing scene: tall, dusty eucalyptus, palms and acacias; dilapidated shops and houses of tin, block, and mold-streaked plaster; people in constant motion—men in shabby western shirts, women wrapped head to toe in bright-colored prints, baskets on their heads—an incomprehensible blur. "Everything's so dusty and brown-looking."

The superintendent turned from the front passenger seat. "It's what they call the *saison seche.* The dry season. Just wait. In a couple of months it'll be greener than you've ever seen."

"I like it already." Val grinned at me and patted the breast pocket of his black jacket. The two little California king snakes he'd smuggled in had made the long trip without incident.

We stopped before a wide blue metal gate that said "TASOK"—The American School of Kinshasa—in sunflower-yellow letters. A tall, dark-blue clad African swung open the gate, and we rumbled down a rutted dirt road past a tennis court to Lower Campus, stopping at the first of four or five old Belgian-built duplexes with corrugated sheet-rock roofs.

When the van was gone and our bags sat on the speckled-stone tile floor inside our door, we ambled from room to room in our half of the duplex. Bamboo-print curtains hung at the windows, which were criss-crossed outside with iron grillwork. The large dining room table and six chairs were of dark wood. "This place is a mansion!" Val marveled. With two bedrooms, a large living-dining space, storage room and big screened back porch, it was more spacious than any place either of us had ever lived. I sank exhausted onto the big worn leather couch and closed my eyes.

"It's a jungle out there!" Val warbled from the porch.

I roused myself to look. A huge sweep of grassy back yard punctuated with palms and mango trees led to a tangled wall of vine-strung trees and bushes. There'd been monkeys in the jungle not many years before, the superintendent had told us.

We would soon learn that a trail led through the mass of greenery to Upper Campus, the site of more staff homes and three rambling sets of old school buildings—elementary, high, and middle school. Upper Campus also held a spacious playing field, an outdoor basketball court, and a large swimming pool.

I would often walk the lush trail to school through the jungle. And most mornings, for years, I would run the trail's mile-long extension, which formed the perimeter of the campus inside the chain link fence.

At TASOK I introduced myself as "Lena," a grown-up version of "Leenie," my sisters' nickname for me as a kid—easier for everyone to read and say than my given name, Eileen, and a stab at overhauling the angst-ridden person I hoped to banish. That first year I worked as an elementary aide in the 5th and 6th grade pod and gave piano lessons on the side. I accompanied school choirs, and because the music score hadn't arrived in time, I played by ear *The Unsinkable Molly Brown*, a musical performed by high school students. "I Ain't Down Yet" would stick with me, words to live by.

Wildly popular with TASOK high school biology students his first semester, Val rarely lectured to an entire class, opting instead for films and individual research papers. He also did chiropractic adjustments on students and discussed Urantia, an obscure theory of "cosmic consciousness," with them. On the rare occasions when I stopped in, students were milling, laughing and talking.

As I made friends with teachers, Val smoked pot with a group of high school students. "You'll get in trouble," I warned. "They're just kids you're messing with."

When he wasn't with students, Val was preoccupied with snakes. He paid the Zairian guards and gardeners to bring him specimens, dead or alive. The live ones became pets: An aggressive python lived in a cage on our back porch until Val had him released off-campus; harmless smaller snakes joined the California king snakes in cages in Val's study, where on a shelf, dead snakes curled in glass jars of formaldehyde. Val's mission was to measure, compare and record the lungs of all species of snakes of the Congo. "Of all of Africa," he glowed. "Eventually of the world!"

Grandiose, unrealistic plans, I thought; he's just plain nuts. But pickled snakes were shipped to him from Australia and Germany; he sent specimens to England and South Africa. His work was all-consuming. At his request, I bought him diet pills from the American Commissary to keep him alert so he could study through the night.

Back then I wouldn't have believed it possible that thirty years later Val would earn a doctorate and complete his book. From Boston he would email me sample pages of indecipherable scientific data, and I'd be impressed.

Val and I had some good times together in Zaire. We drove our school-provided VW van on forays in Kinshasa and the countryside, discovering rivers, caves, savannahs and small villages. We got to know Matadi Road with its batiks, basketry, and wood carvings for sale. Nearby in the other direction from campus were the Kitambo neighborhood's vendors of mangoes, avocados, fresh baguettes, and the guy hawking almost-new *Time* magazines in English. Soon after Val and I parted, I'd be stunned to learn of John Lennon's assassination when the dates *1940-1980* flashed above the premier Beatle's photo on a *Time* cover in Kitambo.

Besides the hawkers, a reputed witch wandered Kitambo streets, her bare, flabby breasts hanging to the waist of her short grass skirt, wild gray hair framing her face. We'd glimpse her sometimes on our drives downtown where we tried local foods: *saka-saka*— rich, dark greens, which I loved; and *fufu*, fermented manioc—the same root vegetable as South America's cassava—perhaps the only food in my life I never learned to stomach.

One Sunday Val and I hiked miles into the countryside to a grassy clearing near the river. After a picnic of nuts, cheese and apples, we fell onto each other on the raffia mat. Clothes stripped off, we were engaged in sex when we heard male voices and looked up: Two tall, T-shirted Zairian men stared sternly from a distance. *"C'est immorale!"* they scolded. *"C'est mal!"* Squelching sheepish mirth, we scrambled into our clothes.

♫

A month after we'd arrived, TAP Airlines delivered from the U.S. Val's new Champion juicer. We wrestled the heavy, expensive machine out of the shipping trunk and lugged it to the kitchen. Then, salivating over the fresh juice he would make with market fruits and veggies, Val left for a meeting with students.

I stared at the monstrosity that took up half the kitchen counter. *For better or worse,* I thought, re-reading the instructions. I plugged in the adapter for 220 volts, which we'd brought for the purpose, loaded in some clean carrots and pushed the on-switch. A *pfft* sounded, followed by a little puff of smoke, and the thing went dead.

When I broke the news to Val, he scowled. He peered at the juicer and its contents, caressed its broad sides and undercarriage, smelled the adapter. Then he turned sad eyes on me. "You should have waited, Lena."

"It was the wrong adapter! The same thing would have happened to you." My eyes stung.

"I would've figured it out." Val sulked, freezing me out for the rest of the day.

We were back to the old pattern: berating, bickering, crying, deadly silence. Then would come relief during a calm, easy period—like the eye of a hurricane—as when we first adopted Fritz, a comfort to us both.

In November we'd found the small black cat reminiscent of Sadie, who had brought us together in San Diego. We loved Fritz's little mew, his delicate batting at cockroaches, his flying after paper wads.

At Christmastime while decking the house with ornaments and bows, I tied a thin red ribbon around Fritz's neck, then went about other tasks. When Val came home he brought Fritz from the bedroom and held him up to me. The poor little cat's mouth was caught open by the ribbon he'd struggled to get off; blood showed around his teeth as he panted. Val glared at me. "You could have killed him."

Filled with pity for Fritz, I reached to untie the ribbon—but Val held the cat from me and took him away, gently extricating the ribbon as he went. Crushed, I apologized, but Val wouldn't talk to me the rest of the day.

We loved animals, and besides Fritz and Val's snakes, we came to possess a little owl and a goat. We nursed the owl with raw hamburger until it grew strong and flew off into the campus jungle. We had a thatched hut built for the goat, who was partial to a red-leafed plant the guard would gather for it. Some TASOK staff began calling our place "the zoo."

As the chiropractor-minister had said at our wedding, when we looked together in the same direction we were okay. Sex was fine for a while, but then things fell apart again. Though busy night and day, Val still wanted sex often—whenever *he* wanted it. "I need more sex than most men. Three times a day, ideally. You're my wife—you owe me." Just plain nuts! The pressure made me pull away.

One night in the bedroom, in a crying rage over his insistence and the mess that we'd become, I punched Val hard in the shoulder with my fist. I drew back howling in pain, shaking my hand; then, afraid the quiet couple next door might hear through the wall, I curled up on the bed and whimpered as Val left the room. Alone with the bleak realization that my marriage was a whopping mistake, I cried myself to sleep.

Back in August, during our frantic, few-hour "honeymoon" in Lisbon on the way to Africa, I'd bought a souvenir postcard: a folkloric Portuguese woman in a full, embroidered dress of black and red—our wedding colors. The day after I hit Val with my fist, I took the card from my drawer and scrawled bold words in pen across the bottom: "Marry in haste, repent at leisure." I propped it on my desk in the storage room and wallowed in resentment.

But the rainy season washed away my troubles. Sheets of water poured down, cleansing earth and sky; the faithful old air conditioner in the living room rumbled on; and the silvery, gulping sound of fruit bats filled the nights.

Val showed me a book about "open marriage." Not myself in this relationship any longer, I didn't care who he slept with—I wanted him to find other partners and leave me alone. Open marriage was worth a try.

Val wrote to a 2nd-grade teacher, proposing sex. She wrote back, "If you write or talk to me again, I'll report it to the superintendent." Undaunted, he tried another teacher with a similar result, this one replying angrily to his face. On occasions when I encountered these two women later, they turned away from me.

Everyone knew that high-class, short-skirted prostitutes hung out under the luxuriant jacaranda trees on Avenue de la Justice, near the ritzy Intercontinental Hotel; we'd see them if we drove by the Intercon at night. Val found a prostitute there he liked and brought her home, twice. I didn't mind; I made sure I never met her. Val said he used a rubber, and I believed him.

I had sex with a couple of men outside the marriage myself that first year. On a post-Christmas trip to Moanda without Val, there was Jake, an American working on construction of the Inga-Shaba dam in lower Zaire. He had flown to the beach with some of us from TASOK. A few people ended up staying in sparse rooms at the old stone Belgian mission there, Jake and I among them. After a teachers' pot-smoking party over a bonfire on the beach, I asked Jake if he'd like to sleep with me. His dark eyes widened. "But you're a married lady."

"Val and I have an agreement."

I was relieved to feel free and easy in bed with someone again. We laughed and snuggled and made love, then spent the night in each other's arms on the white-sheeted single cot.

There was also Parker, a single TASOK high school teacher, a dashing playboy sort who I knew carried on other affairs. We snuck off a few times between classes for sex at his apartment on upper campus.

And there was Thomas, with the British Council; I accompanied his French horn on piano, then accompanied him, occasionally, to bed.

♫

In the spring one of Val's students spilled the beans to his Embassy parents about Val's smoking grass with high school kids. A letter came from the superintendent: Not only was Val fired and ordered off campus; I was dismissed, too. "You will be reimbursed for economy tickets to the U.S.," the letter said.

I had fallen in love with TASOK and with Africa, and I didn't want to leave. I wrote a strongly-worded letter to the Board, who honored my contract: I would stay, on my own, move to single housing and teach middle school English the next year.

Rather than return to the U.S., Val found a house in Kinshasa's *cité*, the bustling Zairian residential area downtown. He got himself a deadly tan-and-purple Gaboon viper he named Ida, a purring ferret from an ex-student, and a steady Zairian girlfriend. I was relieved to be no more to him than a friend. Our marriage was over, though we didn't speak of this.

Instead of a ticket to the U.S., Val's firing netted me a ticket to a wonderful new life without him. I spent the summer in Quimper, France, where I studied French with Europeans in a month-long course. For breakfast in the college dorm I drank bowls of hot, sweet half-tea, half-milk. I took bus tours to castles and cathedrals in Normandy.

In a French class I found a Swedish boyfriend with whom I traveled the Loire Valley; Klas would later visit me in Africa.

When I flew back from France to Zaire for the school year in August, Val met me at the airport. "I was kind of hoping we could patch things up," he said.

Had we never spoken the same language? "There's nothing to patch up. I'm sorry."

♫

My new middle school English teaching job at TASOK was delightful. I loved my small classes of a dozen or fifteen bright students whose nationalities ranged from Vietnamese to Norwegian to Pakistani. We studied novels and short stories, wrote journal entries and essays, and read a drama version of Dickens' Christmas Carol with sound effects.

I still played piano for school musicals, gave piano lessons on the side, and helped arrange public musical events on campus. And freed of Val, I developed easy, rewarding, ongoing relationships with a couple of men. Rich, a Peace Corps administrator, played tennis with me at the American Club on weekends. When I spent nights in his plush, African-art-filled, downtown apartment, he played Al Green and Nina Simone records and fed me foods he'd learned to make in his home state of West Virginia: black bean soup, corn pudding, pickled beets.

At Christmastime I joined my Swedish boyfriend, Klas, in Kenya. We traipsed around Nairobi, then took a train to the seaside town of Mombasa with its huge, arched, elephant-tusk entrance. We went south and camped for days by the ocean in a tent with soft, embroidered-quilted cots and a shower. On my way back to Zaire from Wisconsin the following summer, I spent a week traveling with Klas in Sweden.

I cared for both these guys but was not destined to settle down with either. Living in my new little apartment on TASOK's upper campus and teaching happily for the first time, I felt at home. I played the old upright piano I'd bought, ran the jungle trail, gave dinners, visited with neighbors, partied, and relaxed into being single again.

Fritz the cat had left during the strife with Val the previous spring, and not returned. I learned of a tabby kitten someone was giving away. When the guy delivered the feisty little thing, he said he'd had to pull it from the dryer duct it had crawled into for warmth. Puss-Puss would be my brave, venturesome companion in Africa for years.

In March, just before my thirty-third birthday, I went on a spring-break trip to the beach at Moanda with Lynne, a teacher-friend. She and I lazed at the rambling Mangrove hotel, reading, writing, smoking pot and laughing. Each day we took the stairs down the cliff to the red-earth beach and walked and talked and tanned. Every night back at the Mangrove we ate chicken mwambe or crevettes with rice, and lingered over Castel beers.

When we flew home to Kinshasa, Lynne's husband met us at N'djili. After greetings, he turned to me. "Bad news, Lena. Val's been arrested."

The letter he handed me, bearing the official U.S. Embassy stamp, urged me as Val's next of kin to attend his trial for possession of *drogues dangereuses*—the official Zairian charge.

My heart fell. Though we were still married, I'd been living blessedly free, apart from Val for a year—and now he was sucking me back in. I wanted no more to do with him.

But I knew Val didn't deserve the charge; he rarely smoked marijuana, much less took anything more "dangerous." And I would not have been where I was, teaching happily in Africa, without him. How could I begrudge him my support in court? Two weeks later, I went.

"*Ça femme est là.*" The black-robed Zairian prosecuting attorney pointed to the back row, and a wave of dark faces turned to gape at me, the wife. Val turned, too, offering a grim smile.

"*Voici.*"

At the prosecutor's command, the sea of faces turned back to the front to ogle the small jar of marijuana seeds he held against the light. He passed the jar to the judge in black behind the counter, who examined it. They frowned and murmured to each other.

To all assembled the prosecutor said, *"Il y a encore."* He picked up a small plastic bag of pot to show the court—"there's more." An incriminating drone ensued.

At the prison door on my first visit, a stern, dark-uniformed officer behind a high counter beckoned for the bag of bananas and peanuts I'd brought Val, and the Embassy paper explaining my connection. I passed them up to him. He peered at the paper, then glowered at me. He dispatched someone for Val, let me in and directed me to wait in a dank, cavernous room where uniformed guards, some brandishing rifles, stood glaring at me. The high windows had no glass, only vertical bars; I could see nothing through them. There were no chairs. I stood with my back to a cool, damp wall, not touching it. The place smelled of sewage.

Val was ushered in, looking wan. He smiled, glad to see me and grateful for the food. We talked for a few minutes. I was relieved to go.

During monthly visits I watched Val became thinner, his face more gaunt, but he was always cheerful. Sometimes he reported having diarrhea or a cold, but he kept a positive attitude and was always pleased to get the food. We chatted for a while, but each time I was glad when I'd stayed long enough to say goodbye.

Conditions in the prison were grim for the masses of Zairian inmates, with little food, no beds or sanitation, but Val schmoozed with guards and arranged to get a small single cell. He placed an orange Indian bedspread on the door for privacy. They let him bring in his typewriter so he could continue writing up snake research night and day. He ran and exercised in a large walled courtyard, and twice a week guards escorted him out for visits to the *cité* and to the home of a sympathetic Embassy family who had befriended him.

When school let out in June, I flew to California and stood in line at the San Diego County Courthouse. Having checked out the placard on the counter, I knew I qualified: married less than two years, no children, no joint property worth more than $2000. I could do this short-form thing without a lawyer—though there was a hitch. Upon reaching the counter, I said to the clerk, "My husband's not here. May I take the form home for him to sign?"

Had Val been there, he would have signed. But he was in prison in Africa. That night at Jan's place, I envisioned Val's bold handwriting and practiced his signature on scrap paper. Then I took a deep breath, channeled his brash egoism and wrote *Val S. Heinrich* on the line.

The next day when I handed the completed form to the courthouse clerk she studied it, then scrutinized me. She glanced at the paper again, then frowned at me, as if she knew my crime. Finally she asked for the $65 fee, counted the cash and nodded. "Your divorce should be final within a month."

Back in Kinshasa for the next school year, I paid another visit to Val in prison. "I'm glad things went well with the divorce," he said. His smile was a little sad, and I felt a pang myself.

In October, courtesy of President Mobutu Sese Seko on his birthday, Val was released from prison. He stayed in Zaire, traveling and continuing his research. In November his Gaboon viper, Ida, bit him. His left arm and hand ballooned huge and black. I visited him at his friend's place in the *cité*, where he lay propped up in bed observing the venom's effect and taking notes with his good right hand. Before Christmas he was recovered and on a plane back to the U.S. for good.

Throughout my time with him, it had become clearer and clearer: Val was just plain nuts—as I had been, ever to have married him.

16

Frothy as Foam on Beer

"We're good. Everything's good." Tim's voice is as frothy as foam on beer—as if Haley hadn't just thrown him out in the cold; as if he hadn't broken into racking sobs on the phone two hours before. I'd promised to call him back after our steak dinner at Ron Glasser's, but he seems almost surprised to hear from me.

"What happened?" I ask. "Did you tell her we'd help with rent?"

"Yeah. She says $500 a month is good, my third of the total with her and Abby."

"We can manage that. We'll take it from your ed fund, as long as you're in school."

"Thanks. Yeah, we're good. We both apologized."

"Great! So about the expensive computer.... You're inheriting a few thousand bucks from Nancy this spring. You could pay us for half from that."

"Whoa. I didn't know I was getting money from Nancy."

"Holly too. All the nieces and nephews. You were her only kids."

"Cool. Yeah, sure, I'll pay you back."

♫

"Dental hygienists make $90,000, a year," Tim says, and in January he takes his first bite into a four-year dental hygiene program at Northern Arizona University.

This from a guy who flunked out of community college three times. On the other hand, he passed his last round of rehab with flying colors, is still clean and strong—and he's set on this course. I imagine him wearing latex gloves, delicately poking around in someone's mouth. "You've always been good with your hands." I wish him luck.

He rides Haley's bike to NAU sometimes that winter when she needs the car. "It's so *cold*. I have to keep my head down or my eyes freeze shut. When I get there my water bottle's frozen." He complains about writing English papers and says math is hard. But his tone reflects pride in meeting the challenges. He perseveres.

♫

We arrange to visit Tim in April. Just before we leave for Flagstaff the phone rings, and his words tumble out in a rush. "I'll meet you outside the house. Haley's not going to lunch with us."

When we arrive he's standing out front, arms crossed, shuffling from foot to foot. He slides into the back seat and asks if we can go to Sizzler's. "I never get to eat *meat.*"

As we sit with full plates, Tim fishes in his front jeans pocket for a wad of hundred-dollar bills and hands them to Russ. "For the computer." His inheritance from Nancy has come.

Between mouthfuls of a plump bacon cheeseburger, Tim blurts out the latest: He'd pinched some of Haley's marijuana, and she caught him. "I told her I'd pay it back when I got Nancy's money, and I did. But she says she doesn't trust me now." He hangs his head over his burger like a contrite kid.

I lean back holding my fork and contrive to keep judgment from my voice, aim for curious: "I thought you quit smoking pot." I glance at Russ, who looks away.

"Haley does it a lot, but I only did that little bit. I'm not gonna do it any more."

I won't do it again, officer.... Shit—I'm the Addiction Police again. I know better, but the thoughts just free-fall from my mouth. "Sounds like Haley doesn't want you doing pot?" She seems to be the boss of him.

I know better than this! I put a bite of chicken in my mouth. Like the three C's in my Program say, I didn't *cause*, can't *cure*, can't *control*—and neither can Haley, if she even wants to. I have to stop reacting.

"She doesn't care. We smoked together in Prescott when we first met." I chew my chicken slowly. "It's just she didn't like that I stole it."

Russ asks, "Do you think she'll get over it?"

"She's still pretty pissed. She's shut me out." He bites at a fingernail. He has very little in the way of fingernails; since elementary school they've all gone to appease his anxiety. But Russ bites his nails too, always has, as far as I know: like father, like son. And who am I to talk? My acid reflux has been acting up.

On the drive to Sizzler's I'd asked if we could visit Haley and the cats. As we finish our food Tim texts Haley. "She just took a shower, but she says you can come over any time."

Haley sits on a high stool at the counter that divides the living room from the kitchen. She's talking on her cell phone. Her dark, golden hair is damp; she runs her fingers through it as she swivels, legs crossed, on the high stool. When we come in she gives us a quick sideways smile, then lets her hair form a curtain between us and keeps talking. I sit on the rocker, Russ and Tim on the couch. Black-and-white Tux leaps onto my lap, campaigning for attention, which I gladly give him. Tim and Russ pet long-haired Caffrey, the household favorite, who sprawls between them. We prattle to the felines, and about them, while Haley talks on the phone, her back to us like a wall.

Finally Russ and I raise eyebrows at each other. He cocks his head toward the door, and I nod. "Can you make us some coffee before we go, Tim?" Russ asks.

Haley closes her phone and turns. Tim rises and strides past her into the kitchen without speaking. As he makes coffee, Russ and I carry on a stilted conversation with Haley about school, the cats, the weather, until Tim comes back with full cups. His coffee tastes bitter compared to last time, as if he's brewed it with the rancor between him and his mate. Russ and I sip steadily, steering clear of the frostiness in the room.

As our cups empty, the doorbell rings and Haley swings off her stool to answer it. Someone with a flyer or survey. Haley returns brashly cheery. "He asked if I had a boyfriend—then he said, 'Is his name Lucky?'" She laughs.

A little grin tugs at the corner of Tim's mouth.

At the car to see us off, Tim's words cascade. "I'll be sober for a year in May. I think about going to a meeting to get my chip. But it would be kind of a lie, 'cause I smoked that dope."

"You're doing good, Timmy." I hug him tight. "Love you."

"Love you," he repeats, like the stuffed parrot with the battery in it he had as a kid. Russ hugs him goodbye and the parrot speaks again.

We're quiet as we drive away. Tim seems at loose ends, his situation precarious—but my Program has taught me to release with love. Worrying won't protect me from the future; it only ruins the present. As a Program book says, I'll do better to let "pieces of the here-and-now" save me from useless "what-if's" that may never come. As my stress recedes, so does my acid reflux.

Cruising through the ponderosas down I-40, a.k.a. the Purple Heart Trail, we reach the swath of yellow flowers that blanket a wide meadow outside the town of Williams. A raven cuts through blue sky and glides strong and sure over the field of yellow in the here-and-now.

♫

By mid-May Tim's roller coaster is climbing to the top. He and Haley are "better than ever," he reports. With money from Nancy to pay for summer rent and food, he doesn't think he needs a job. And he's got a semester of college under his belt. "I flunked math," he says with mild chagrin. "I'll retake it in the fall." His determination heartens me.

When Haley finishes her teaching year at NAU, she takes off

for an intensive, two-and-a-half-month Bikram yoga training in L.A. Tim is left in charge of eleven-year-old Abby, who's just twelve years his junior. A month in, we talk on the phone. He says, "It's weird. Our relationship is *better*. We've gotten closer. I guess she doesn't have to compete with me for Haley's attention now."

Sweet words. Tim and Abby have bickered like kids sometimes. Now he's the adult.

He cooks for Abby, "mostly pizza or mac and cheese with salads." He takes her to movies, drives her places. He posts a photo on Facebook of him and Abby wrapped together in a plaid wool cape at a Native American gathering in the mountains. I click "Like."

Russ and I drive up to Flagstaff one day and take our son and his pro-tem daughter out for lunch. As we walk downtown Abby bounces around Tim, clinging to him, hugging him. We eat at Diablo's, where the food is local and organic. I have salad, Tim and Russ order burgers, and Abby has the rosemary fries. "I always have just those," she chirps. "I *love* 'em."

As we sit outside at a picnic table with our food, Tim says to Abby, "I know you'll tell your mom I'm having meat."

Abby smirks.

"You're such a brat. I'm gonna tell her myself." He texts Haley and confesses. "There." He's smug. A small relapse into not-so-grown-up.

After lunch we wander through a cavernous indoor shopping center and stop at a candy place. Abby hangs on Tim's arm and begs for a caramel apple. "I just bought you all that candy a couple days ago," he says.

"*Please....*"

"I'll buy one for you, Abby." Pulling out the money at the counter, I turn to Tim. "I don't mind. You've probably spent a lot on her since Haley's been gone."

"She's spoiled," Tim says.

I hand the treat to Abby. "Apples are good for you."

She hugs me. I lift her long blonde hair out of the way, pull her gently close and pet her head like she's a kitten. "I bet you miss your mom."

"Yeah...." Her voice is mournful.

I keep my arm around her as we walk out. "You're kind of like a grandkid to me, you know."

She offers me a bite of candy apple. It's delicious.

At the end of Haley's yoga course, Tim and Abby drive to L.A. to bring her back. Tim posts photos on Facebook of him and Haley, radiant, sitting on a bench under a tree, their arms around each other, the blue ocean behind. Abby must have taken the shot. "Like," I click.

♫

The little Flagstaff family cruises through the rest of summer and back to school in August. We pay Tim's tuition from his fund. He's still in the dental hygiene program, but we hear little about his studies except that he likes an elective psychology course.

They come for Thanksgiving again, Haley with her signature baba ganoush and vegetarian stuffing. Besides Tim's three and our daughter Holly from Tucson, we have Russ's sister and brother; Nancy's still-bereft husband Ken, with his wayward thirty-something son and the son's physically-challenged partner; and a VISTA worker from Massachusetts who has nowhere to go. It's a motley crew, but everyone seems at ease—except Haley. Before dinner, she is on edge. She fidgets, acts too cheery.

As Russ makes turkey gravy and the others pick at hors d'oeuvres, I invite Haley on a tour of our house—she hasn't really seen it. We start with the plant she gave me the previous Thanksgiving, which is thriving on the piano, and end in the sun porch, where my supplies for making stepping stones are strewn. She *ooh*'s and *ah*'s appropriately. "A good friend of mine does mosaics on tiles and flower pots," she says. "She sells them and gives half the money to Native Americans for Community Action."

"Nice," I say. Haley looks at the ceiling fan.

I can't help wanting to like this young woman. I feel we share deep similarities: both from rural Wisconsin, both into social justice, both committed teachers, cat and nature lovers—and I so appreciate her attraction to my son. But she speaks to me through some wall she's thrown up, and I can't crack through.

When people are lolling in the living room after pie, I ask Haley privately if I can bum a cigarette from her when she's ready to have one; I know she smokes two or three a day. She follows me out to the front porch and stands near a support post, looking at Granite Mountain in the distance, as I sit on the swing. It's cold out; we clutch our arms. Haley takes a little bag from her purse. "I roll my own. I don't like all the chemicals in regular cigarettes." She extracts tobacco with her fingertips and deftly rolls it into a Zigzag paper. "These are cheaper, too." She flicks her eyes at me. "But they're pretty strong...." She licks and seals the paper.

"I sometimes rolled my own back in the day." I haven't smoked a cigarette for years and was looking forward to a Marlboro or a Winston, but I delicately take the little twisted thing from her and she helps me light it, cupping the match's flame. She steps back to her post and gazes out, and I ask her about composting—I've just begun; she's been doing it forever.

"I mix manure in with the scraps once in awhile," she says. "And yard clippings."

I take a drag on the cigarette and suddenly feel my stomach rise. I swallow hard.

"I just like putting good stuff back into the earth, not wasting it," she muses.

"Yeah. I like that too." My guts are roiling from the cigarette. "Do you put in egg shells...?" I'm shivering, becoming sicker and sicker, but I don't let on.

"...You have to keep it moist," she says. "Then it really doesn't take long to turn to actual dirt."

Desultory talk drags on as I go through the motions, trying not to inhale. I want Haley to like me—to feel easy with Tim's hip mom, to share confidences—but it's not happening. I feel worse and worse.

Finally Haley heads inside out of the cold, and I follow, dizzy, my guts churning like a cement mixer. Haley sits down near Tim, but I keep moving, picking my way through the others sprawled in the living room. Then I walk quickly through the dining room and the kitchen and the sun porch and out the plate-glass door into fresh air, out of ear-shot, where I throw up my entire turkey dinner behind some bushes.

Bad idea, faking "cool" when I felt like crap. No wonder Haley wasn't open with me. I wasn't with her.

17

I Have You to Thank

OVER CHRISTMAS, Haley, Tim, and Abby drive across the country in his Honda to visit Haley's dad and step-mom in Wisconsin. Tim posts idyllic photos of them near Haley's folks' rustic barn, with cats and horses. We talk on the phone on Christmas day. "They're really nice," Tim says. "Haley's dad reminds me of Dad, and her step-mom's a lot like you. They had presents for me and I felt kinda bad 'cause Haley had presents for them, but I didn't."

Our daughter Holly and her boyfriend Rick are with us from Tucson; they came late on Christmas Eve and stayed the night. I'm amazed at the gifts Rick has brought us—an M.C. Escher book for Russ, a Putumayo CD of Bossa Nova music for me. "How did you know what we'd like?" I ask. Holly admits she helped him. She has nice presents for us, too.

I can't help comparing my adopted kids: Holly now gives presents on traditional occasions; Tim does not, though he shows appreciation in other ways. More and more I simply watch in fascination, admiring and not judging these children who are mine, but not-mine, whom I love so much.

"Talking with you is like a Christmas present," I tell Tim on the phone to Wisconsin.

When we visit Flagstaff after New Years, Tim says he's changing his major. "Too much math and science for dental hygiene. I really like psychology. I'm gonna try to major in psych and minor in music."

"That's my bachelor's degree, exactly," I say. "You're really good at guitar, but can you minor in music without being able to read it?"

"Dunno. Maybe not. I'm gonna try for it, though."

He's retaken the math class he flunked, and passed it this time—"barely," he says. "I need to work harder. I played video games too much." For the new semester he has classes that appeal to him. "Haley's sort of my counselor now. She's better than my official one."

He's letting Haley call the shots, making her his Higher Power, I'd say—but it's his business. We pay his tuition on-line from his dwindling ed fund, and have access to his course and grade records, but we don't look to see if he's got a music minor, or what his grades are. I'm curious; I think to check, then catch myself and don't.

On a Friday in April Tim calls, his voice buzzing like high-tension wires in a storm. "Will you be home tomorrow? I'm coming down. I wanna visit."

"What's up, Tim?"

His words slam into each other. "A professor friend of Haley's, this Dan guy, is going through a divorce and she's helping him with it. She's always with him. She stayed over at his place till 4:00 this morning...."

My heart thuds in dismay. "We'll be here, Tim. Come on down."

"I'm spending Friday night with Joe. I'll call you Saturday."

This spring Russ and I are leaving our big family house of twelve years, out in a country sub-division, for a smaller place in Prescott. We bought the little old house on Garden Street four years ago with the idea of downsizing and living in it. It is without a renter now, time to make the move. Each time I drive the ten miles to town I take a load of stuff. When Tim calls on Saturday I invite him to meet me there.

I'm standing on a stool by the high plate rack between the living and dining rooms when a deep male voice says, "Hi."

"Tim!" I set the blue cat plate in its place, down the line from the bigger deer-in-the-woods one in the center—I'm arranging the thirteen plates in descending size from the middle, going for symmetry and a balance of size and colors. I leave them to get down slowly and hug my son. I feel the stiffness in his body. He moves away and stands straight by the dining room window, his girth and posture resembling the strong ponderosa trunk I glimpse behind him through the wavy windowpane.

"I'll be finished with this in a minute, Tim."

Returning to the stool with Russ's grandmother's old Venetian plate, I hear a long, shuddering breath. I place the fragile plate next to the cat plate and ask casually, "How's Joe?"

"Fine. He's getting married in October."

"Wow."

"I'm never getting married. Anyway, I might be on my own again any day."

"Things are bad with Haley, huh?" I move the Venetian plate a quarter of an inch to the left.

"She's never home now. She's always over at Dan's."

The plate's too far left. I nudge it back to the right. "How long's this been going on?"

"Maybe two weeks. We fight about it. She says she's just keeping him company 'cause he's so messed-up over the divorce. But I don't know.... It's too *much.*"

I hear a gasp, turn and see his finger wipe a tear. I climb down and go to him. "Oh, Tim." As I wrap him in my arms he falls into me and leans his head against my shoulder, his sobs loud and natural, like a baby's—but in his deep, twenty-four-year-old man's voice. My body quakes against his as I weep with him.

He pulls himself up straight and rubs his eyes with a fist. "I thought I was over this."

I grip his firm upper arms. "No. It's okay, Tim. You're strong to let it out. *I* wouldn't put up with that crap. It's good you got away." I release him and he sinks back against the window frame.

"I hate to think about packing everything and moving out, leaving the cats.... And Abby. I'd miss her. I don't wanna be single again...."

His cell phone jangles. He reads the text and looks up. "Haley wants me to come home."

♫

Tim has finals in a week or so, just before Mothers Day. I wonder how he'll do, with the stress he must be under. I pray to the Universe to guide him.

Holly's graduation *cum laude* from U of A in Tucson is the Saturday after Tim's finals, and he wants to go with us. "I need another break from this place anyway," he says on the phone.

"Haley's still seeing that guy?"

"Yeah. But not so much. Dan texted me and said they're just friends. Anyway I don't care. He's kinda dorky."

Tim comes down to Prescott and rides with us to Tucson Friday afternoon. There's a picnic at the Marriott—Thai food with Holly's roommates and their families. The roomies are attractive young women who are graduating with her. Their boyfriends are there too, as is Holly's Rick. Tim meets Rick for the first time, and they get along easily. After we eat, the young folks sit at a round table outside and play Snap as the sun sets. I enjoy being among the proud parents and seeing my two kids interacting so well.

Commencement is a flurry the next morning. Holly goes early, getting ready to march with her College of Social Sciences. We park blocks away and hustle along the sunny sidewalk with the mass of people. I stop by a table and buy red roses for Holly. Rick is saving us seats in the stadium; we communicate by texting and scramble up the clanking bleachers to join him. Spirits are high; the speakers are great. We search for Holly with binoculars and think we spot her.

I'm so damn proud—of Holly for graduating, and of Tim for being there. Here's his little sister, three school years younger, graduating from college with honors, while he's scrabbling to get through his third semester—and I don't perceive a shred of the old childhood jealousy in his soul, only gladness to be with us.

After the ceremony we meet up and take photos. I'll later post one on Facebook of me and Russ and Tim and Holly on an outside stairway landing, Holly in her blue cap and gown holding the roses, all of us beaming. Many friends will comment and click "Like."

The four of us have lunch out with Rick and his mom, who's from Chile and always brings us a present—as I do now for her; I exchange our California dates for her Chilean wine, spoils from our respective recent trips. She's twenty years younger than I and has a degree in psychology, like me. It's fun catching up on the status of her job, her travels, her cats and dog.

Munching on my salad I flash on the word *serenity*—how I used to dislike even the sound of it, because I didn't own it. Now I'm floating in it.

Rick and Holly leave the restaurant before the rest of us, and when we get out to our Honda, I see perched on the silver hood a small plant with a bright red bloom. "Happy Mothers Day," Holly says. "Love you."

On Sunday morning back home in Prescott, as Russ makes breakfast and I sit in bed reading Program meditations, Tim comes in tentatively and says, "Happy Mothers Day." I put down my book. He moves close and blesses me with a hug.

I'm playing piano for the Unitarian Congregation service at 10:00, and Tim attends with me and Russ. Afterward he chats with some of our congregation friends. His social ease with older adults surprises me, seems new.

The three of us have time for lunch downtown before Russ, who's lent his resonant bass voice to the Yavapai College community choir for years, must leave for a pre-concert rehearsal. Tim and I will go to the concert, but we have time now to linger over coffee at Cupper's. I ask Tim how his finals went, and he winces. "Math was really hard."

I point out his progress on other fronts: "I'm glad you're not so bothered by Haley hanging around that Dan guy. You're doing good."

"I don't pay attention any more. I keep busy with other stuff."

"Sounds like you're detaching. Maybe you learned some

tricks from your old Program for alcoholics." He stopped going to meetings after Providence House.

"I think of Program stuff sometimes." We sip coffee. Then he sits back and looks at me. "You've really changed."

I smother a grin and cock an eyebrow. "What do you mean?"

"You're more laid-back. Stuff doesn't bug you like when I was in high school."

"I have you to thank, you know. I'm sorry you had all that trouble with booze, but it got me to those meetings."

We finish our coffee. "There's an art fair on the Square," I say. "We have time to walk around before Dad's concert,"

Sun glinting off our heads—his bald, mine silver—we link arms and cross the street.

Holly's graduation from U of A

Tucson, AZ - May 2012

18

Neighbors in Africa

"...AND HE HAS a really long red beard."

The TASOK superintendent's description of the new assistant administrator, due in the next day from Portugal, made me conjure a guy who looked like ZZ Top: skinny beard down past his chest, but mindful eyes—a Buddhist type, like a history prof I had back in Wisconsin. But when Russ Erickson appeared at the staff get-together, he looked more like a well-tended woodsman: tall and substantial, his brick-red beard as full as it was long, just covering his neck. Strawberry-blond hair curled to his collar. Behind wire-rim glasses his blue eyes searched for a place to settle.

I left without meeting him. He was surrounded by staff, and I needed to get back to my friend Jan, visiting from San Diego. She and I had just returned from Burundi, where we'd spent a few days lazing near Lake Tanganyika with my boyfriend Rich, who had transferred with Peace Corps to the little neighboring country. In a couple of days Jan would go home to her teaching job. I wanted to take her to dinner at my favorite Chinese restaurant, and, tomorrow, to Beaux Arts, the African art school, with its sculpture garden.

The next morning we heard rattling hangers through my bedroom wall. Someone had moved in behind me in the quadruplex. After breakfast Jan and I went around the back of the building, past my favorite campus tree—a towering, smooth-skinned, double-trunked ficus—and up the gravel path to welcome my neighbor in 98C.

At my knock the new inhabitant pulled open the door and blinked through the screen, then rubbed his bearded chin and smiled.

"Oh—it's you!" I blurted. "Sorry. I'm Lena Hubin. In 98B. I heard you through my bedroom wall."

He grinned. "I'm Russ—"

"Erickson. I know. From yesterday." I introduced Jan.

"I'm still unpacking, but come on in." He pushed open the screen door. "I've got coffee on."

Both Jan and I drank tea, not coffee, but Russ's brew smelled tempting—and this day would prove to be the beginning of my hot-beverage conversion. We perched on either end of the couch, which was covered with the same beige and green bamboo-print fabric as mine. In fact, the apartment was a mirror image of my own train of little rooms—bedroom at the back, then living room, dining room with tiny bath, and kitchen. Russ had placed a wooden desk with a red gooseneck lamp near the door. My piano stood in the corresponding spot in my apartment; I wondered if he'd hear me playing as he sat at his desk.

Jan and I had a clear view of Russ moving about his new kitchen, loading a tray with a carton of long-life milk, sugar, some spoons, and small, green-trimmed Corelle-ware cups identical to mine. "Is that a coffee grinder?" I asked. The little upright appliance sat beside the coffee maker, both pieces connected to adaptors. "I've never known anyone who grinds his own coffee."

"Yep. I make it from the ground up." He brought the tray to the table at our feet and poured our coffee, then sank into a side chair. He set his cup beside him, next to a curved wooden pipe in an ashtray. As he leaned back, his blue Feed-and-Read Bookstore t-shirt crept up, revealing a bit of hairy, bulging belly and an ample sense of ease.

We learned he came from a small hog farm in Illinois; I was from a small dairy farm in Wisconsin. "We were neighbors in the

Midwest," I said, "and here we are, neighbors in Africa."

Too bad Jan and I had plans. Visiting with Russ was so comfortable I could have sunk into his couch and spent the day.

As the school year kicked off, Russ and I began hanging out together. I'd go around to his apartment and have coffee with him before I headed to my middle school classroom scant yards away, and he crossed the playing field to the admin building. After school we'd sometimes change into shorts and haul rackets, balls, and water bottles to lower campus, where I taught him the rudiments of tennis.

The cracked and shabby campus court lay like an island in the middle of a grassy field, isolated by a dirt road that ran along a vine-laden chain link fence on one side; on the other, further away, an exploding stand of bamboo held back the jungle. Russ and I would whack balls back and forth on the court's faded green concrete for a hot, humid hour. Then, standing languidly at the net across from each other, we'd mop sweat, suck water from our bottles, laugh and talk.

Afterwards at one of our apartments we'd share a frosty Primus, the pungent local beer with the outline of Zaire embossed on the giant brown bottle. "There's a rumor that they brew this stuff with formaldehyde," I told him.

"Must kill what ails you." Russ took another swig.

He and I had a lot in common. His parents, like mine, enjoyed history and literature and music. Unlike most farm women of their generation, our mothers both had degrees beyond high school—his mom's in nursing, mine in teaching. Both of us had been baptized and raised Methodist. We'd both taught in foreign countries before Zaire—I in Nicaragua; he in Australia, Yemen, and Portugal—and we loved traveling. We'd each weathered a divorce while living abroad, and now had lovers in far-flung places. His diplomat girlfriend, Juliette, lived in Johannesburg; I had Rich, my Peace Corps guy, in Burundi.

One day as we rested at the tennis net I asked Russ, "Are you the brother I never had?"

What we didn't have in common was body types. I was fit and thin, and he had that belly.

A couple of months into the school year, Russ and I, along with several other staff, went out for dinner at the Kozy, a little restaurant on the main boulevard, run by parents of some Pakistani students. They pulled tables together for us and brought out little bowls of raw, curried, julienne carrots. "Mmm, I love these." I reached across Russ, at my left, to extract one.

Russ leaned into me and said quietly, "Nice arm."

"Oh. Sorry."

"No, I mean, *nice arms.*" He rested two fingers near my bare left shoulder for an instant, making me tingle—or was it the air conditioning? I pulled up my shawl as he lifted the little bowl of carrots, forked some onto his plate, and tasted one. "Mmm-hmm. Spicy."

During dinner I felt his leg brush mine. Was I crowding him? I moved my leg away, only to feel his against me again. I glanced at him; he flashed an innocent grin.

Back on campus Russ walked me around to my apartment, where he stepped close and fingered a strand of hair near my cheek. I leaned into his hand and his thigh slipped between my legs.

"Oh God, what are we doing?" I groaned. We had other people in our lives. Rich was coming from Burundi for Thanksgiving; Russ would fly to Jo'burg to see Juliette at Christmas. Our having sex would make things more complicated than they already were.

He raised my face with his hands, and I melted into the kiss.... then pulled away. "I can't."

He stepped back with a sigh, said goodnight and quickly left. In my apartment, my heart pounding, I swooped Puss-Puss from the floor and held him close. Three taps sounded on my louvered bedroom window, Russ's ritual signal as he passed to go home. "Damn," I breathed, and slumped onto the couch with Puss. "What would be so wrong...?" I mused to the purring cat. Yeah, I had Rich out there—but things weren't likely to get more serious with him; he worried about our color difference—his black to my white—and claimed he wasn't the marrying type, over forty and never wed. Anyway, would having sex with Russ need to change my relationship with Rich?

I petted Puss's head and searched his eyes. Okay, say I fell for Russ: Worst-case scenario, he'd end up throwing in his lot with Juliette; then I'd be out in the cold....

But right now I was hot for Russ, his belly just part of the package. Pouring Puss-Puss from my lap, I sprang from my chair and out the door. I went behind our bedroom windows, past the smooth ficus with its two slim trunks entwined, and up the pathway, where I saw the candle-glow through Russ's living room window, smelled his cherry pipe tobacco. I rapped lightly and let myself in the unlocked door.

That night next to Russ I dreamed of lying entranced beneath a shimmery, sparkling Christmas tree. Basking in bed the next morning, I smelled the coffee and felt an overwhelming sense of home.

"Hello, Killer." Rich's pet name for me rekindled affection as I picked him up at N'djili Airport the day before Thanksgiving. I was glad to to see this kind, modest man again and shrug off what had come to feel, in the past month, like too-quick, hazardous enmeshment with Russ. Rich stayed with me, and we had familiar sex on the other side of the wall where I knew Russ was sleeping. I squelched myself and hoped Russ couldn't hear the creaking bed.

Thanksgiving Day was pleasant and relaxed. I knew Russ was having turkey dinner with a group of teachers on Lower Campus; Rich and I dined in town with Peace Corps friends. During the next few days Rich and I visited old haunts in Kinshasa and took drives out of town. I managed to avoid encounters with Russ.

On Rich's last night in Kinshasa, as we sat at the bar at Chez Nicola nursing pre-dinner drinks, I said, "I've started playing tennis with someone...."

Rich looked at me, and my eyes dropped to the lime in my

gin. "'Playing tennis.' That's what you call it?" He jiggled his glass of Coke, rattling the ice.

I kept quiet. I thought Rich should know about other men—but I'd been tactless and unkind.

"*Vos table est prêt.*" The white-clad African waiter led us to our table.

We ordered with rigid manners. Rich maintained a chilly distance over dinner.

Sex that night was perfunctory. Rich seemed driven, and I let him drive. The next morning I took him to the airport. "Goodbye, Killer." He hugged me quickly, drew back and was gone.

On the long drive back to campus, passing straggly eucalyptus and crumbling city buildings, I felt an emptiness. Had I lost Rich? I had not yet "won" Russ; there was still Juliette. Though I wasn't sure I wanted either Russ or Rich for keeps, the possibility of losing both unnerved me.

I wrote Rich a warm letter thanking him for coming, for the good time we had; I hoped we'd meet again, at least as friends; my tennis partner and I were just friends. "I'd like to stay in touch." He wrote a cordial letter back, thanking me for my hospitality.

Russ and I, pulled together on our home turf as if by a magnet, resumed the casual sex and dating pattern we'd begun. But his Christmas trip to visit Juliette loomed.

♫

I'd made plans to surprise my parents in Wisconsin for the '82 holidays, and in December I flew home from the tropics to a magical white Christmas. My sister Chrissie picked me up at the Minneapolis airport and drove me to our old farm two hours east on snowy roads. When I appeared in Mom's kitchen in my white down jacket, her brown eyes brightened almost conspiratorially: Had she caught wind of my visit? From far away, through letters, I'd come to appreciate a savvy intuitiveness in my mother. When she'd learned of my divorce from Val she'd written, "I knew things weren't right when there were only snakes for wedding décor, no cats or music notes." I suspected Mom had caught some hint of my visit in a letter—but choosing to believe I'd surprised her, I never asked.

Since her Christmas break hadn't started yet, I visited Mom at Riverside Middle School. In the smoky teachers' lounge she beamed as she introduced me to her colleagues as her African Queen. I spoke with the young music teacher, who had done a production of *H.M.S. Pinafore,* a musical in which a captain's daughter loves a lowly sailor and all goes awry. I would produce it with my middle schoolers at TASOK the next year.

Trussed in my down jacket, jeans, and tall boots, I traipsed the two short blocks of wreath- and holly-bedecked stores to shop in my hometown. Dazzling snow lay on the ground along the sidewalks. People I met smiled and cast vaporized "Merry Christmases" into the crisp air. The little town overflowed with Christmas cheer; I couldn't help but catch the spirit.

Beside our old barn I built a snow woman with snow breasts and dried-flower hair, and romped with Suzy, my folks' little white mutt. Mom took photos of me in the snow. I celebrated Christmas in gatherings of relatives and met with an old high school friend home visiting, like me. Mom had been making windsocks that year, and she gave me one with a line stitched across a blue ocean connecting outlines of the U.S. and Africa. It would fly outside my apartments in Zaire until it began to disintegrate in the tropic air.

Home in the U.S., my life drew snug and warm around me like my down jacket, crowding out worries of the future, of what might befall with Russ or Rich in Zaire.

My first night back in Africa, Russ and I went out for dinner at *Plein Vent*—"Full Wind," in French, for its broad, breezy veranda. Outside the tall, skinny building that housed the fondue restaurant, a legless man sat beneath a fire-red blossomed *flamboyant* tree playing intricate rhythms with sticks on cans and bottles. We applauded and dropped some coins for him, then let the lumbering elevator take us to the seventh floor. At a table on the veranda we ordered cheese fondue to share. Then Russ took a sip of wine and cleared his throat. "I found some other guy's shoes under Juliette's bed." But he and Juliette would keep in touch. "If I'm reading her right, she wants to see me again."

Rich wrote to me. "I'm seeing a Burundian woman. She's nice, but it's just for now. Maybe you and I could meet this summer in the States."

Russ and I continued playing tennis, going out to eat, taking drives, spending nights together. Whether we stayed at each other's place or not, I'd join him for coffee many mornings after I ran and showered. Sometimes Puss-Puss trailed me and sprawled on Russ's couch.

But Russ and I maintained our separate lives, allowing each other space for other friends. Cocooned together on forty-three scant acres in Africa, we TASOK staff members had an instant bond, like family, and our lives spilled into the always-warm outdoors. We'd see each other walking to the pool or tennis court or classroom; we'd meet traipsing through the jungle. We shared Zairian houseworkers, gardeners, vendors, and French tutors. Having no phones, we'd pop in on each other for drinks and chats and school business. I hung out with the music teacher, who lived next-door with her little dog in 98A; I played piano for her high school musicals. Russ took up playing squash with the middle school science teacher; he also spent time with a guy he'd taught with in Yemen who now lived in the next quadruplex and taught 6th grade.

The second semester sped by.

♫

In summer, Russ picked me up at O'Hare in Chicago in a slick, black, borrowed Corvair. He was working on a school admin program that summer at ISU in Normal, Illinois. I stayed with him for a couple of days, tripping down the warm, humid streets in a flared, flowered-cotton skirt and matching spaghetti-strap top I'd bought at Goodwill in Wisconsin. As I flung my arms around him on the sidewalk, Russ said, "You must be Rebecca of Sunnybrook Farm." We drove south to grand old Pere Marquette Lodge in a state park on the Illinois River. The place had a giant chessboard painted on the floor with life-size knights and rooks and royalty. We took photos as we made chess pieces of ourselves and played a game or two. After dinner we lounged on our bed's pine-and-maroon quilt and fell into sex beneath huge timbers crossing overhead.

Russ was the first of many friends and lovers I visited in the States during that summer of '83. I had lucked into an Eastern Airlines pass that for $399 allowed residents of foreign countries unlimited trips anywhere Eastern flew in the U.S.—as long as you didn't mind going through Atlanta, the hub. I had flown to Minneapolis and visited family in northern Wisconsin before whizzing off, via Atlanta, to see Russ in Illinois.

At Dulles Airport in Washington, D.C., Rich met me in his refurbished blue MG and whisked me through green mountains to his old, two-story, dark-wood-lined house in West Virginia. The house was walled into two living spaces; a man in his eighties lived next-door. "I've let Hank live here for years. He pays token rent and keeps me company when I'm home."

That night I slipped off my long, lacy cotton robe and slid naked next to Rich in his old four-poster bed. "Lookin' good, Killer," he said, pulling me to him. Hank was old; he probably couldn't hear much through the wall.

Flying high that summer, I jet-setted on to visit my sister Carol in Denver, and friends in Cocoa Beach, Missoula, San Diego, and San Francisco. I went hiking and rock climbing and horseback riding; I trekked around old city squares, parks, and Chinatowns, and dipped into the waters of American lakes and oceans.

In San Diego I ran into Sarah, Nate Collins' sister, from my old Chicago neighborhood. "Nate's in town," she said.

Nate, who had broken my heart on West Buckingham, wanted to see me. We met for dinner in downtown San Diego, then put on swimsuits and sneaked into a ritzy housing complex he'd worked at in La Jolla. We passed a bottle of wine back and forth in the hot tub. Afterwards, the top down on his old marine-blue Porsche, we cruised in moonlight to Presidio Park, where we smoked a joint, stripped off some clothes, sprawled on a broad old cannon—*El*

Jupiter, I think—and made love under the stars. "Where've you been?" Nate moaned, as if *I* were the one who'd left.

I had wonderful visits with women-friends, too—in Florida, Colorado, and California—and by the end of summer, the U.S. had come to feel as comfortable as my favorite jeans and T-shirt.

Toward August, on an Eastern flight's descent into Atlanta, we hit major turbulence in blue sky. Two young tow-headed boys beside me, their parents across the aisle, whined and whimpered. "It's okay," I soothed, and patted the knee of the tyke next to me. "Just ride the bumps."

This from someone whose heretofore deathly fear of flying had driven me to Valium and large amounts of alcohol to survive long flights. Perhaps all those summer trips in and out of Atlanta had conditioned the terror out of me. My entire life felt smoother, the bumps gone; I was not about to crash. Come to think of it, through much of that summer of '83 I felt freer than ever—floating on air, and at the same time, grounded.

♫

On the second leg of my trip back to Zaire, we reached flying altitude over the Atlantic as the sun dropped. I sipped a gin and tonic, had dinner, and went to sleep. Somewhere over mid-ocean, turbulence made my heart thump. The middle-aged Belgian man next to me snorted in his sleep and shifted to face me, and the sky smoothed out. I reclined my seat, and as I gazed out the window at bright, pin-prick stars against black, my thoughts drifted from one blithe summer encounter to another. It was clear that *friends* were important, loner though I was. They'd helped me glide through this vacation. I could depend on them for companionship, support and understanding. I'd said to Rich about Russ, "We're just friends," and it was true. Both men were my friends, and along with women friends, that could be enough, for now. Settling on one man would only lead to marriage. What was the hurry? It had been just three years since I'd left the disastrous one with Val. I was thirty-six, but my biological clock—if I had one—wasn't ticking. I'd decided long ago that if I ever wanted kids I would adopt.

My summer travels had afforded me a chance to breathe and coast and let things sort out on their own. I would cruise through my sixth year in Africa, then go to grad school in California—*California*, my alma mater, where I was a resident. I'd love living there again. I would apply soon to several universities, to study English—maybe writing.

When I awoke, soft layers of pink-tinged sky filled the window. "Good morning, ladies and gentlemen," the announcement blared. "Before we land in Brussels we'll be serving breakfast."... *"Bonjour mesdames et monsieurs.... petit dejeuner."*

I straightened my seat back and put down my tray table. A flight attendant was already pouring coffee. It would probably taste bad—but I'd be home in Africa that night.

In TASOK apartment 98B

Zaire, Africa

19

Maybe a Second Cat

In March, a long-awaited letter landed in my TASOK mailbox. I tore into the envelope and scanned the lines—and breath left me like a punctured tire. The letter tight in hand, I left the admin building and stumbled across the field to 98B, where I swooped up Puss-Puss and slumped onto the couch.

San Francisco State had turned me down. I felt like one of the wads of paper I'd hurled at the trash while wrestling unruly words into the required writing sample. I was a shitty writer—not good enough for the City by the Bay. Holding Puss close, I smoothed the wrinkled letter and read it through: "*.... recommend that you pursue an undergraduate program....*"

What made me think I could write? Winning that contest in 8th grade a hundred years ago? Mrs. Carlson's misplaced faith in me? Articles I got published without pay in overseas teaching journals? Certainly not my years'-worth of rampant journal ruminations.

I put down Puss, washed my face, and went around to 98C.

"That's not the only program for writing in California, is it?" Russ poured beer into mugs frosty from the freezer. "You applied to others, right?"

"Not many have *creative* writing. I was accepted by Cal State Irvine and Fresno...."

"So—"

"I wanted San Francisco! Irvine wants me to make up a bunch of courses, and anyway it's part of L.A. and I don't want to live there. And Fresno's just hot, boring cropland—I might as well go back to the Imperial Valley." I gulped cold beer like a palliative. "This was a dumb idea anyway. Just because I like writing doesn't mean I'm any good at it. Obviously."

"Isn't there some famous writer at the U in Fresno?"

"You mean Phillip Levine?" Did Russ know this because of his own masters in English? I'd never heard of the poet until I got CSU-Fresno's application for the program. "But he left."

"Hey, you've been accepted, you've got options. What could be so bad about living in *any* university town in California?"

♫

By the time the plane touched down at N'djili the previous August, I'd transformed into a grad student. The following spring I was shedding my TASOK cocoon and opening my wings—enrolling at California State University in Fresno.

In the cramped stacks of the Kinshasa Library Club I rummaged through books and encyclopedias to learn about my California home-to-be. *Fresno* means "ash tree" in Spanish, named for the trees along the San Joaquin River. Plums and oranges and peaches were among the major crops: Trees! Trees, full and green, inhabiting the sky—unlike the low-down cabbages and lettuce and alfalfa that had crouched in the dust lining the road to school in the Imperial Valley. Fresno was three hours' drive from San Francisco and just two from Yosemite. How bad could it be?

In late July my parents helped me load a U-Haul truck with my childhood wash-stand dresser, a rocking chair, a double bed, and a big, round, etched mirror donated by Mom. The dark, wenge-wood bar carved with a village fishing scene, which I'd shipped from Zaire, went in the truck still in its wrappings, along with the old Sears bike that had been my major means of transport in past lives. Into the cab I plopped Maizie, a gray-striped kitten who during my Wisconsin stay had wandered in from the cornfield. I aimed the bulky truck toward California.

I spent my first night on the road on the far side of Iowa in a bleak Motel 6. Staring at the TV, I thought about the bright little hotel where Russ and I had stayed in Kikwit. After the nine-hour drive along the asphalt road from Kinshasa past rushing rivers and tall, encroaching grasses, we'd settled into our cozy room. The next day, for a few *zaires*, an adroit African stood in his *pirogue*—a canoe hewn from a single log—and poled us along the shade-dappled edge of the wide Kwilu River. Seated single-file on planks in the little boat, we glided over silky brown water beneath a fringe of tropical greenery. Back in our room after dinner in the Lebanese pine-and palm-lined courtyard, I had been more eager for sex than Russ—a rare event.

Here in Iowa, the drab-clothed double bed sat empty but for Maizie snoozing nose-to-tail on a pillow. The standard cityscape on the wall and the droning TV made me feel as lost as my kitten when she'd tottered out of the tall corn. I picked up the phone on the nightstand and called my sister Carol in Denver, collect. "I'll pay you when I get there." I twiddled the coiled rubber cord. "I just feel kind of lonesome."

"Not for long, Eileen," Carol said. "Relax!"

"I've had a stomachache since I left Wisconsin. Maybe I'm sick with something I picked up in Africa...."

"You'll be fine." As if *she* were the big sister. "I'll see you Wednesday!"

The truck had no air conditioning, and I drove through the sweltering heat of summer with the windows down, squirting myself with water from a spray bottle. Maizie rode shot-gun without a carrier, and when she began to pant I leveled misty bursts of water at her, which she accepted with amazing equanimity.

In some small Colorado town before reaching Carol's in Denver, I stopped and got out for a Big Mac, leaving the truck's windows part-way down for Maizie. When I returned she was gone. Panicked, I walked through the neighborhood calling and calling, until a woman working in her yard shaded her eyes and pointed. "I think she went under my car." The woman stood on one side of her sedan while I slithered part-way under the other and maneuvered Maizie out. We were soon back on the road.

When I'd flown to California earlier that summer looking for a place to live, I'd happened upon Clovis, a town on the northeast side of sprawling Fresno. Swinging on cables over Clovis's old main street was a faded green art-deco sign proclaiming the city "Gateway to the Sierras"—a breath of fresh air compared to Calipat's "Lowest-Down City" label. I'd rented a one-bedroom apartment near the pool in a complex on West Alamos.

A month later, when the U-Haul's contents were emptied into my new Clovis apartment and the truck returned to its depot, Maizie and I were home.

For weeks, I took the daily twenty-minute bike ride down Shaw Avenue to school. And Cheryl Riordan, a grad student fifteen years my junior who owned a car, didn't mind driving me to night classes. But one morning I tumbled off my bike and fell hard onto the curb. "Dammit!" I fumed, a hand on my pained hip. I stood up, wrangled my backpack heavy with *The Complete Works of Shakespeare* over my shoulders, and got back on the wretched bike. As I rode on to school, it sank in: Enough of this hare-brained plan for exercise and saving money; I'm too old for this. I bought a ten-year-old, repainted Datsun.

My new ride proved a mixed blessing, morphing from dazzling silver to an abysmal charcoal, depending on the light, its behavior, and my emotions *du jour*. It eased my grad school transportation needs, but extorted money and attention for its upkeep.

Toward November the dreaded annual *tule* fog crept in like a stealth bomber and settled over the valley. Thick fog obliterated everything further than four feet ahead, creating disorientation and traffic pile-ups. One day I got lost driving home from Vons grocery. I nosed down unrecognizable streets, turning corner after corner, expecting some familiar landmark to appear, until tears of frustration blurred my eyes. I pulled over near a rangy tree I hadn't seen till I was parked beneath it. I wiped my eyes, got out and found my way to the nearby corner, where a street sign said Los Alamos. A miracle: I was home.

Each fog-wrapped morning, in my drab sweatpants outfit, scarf and gloves, I ran down neighborhood streets for exercise, engulfed by dense, bone-chilling vapor. On Tuesday, November 6th, I looked for a sign along my route. When it popped into view, pointing out my precinct's polling place, I stopped mid-run to vote for steely-haired, eminently forgettable Walter Mondale for President. Then the fog enshrouded me again.

In the midst of Fresno's dank winter, stress sat as heavy on my shoulders as my backpack full of books. I was drowning in arduous reading and writing, never able to get my head up long enough for a deep breath. Dr. Ziegler, my autobiography prof, had us unearth rough gems from the pits of our subconscious, then use writing to scrub and polish and expose them to harsh light upon the page. "Think *deep*. Let the *truth* of your experience emerge!" he said. Urged to bare our secret lives in class, some students broke down sobbing. "That's good. Dig *deeper!*" Dr. Ziegler said. "If the material feels too raw and recent, you'll just have to wait and write about something else." Some students dropped the class.

Dr. Z met with survivors one-on-one. A Scottish flat cap perched on his bald pate, he sat across from me at a picnic table near ag department cows munching alfalfa in a field. Dr. Z's eyes, hard coals set within his sharp tan features, bored into me. "How did it make you feel when your dad shooed you out of the barn during the insemination of the cows? What impact did that have on sex for you when you hit puberty? There's a connection...."

God only knew. Why had I written that stuff? I didn't want to think about it any more. I dissolved in tears at Dr. Z's impossible queries. Then, back at the drawing board, I ground out ten new pages—deeper ones, I hoped.

I was equally confounded by dour Dr. Simons' advanced fiction writing course. I cranked out rambling stories whose woeful plots, based not-so-loosely on events in my own life, dredged up more angst. Hemingway was Simons' idol, and the prof was never satisfied with my work. *Prosy*, he would scrawl over a passage. Or *banal*, or once, *clear as mud*. Sometimes I felt trapped by his acerbic suggestions for revision: Should I acquiesce, or risk a bad grade? Like a trembling rodent, I gave in for the reward.

For British Lit I chose to report on Margaret Drabble's *The Realms of Gold*, which I'd read before, having discovered Drabble's books in a London bookstore. When I presented my report to the class, describing the bit set around a table in Africa made me giggle so hysterically that I teared up. Studying the scene had hauled up thoughts of Zaire: the sight and smell of *saka saka* and *fufu*—Zairians' staple meal of greens and that abominable, fermented manioc. One evening our Zairian hosts in the remote village of Seke Banza had served it to a dozen TASOK middle schoolers and me, on a trip to help a Peace Corps worker build a school. When 7th-grade Amin Dewji was handed his plate of *saka saka* and *fufu*, he rolled his eyes. "Eat, Amin. People in Third World countries are starving," I said, no irony intended. I choked down my own plateful.

I wanted to taste that dish again and traipse with those kids through the brush to whack off chunks of towering termite mounds with machetes and drag them back for use as mortar—"termite spit makes it stick," the Peace Corps guy had told my kids. On the ride back to TASOK we ate sweet ripe mangoes sent with us by the villagers, juice dripping down our chins. Sixth-grade Todd Lerner's mango allergy flared up, reddening the skin around his eyes. "It's happened before," he said, rubbing at it. "I'll be okay."

In Brit Lit class that night, mid-report, I passed a hand over my eyes. I had no time for nostalgia. I needed my psychic energy to succeed in school. I wanted A's.

♫

During winter break, my best grad school buddy Cheryl Riordan and I drove to Yosemite, her yellow Camaro's radio blasting "Red Red Wine." We holed up in a cabin for two days, and lolling by the fire, let flow a stream of consciousness. "I'm pretty sure I'm in love with Jaime." Draped over the loveseat, Cheryl sipped deep from her cabernet. "He doesn't belong with Nikki. She's so crass, and he's so *sensitive*...." She sighed.

"I think about Doug a lot lately." Cross-legged on the braided rug, I tossed a log into the crackling fire. Doug Lindley, the musician I'd fallen for and been dumped by in San Diego seven years earlier, had reappeared. This time around I wasn't crawling through his windows or backing him into corners. He'd come to visit me in Clovis in November. We hiked among the sequoias of Kings Canyon, then made love beneath the comforter my mom had given me, with its music staff and notes. "I fantasize about him."

"What about Rich?" She knew my West Virginia Peace Corps boyfriend had been to visit, too.

"He hasn't written in ages. Anyway, things haven't felt the same with him since Zaire." I finished my wine and poured more. "I do miss Russ, though." I'd come to depend on his companionable, newsy letters from Zaire. *"Puss-Puss has learned to catch beer coasters out of the air,"* a recent one said.

I'd put aside the quest for a perfect mate, settling for long-distance, part-time lovers—but this left my days bereft. Thank God for Cheryl, my friend and confidant. Grad school would have been unbearable without her. But at home, loneliness was my companion.

"You and Russ'll probably have a dozen kids and live happily ever after." Cheryl grinned at me and took a sip of wine.

"Hah! *You're* more likely to have a bunch of kids." I was in my mid-thirties, Cheryl just twenty-one. I knew she wanted to get her doctorate and then have babies.

I'd never thought I wanted children, but in my Los Alamos apartment complex, I caught myself noticing them. One day by the pool a mother was encouraging her little kid to swim to her. When the tot emerged at her feet, his mom swooped him wet and giggling into her arms, and I felt a tug.

A flute-playing grad student who lived in the apartments was a single mother of two cute, lively young kids. I toyed with an idea: Could I create a family without a man?

Relationships with men had been complicated and exhausting. Loving a child seemed simpler. Wasn't I independent and mature enough to care for a baby on my own?

Thoughts of adoption surfaced, and a dream took hold: I could save some precious little being from a life of poverty in China or India. I would love the baby into becoming my closest ally—

as fulfilling as a man, far better than a cat. My child and I, with Maizie, would be a family.

In October I'd embarked upon the plan. I made calls, wrote letters, filled out applications. In a few weeks I was accepted as a potential single mother by an agency in Minnesota. I'd passed! I'd be a mom! I imagined rocking my baby, singing to her, hearing her first words, helping him toddle around Maizie as he learned to walk—boy or girl, it didn't matter.

"Oh, Eileen, *don't*. Not on your own. It'll be so hard," my mother said on the phone.

Here was her damned advice again. Could I do nothing right in her eyes?

Between coursework and classes the next few days I mulled it over: sweet babe in arms vs. Mom's warning. I'd often shunned her counsel and later realized she was right.

Doubts of my own seeped in: A baby would take *time*. And childcare...?

I'd thrown away the letter from Minnesota.

"We should move." Cheryl reached for her boots. "Let's go for a hike."

♫

Soon after my aborted foray into adoption, I'd started accompanying the flute-playing grad student-mom, regularly getting my fingers on the music department's old Steinway grand pianos. Then I was asked to teach Basic Writing second semester as a grad assistant—which delivered me two classes of fifteen interesting young adult students like Lily from Hong Kong and Bahar from Indonesia and others from Iran, Guatemala, Pakistan. The rich mix of nationalities catapulted me back to the cozy familiarity of my classroom in Zaire.

There were these and other diversions from my grad-school labors—but home was still a loveless void. If I wasn't going to adopt a child, maybe a second cat would relieve me and be a companion for Maizie. After Christmas I rescued a large, plush, gray adult female. Pandora and Maizie got on well, though Pandy was more skittish and reclusive. She ventured only onto my tiny fenced-in patio, whereas Maizie ranged far from the apartment, coming back each night. Less needy than her new sister, Maizie remained my favorite.

♫

One week in foggy February I fumbled with a Faulkner paper for American Lit, frustrated by the obscurity of *The Sound and the Fury*; the thing was due on Friday. Then in Wednesday's fiction-writing class Dr. Simons rode hard on a short story that I'd revised to near-perfection. I was crushed. Cheryl was teaching a Shakespeare class and had little time to listen to my academic plaints.

That week I was also hammering at a difficult Mozart piano accompaniment for my flute-playing friend's upcoming recital. I ran to the music department every chance I got to practice the complex measures; the twisty tune coursed through my brain in bed at night.

To top off my distress, a kid in one of the writing classes I taught was disrupting class with wise-ass comments. On Thursday he flung out the *F*-word, and I wanted to throttle him.

Life was a speeding train threatening to derail, and Doug in San Diego wasn't answering his phone. Was he through with me again? I longed for another letter from Russ. Could he be seeing someone else? In the middle of the night, worries haunted me. I wouldn't make a living as a writer; that romantic fantasy had been laid waste by the slogging, never-finished nature of actual writing for my classes. Maybe I could teach at some community college—but I had a friend doing that in Illinois who traveled between two schools and worked her butt off for little pay and no benefits. And after my wonderful positions in Nicaragua and Zaire, could I be happy teaching in U.S. public schools? I feared not. Maybe I'd go overseas again—but alone?

On Friday night I came home late from Cheryl's, and Maizie wasn't there. I called; she didn't come. I went to bed, but awoke several times and went outside in the dark to search, walking around back to the parking lot. I got up at dawn and looked outside again; still no little gray feline. The most comforting being in my life was gone.

The next day a letter from a friend in Zaire said the Peace Corps director had died of AIDS. The words shot fear through my body like high-voltage current. When Rich and I had eaten Thanksgiving dinner at his house, this personable, fortyish, non-gay guy had been healthy and happy!

In Zaire I'd heard locals were dying from AIDS, though I knew of no one who'd contracted it. There was no TV at TASOK, and little access to news. It was easy to regard AIDS as a foreign menace to which we outsiders were immune. But my friend's letter had brought word of an American victim, someone I'd known. AIDS could obviously happen to anybody. Why not me? I probably deserved it. And a recent headline at the Vons grocery check-out line had said, "1500 Dead of AIDS in U.S."...

On emotional overload, I made an appointment with a psychologist and confessed my fear at the first session. "I'm too scared of AIDS to even go for the test. What if the results are positive?"

The therapist gave me an assignment. Always the good student, I did as she asked: For ten minutes each day I sat in my rocker and breathed. As Dr. Goldberg had taught me in the psych ward years earlier, I breathed in, tightened my muscles, then breathed out. Over and over. A flood of thoughts rushed in, causing tears, dislodging the stress that had been living in the basement of my brain for weeks, for *months*.

On Thursday of that week, I came home to find Maizie strolling toward me across the grass as if she'd never left. She'd been AWOL for six days. "Where've you been, poor puss?" I swooped her up, stroked her, and removed her broken collar. I took her inside and fed her, then settled her on my lap in the rocker and breathed.

20

On That We Concurred

THE SECOND SEMESTER at CSUF rushed on, smoothing away the sharpest edges of my anxiety like a river polishing rock. A torrent of work and commitments rolled along, but I'd learned to navigate grad school currents. I was earning *A*'s. Though news about AIDS could still pull me under, sessions with my therapist, Myrna, and her breathing lessons, kept me afloat.

Letters between Russ and me crossed over the Atlantic. I shared details of my classes, my friends and cats, my days. I loved his news from Zaire on tissue-thin stationery with tiny colored village scenes on top. *Remember that tall mango tree by our apartments?* he wrote in his left-handed print. *Yesterday a mango fell through my roof and broke off a chunk of the Eternit tile up there. It scared the hell out of me.* And at the end, *I really miss you, Lena.*

Things are fine here, I wrote back, *but Fresno is gray and boring. I miss Zaire.* Then in March, *I'm thinking of doing the five-week California Writing Project here this summer. I could get a fellowship.*

He wrote, *How would it be if I came and stayed with you in July?*

Myrna pursed her lips and nodded. "He smokes a pipe, he

whistles, he talks too much..."

"I don't mind the pipe, but I don't know if I want him smoking at my place for over a month. Even outside on my tiny patio."

Myrna smiled and nodded some more.

"Russ made fun of my running at 5:30 in the morning," I'd told her at an earlier session. "*He* should be running. His belly always bothered me...." And, "He can't seem to be quiet for long. If he runs out of things to talk about he *whistles.* It gets on my nerves."

"I know," Myrna said. "He whistles, he smokes a pipe, he talks a lot...."

I finally felt the comfort in her refrain. What did I expect, perfection? I breathed, and focused on Russ's kindness, his gentle wit, the fun we had together.

But fear would sneak back. My three previous attempts at cohabiting with a man had not ended well. Maybe I simply wasn't wired for it—was too independent, as my dad had once said.

In April Russ wrote, *I've started running in the evenings, two laps of the jungle. Fruit bats swoop across the path. They're HUGE. They must be 5 feet across. I remember how you liked their gulping sounds.*

Bonnie, a TASOK teacher-friend, wrote, *Russ talks about you a lot. By the way, he's looking really good these days.*

♫

Tall and confident in a dark green polo shirt, Russ looked great when I picked him up at the Fresno airport. Had he lost weight? His hug brought back the warmth I remembered. We soon fell into an easy rhythm together, in bed and out. He liked my two gray felines, inside all the time now due to complaints of cat damage to flowerbeds. I kept the litter box in a closet, and Russ cleaned it more often than I did. He would sometimes take a cat out to the enclosed patio and keep her close while he lay in the hammock smoking his pipe and reading. I left the glass sliding door open to let the smell of his cherry tobacco drift inside.

We studied together at home, sharing details about our courses. In Russ's admin counseling class, they did therapy exercises on each other behind one-way glass while classmates watched. One evening as he laid a big textbook open at the table, he told me that a woman he was practicing on had started crying and couldn't stop.

I looked up from washing dishes. "You made her cry?"

"I don't know. She got talking about her dad, who died when she was seven. She thanked me afterwards." He smoothed the pages with his palms. "The teacher criticized me for not going into 'that dark hole' with her. That's what he said—*'that dark hole.'* I guess I didn't empathize enough." His eyebrows furrowed.

That Russ might not have been able to empathize with this woman would stick with me like a pesky gnat I couldn't swat away.

I became well-acquainted with the people in my 9:00-to-5:00 Writing Project. In a small critique group, I got to know Jordana, a tall blond middle school teacher. She liked my narratives about Zaire, and I was intrigued by her dramatic fiction writings—which she soon confided were really non-fiction: Her lawyer ex-husband had hired someone to kill her with a baseball bat. After his attack, when she came out of her coma, she could speak only her first language, Dutch; she had to relearn English.

"She's still scared her ex will find her," I told Russ over gin and tonics on the patio. "She had a high-powered burglar alarm system installed in her house."

Russ shook his head. "Weird."

"And I thought *Val* was nuts." I felt a rush of gratitude for Russ's pacific nature.

One night in July, eating supper at the table, we heard rustling in the living room and found Pandora trapped in a plastic bag, a handle caught around her neck. She threw herself across the carpet—a frantic, shrink-wrapped lump of gray that stopped, then jetted in another direction. Russ and I squelched laughter as I dashed to the rescue. When I released her, my poor cat's eyes gleamed large with fear, and I felt bad for having laughed.

On weekends we drove my Datsun—the *Silver Streak,* Russ dubbed it—to Woodward Park to walk and jog and throw a Frisbee. For the 4th of July we went to the university to hear Tchaikovsky's *1812 Overture* performed outside with fireworks and cannon fire. "Not so different from when a jet flew down Boulevard Treinte

Juin for Zaire's independence day, huh?" Russ said.

"Maybe safer."

Neither of us had been in Kinshasa when this happened, but we'd heard tales of Zaire's outrageous independence celebrations back in the '70's.

After the concert we walked around the old Tower District and had a beer outside at a corner cafe.

Fresno had its charms after all.

♫

The end of July, over drinks in a booth at the Acapulco on Blackstone, Russ said, "I was kind of hoping you'd be interested in planning a wedding." He slipped a hand into his pocket. "I brought something from South Africa."

Sheer terror struck me. South Africa was Diamond Land. I caught my breath and drew back—Pandora in the plastic bag.

"I realize this summer is just an experiment," Russ added, "but I like how things are going. I thought maybe you did too."

"I do.... But *marriage*?"

His hand came back empty and grasped his margarita on-the-rocks.

I'd been pretty sure Russ had the *M*-word in mind when he asked to stay with me. And his presence had become such a cushion of comfort that I felt weepy now, denying him. But his sudden proposal had triggered my anxiety like a burglar alarm. I steadied my hand on my frozen margarita.

♫

When our course work finished in early August, we took a vacation. First we drove to L.A. to see the musical *Cats*. I sat on pins and needles in the dim theater, pushing back bleak imaginings of my unknown future as the eyes of the sinuous feline impersonators blinked bright in the dark.

Then we drove up Coastal Highway 1, through the giant Redwoods and on to the Shakespeare festival in Ashland, Oregon.

In that little town we saw outlines of dead bodies chalked on the sidewalks, each labeled with a name and date. "Nagasaki," Russ said. "August '85. This would be the fortieth anniversary." We learned the city commemorated the bombings every year. The artistic tribute impressed Russ to the point of tears. His sensitivity amazed me. He certainly had no problem going into "that dark hole" in history, and expressing his feelings over it.

At Ashland's Elizabethan Stage we attended *The Merchant of Venice,* in which Portia's pure, compassionate mercy drops like gentle rain from heaven, and all ends well for the lovers.

The long drive back to Fresno passed quickly.

On Russ's last day in town we waited for the cool of dusk before sitting with illicit bottles of beer by the lake—alcohol forbidden in Woodward Park. His left arm whipped forward to skip a flat pebble across the water. "Four," he counted. "So you're not ready to say yes, are you." A flat non-question.

I sat straight and sipped my beer. The summer had been as perfect as could be. There was no one else I'd rather be with than Russ; I knew that, now that we'd spent weeks under the same roof. It wasn't marriage that held me off; I'd begun to think it might be worth another try. But my free-floating angst put barbed wire around me, fencing Russ out. I squeezed his hand. "I'm sorry."

♫

One day in September, getting out of my car to buy a can of tomatoes at Vons, I saw a tiny plane dive straight down, clipping a wing on the store's back roof, sending fragments flying. "Holy shit!" I blurted to no one, and ran around to see.

The plane sat silent, tipped onto its unbroken wing. The pilot, hovered over by a couple of guys in Vons aprons, stood dazed on the asphalt, brushing himself off—*alive.*

At home there was no one to tell about the crazy crash. I made my chili and ate it on my own and had leftovers the next day, and the next. Russ made better chili.

That fall, in my third semester at CSUF, I began work on my thesis, a collection of short stories. I would entitle it *Making Time,* the story about a depressed and lonely young woman who "made time" with guys, but never felt there were enough hours in the day for real, meaningful living. I felt superior to my main character: I no longer fell into bed and bad relationships. But like her, my days were filled with too much to do and too little fulfillment.

An epiphany on a bridge one day triggers my protagonist to ease up on herself, and at the end, a healthy love relationship sits on the horizon. Was I foreshadowing my own future?

♫

Two months after Russ left, I was in my rocker revising a story, facing the TV evening news, when Rock Hudson's handsome face filled the screen, the famous actor dead of AIDS. Scribbled pages fell from my lap.

I cried out fears to Myrna the next day at my appointment. "How can I *think* of getting a life if I still panic every time I hear that Goddamn A-word?" I let out a quivery breath. "I never should have had sex with all those guys."

"Sounds like you're letting old guilt creep back to punish you."

"Why shouldn't it? I was stupid. I still am." I wiped tears.

"Lena, no." She drew her chair close. "This is a stressful time for you, lots of uncertainty. Relapsing into worry is allowed! And you have permission to ease up on yourself. Keep breathing."

A few days later a letter came from Russ. *I've started dating a woman who's with the Swedish Embassy. She's not* you, *but it's somebody to go out with.*

The thin stationery wrinkled in my grip. We'd talked of seeing others, decided we must keep things "open." I had men-friends in my classes at CSUF. One had helped me haul a daybed in for my living room. I had coffee with another occasionally before our class. But I was not dating; I'd told Russ that.

"I don't want to lose him," I said to Myrna. "He's not worried about AIDS. He doesn't think I have it. He's probably right. Right?"

I was lying in the hammock on the patio in early November when the UPS man came with the little box. I extracted the dazzling solitaire diamond, perched tall on its thin gold band. I held it up to sparkle in the hazy sunlight before easing it onto the ring finger of my left hand—a perfect fit.

At school Cheryl hugged me, exclaimed over the ring and spread the news. Flashing the diamond in the following week, having it inspected, accepting congratulations—I loved all of it. Glitzy and traditional, the engagement ring wasn't really my style, but it delivered a dose of rapturous calm each time I glanced at it.

I stopped in to see Dr. Z, on my thesis advising team. "So you're going to wash dishes wearing that?" he said.

Speechless, I could only beam.

"Seriously. What's the plan?"

"We'll be married in Illinois just after Christmas, then go back to Zaire. Dr. Simons says I can send my thesis stories from Kinshasa for you three to critique next semester. I'd like to finish by June." I didn't tell him I'd been promised a teaching job at TASOK the following year, if I wanted it.

"Don't go blind looking at that rock." Dr. Z winked.

My flute-player friend would take Pandora. Maizie would go on the plane with me back to my sister's in Wisconsin. I relaxed into planning a simple, cozy wedding. I'd have the white cake trimmed with red frosting roses. December 28th would be snow-covered winter in Illinois; I would pick up something like an off-white sweater and wool skirt to wear, perhaps at Goodwill.

"*What?*" Cheryl was appalled.

She waited outside the dressing room at Marshall's as I slipped into a mid-calf, three-quarter-sleeved, cream-colored, chiffon-feeling dress whose bodice was studded with tiny pearls and drawn in at the waist by a pleated satin cummerbund. Cheryl gasped as I emerged smiling, the skirt swirling around my legs.

I bought pumps to match.

Russ's sister Nancy arranged for us to be married at the old Swedish schoolhouse in Bishop Hill, not far from where Russ had grown up, near where his parents still lived. An old neighbor made the white cake with red roses.

Near the back of the schoolhouse room at 2:00 p.m. on Saturday, December 28th, I switched on the tape of "Variations on the Kanon by Pachelbel" from George Winston's *December* album, then walked up the aisle on smooth old wood. I smiled at Russ, who waited beaming in his brown tweed suit and vest. The thirty friends and family members who'd driven through snowy hinterlands watched from folding chairs. Russ and I faced the minister in front of the blackboard, flanked by our attendants, my sister Chrissie and Russ's dad Ivar. George Washington bore witness from his framed portrait on the robin's-egg blue wall.

After the vows we opened gifts. In a photo I'm glowing as bright as the large white dinner plate I'm showing off—from a set of eight called *Sonnet*—made in Japan and "oven to table to dishwasher, microwave oven safe." Bless my mom for remembering I'd always wanted white stoneware. The entire set, small chips on only a single cup and saucer, resides with me today in Arizona.

Everyone pitched in to heat casseroles and arrange salads, and we sat down at Christmas-cloth covered folding tables. Russ and I cut the cake and served each other a plate—but we skipped the exchange of forkfuls; I could feed myself, thank you. Then I played the ancient upright piano for a sing-along of old familiar songs like "Love Me Tender" and "Everything's Comin' Up Roses."

Russ and I bundled up in winter coats and hustled through a rain of birdseed instead of rice—my bird-lover mom's idea—to the old red sedan we'd borrowed from Russ's dad. When we opened the car doors, a multicolored tumble of balloons drifted out into the softly falling snowflakes. We drove off with a clatter: Besides piling in the balloons, sister Chrissie and her daughter Jenny had tied pop cans to the bumper. On the way to the hotel we drove to the local cemetery, the most scenic place around. In the twilight we gazed at snow-frosted gravestones and pondered life and death from our newly-married perspective.

On December 31st, in borrowed boots and old coats, we toured Russ's brother Roy's pig barns in the icy cold. The dust and smell of the grunting, squealing animals in their close quarters appalled me. I caught a nasty head cold that would stay with me all the way to Zaire.

Early in the new year, dipping and screeching, our plane set down off the ocean onto the scant landing strip in Funchal, the tropical capital of Madeira, site of our honeymoon. We left the warm city behind and drove our little rental car up winding roads to the frigid, windy tip of the mountainous Portuguese island, stopping to hike along old sections of the famous *levadas*—aqueducts—some of which are still used to transport water. Wracked by my cold, I was glad I'd brought my warm red sweater and leather jacket.

Our spartan hotel, near the top at 6,000 feet, had no heat—and I was miserable. The proprietor spoke some French, so we were able to communicate our need for a *"truc pour chauffer la chambre"*—a *thing* to heat the room. The kind man brought us the perfect *truc*, a portable heater, which saved me.

We drove back down to Funchal along the treacherous narrow roads. Thin waterfalls trickled over the car from mountainous walls above us, then down the cliffs on the opposite side and into the sea below. Panic grabbed me. "Can you go a little slower?" I begged Russ. "It seems slippery."

He smiled and slowed a little. "Don't worry, Lena. We're fine."

My hands stayed fastened to the handle on the glove box.

We stopped at the world's second highest point above the sea and stood holding hands near the precipitous edge—but I soon pulled away and walked back to a souvenir stand piled with embroidery, painted gourds and snow globes. When Russ joined me I told him, "Val said people on cliffs have three fears: falling, jumping, or being pushed. He said he always thought he might jump. Just now, I was scared I'd fall." I shivered. Would Russ notice if the ground started giving way beneath me? Would he catch me?

He took my hand as we walked to the car, afraid of none of

the above.

Back in tropical Funchal I breathed easier. We went to the finest restaurant, where we sat on the rooftop patio sipping wine and laughing over the menu, which, in English, featured such delectable entrees as *Fish Jump-in-the-Mouth*. After dinner we perused the main souvenir shop, whose only salesperson wore a brown leather jacket and jeans. As we cruised the aisles we speculated about this androgynous-looking character. At the sales counter we studied the person close-up for clues, and when we left, we disagreed: man or woman? Some combination? We'd never know. On that we concurred.

After an abrupt take-off our plane settled into a smooth flight to Zaire, and we sat back with drinks. Relieved to be finished with the month's dramatic ups and downs, I looked forward to settling down at TASOK and getting rid of my cold.

Our wedding in the Swedish schoolhouse

Bishop Hill, IL - December 1985

PART II

21

But It's Warm in Bombay

OUR SON TIM stands at the altar in a white shirt and tie, more handsome than I've ever seen him. Vows are spoken; then Tim pulls the ring from his pocket and grins as he hands it to the groom, his best friend Joe, who slips it on bride Cathy's finger.

The October 22nd afternoon wedding has a Halloween theme and is staged outdoors in crisp, pine-scented Prescott air. On a friend's high deck, a trellis wound with orange and black flowers frames the couple—Cathy in strapless, lacy white and Joe in a black suit. Four bridesmaids in long black dresses stand at the left; the groomsmen, Tim and his old roommate Ryan, flank the couple on the right.

After the brief ceremony we go inside where the three-tiered cake sits on a counter. Its white frosting is adorned with orange and black pastry flowers, but the show stopper is on the top: The formally-dressed plastic bride and groom are *skeletons*. "Wow. Looks like a *Dia de los Muertos* thing," I say. "Works for me. A wedding's a good time to contemplate life and death."

Beside me, Tim eyes the bony couple on the cake. "They're supposed to be zombies."

I don't ask what that means. But this wedding's flaunting of tradition brings back my own with Val thirty-five years ago: the black dress I wore, the snake decorations on Val's shirt and the cake. That marriage had unraveled quickly. Will this one hold? It seems haphazard. Russ and I didn't receive a real invitation for the event, just word from Tim that we were invited. We waited into the afternoon for his call to tell us the estimated start time, wondering if the event would come off.

But now the deed seems happily accomplished. Before the newlyweds cut and serve the cake, the maid of honor reads a statement. Then best man Tim extemporaneously praises his friend Joe. "He's always been there for me. I would trust him with my life."

Tim sits with us as we eat cake, and Russ asks how things are going with Haley. Tim takes a long drink of Coke, comes up for air and smoothes his tie. "Fine."

♫

"Haley's freaking out in the bathroom right now." It's a week after Joe's wedding and Tim has called from Flagstaff. "She asked why I'm so calm, don't I even care? I kinda don't. I told her I still love her, but not romantically any more."

"Wow. Big change, Tim." If it's real. They've come close to breaking up before. As for Haley's "freaking out," I know how he exaggerates. She probably cried a bit, or cursed, and is over it by now.

"I'll pick up Abby from school today. Then I'm gone."

"Poor Abby. She'll miss you...." I'm wondering if this is real.

"We can text. I feel sorry for her. She's got a crazy mom."

This sounds sincere. They've really broken up. I feel bad for Abby too—and panic streaks through me for my son. I take a deep breath. "So what's the plan, Tim?"

"I can keep my job at Cracker Barrel till I find a better one. I'm gonna move out by November so I don't have to pay Haley another month's rent."

"That's in two days, Tim. Not much time."

"She's letting me leave some stuff in the garage. I'll sleep in my car for awhile if I have to."

In November, in Flag? "It must be getting cold up there...."

"Ma? Would you and Dad be willing to lend me the money I owe Haley? Then I could make a clean break."

Last we knew, Tim owed Haley upwards of $2000 for repairs she had done on his car, and rent, when his ed fund with us ran out. He'd opted not to return to NAU in the fall, and had been working at Cracker Barrel since July—going on four months—but was apparently still in arrears.

An image flies to mind of my son snuggled up in his car with a bottle of Jose Cuervo. If things don't go his way he might get plastered and freeze to death....

But my Program for families of alcoholics has taught me that I can't save him. I switch the phone to my left ear and hold it with my shoulder as I pour a cup of coffee. "Sorry, Tim. Dad would agree, we can't lend you the money." I take a sip.

Tim clears his throat. I hear a door slam in the background. Haley?

I'd like to pony up the $2000 and anything else Tim wants—but I'd be taking on his responsibilities. He's twenty-five years old. I must detach, but it's not easy. "I'm really sorry."

"It's okay."

"So, I guess you don't know if you're coming down for Thanksgiving this year...." He's always been with us on Thanksgiving. I'm hoping he'll shoot for the usual get-together, now just a few weeks out.

Two days later, Tim makes a reconnaissance trip to Prescott. He spends Friday night with Russ and me, and over pizza the three of us watch TV news footage of Hurricane Sandy. Leaning forward, Tim stares at shots of the devastation. He hasn't heard about the brutal storm which slammed the east coast days before, killing scores of people. Now it seems a riveting distraction from the chaos in his life.

For entertainment after the news, Russ puts in a newly-made DVD of Tim's first year with us: We're in Africa. We've recently adopted him; he's fifteen months old, a bright-eyed cherub. I can see where fine dark hair is growing out over the patch of head that was shaved for the IV tube, after he arrived in Illinois with pneumonia and malnutrition. He babbles cheerily in his car seat, crawls nimbly around our TASOK screened porch, experiments with blocks, pats at Puss-Puss.

Oh, there I am in that long Indian dress, tossing our new son in the air one minute, helping him walk the next. And there's Russ, snuffling Tim's neck, making him grin. Then we're taking turns carrying him on our backs down the jungle path, around the school grounds, narrating from behind the video camera—enthralled by our happy, growing baby boy.

Watching from the rocker, I'm buffeted by a sudden desire to have my sweet babe back—have my own young *self* back and do this parent thing again; I'd be so much better at it. I glance at my grown son on our couch, his shaved head inclined toward the TV, and the notion washes away like water over Congo River rapids, replaced by gratitude for his adult presence.

Watching himself as a baby, Tim says, "Wish I could've warned him."

I feel another pang of sadness and don't speak.

In the morning I pass the guest room, noting Tim's guitar propped against the bed where he slept. Three quilts lie rumpled on the sheets—I hadn't realized how cold it is in there; Russ will buy a heater today. Old friends are coming for a night soon, then family for Thanksgiving.

Over coffee this morning Tim's a cocktail of emotions: staring at his MacBook from the loveseat one minute, then jumping up to pace and blurt out thoughts. Only his compulsion to get on alone seems to ground him. "I'll be glad to get my own place." He rubs his eyes and blinks. "We finally cleaned out the garage and got everything arranged the way we want it."

I feel for him, wish I could ease the pain. As the song says, breaking up is hard to do. It always was for me.

Harder than leaving Haley and the house, it seems, will be extricating himself from Abby and the cat care and the ease of the familiar routine: days and weeks and months—two years—of tending these live, needy creatures; of meals and housework and transportation and bill payments orchestrated by Haley, executed by Tim.... Perhaps he'd needed to be in the box where Haley kept him, until he got strong enough to tire of it and escaped for good.

He's on his feet now, pacing the old wood floor. "I'm glad to be outta there, really. Haley and Abby scream at each other now. They had an actual fist fight two days ago. Haley told Abby she would've aborted her, but it was too late at five months." He shakes his head. "Abby's a casualty."

I feel sorry for the little girl. But Tim's statement has come out as a cold, hard fact. He's batting verbalized thoughts off the walls like squash balls, *wham, wham, wham*. "I think I wanna leave Flagstaff and move back to Prescott. I can prob'ly transfer to the Cracker Barrel here. They'll transfer you anywhere." Or Joe's new sister-in-law could get him in at True Value, he says, or Libby's daughter at Goodwill. "I'd like to get away from the food industry." He plops back on the loveseat.

My breathing speeds with his compulsive ramblings. I reach for the *Courier* and try to focus on front-page news as I rock in the chair nearby.

"If I make $9 an hour, that's almost $1400 a month." Now he's probing his Mac for apartments in Prescott. "I can afford $500 to $700 for rent...."

I stop rocking and peer over the paper. "Would you make that much at Goodwill?"

"I dunno."

"I doubt it. Putting the cart before the horse." I can't help it, I've stopped minding my own business to rein him in. Even if he makes that much, he hasn't factored taxes....

He plans to be in Prescott three nights, maybe four. Russ and I invite him to stay with us.

Tim helps with dishes, jokes and smiles, picks at his guitar, thanks us for our support. Though at loose ends, he seems optimistic about sorting things out. Best of all, I am convinced that he won't drink—he's stone-sober and seems likely to remain so—and for this I feel boundless gratitude.

But he's smoking dope again. He confided this to Russ at Joe's wedding reception. And he'll smoke more and more, if he gives way to his addictiveness—won't he? Could marijuana cause his total disorganization and collapse? I hope he'll Think, and put First Things First, as my Program advises. But his First Things may be way different from mine. I'll need to work my own Program: Let Go and Let God—or the Universe, as I prefer to say.

As I click words into my Mac now, I feel nagging, burning discomfort near my left shoulder. I stop, close my eyes and ask the Universe to help me detach from Tim's actions. If I don't, they'll weigh me down like my grad school backpack full of Shakespeare.

I open my eyes and stare at the screen. Through his school years I coddled and cajoled Tim: attended diligently to each whacky thought he uttered, took it at face value, was crushed and heartened in quick turns. I would react, form judgments, blurt advice. I'm finally learning there's no point trying to make sense of all his bobbing pronouncements.

I take a deep breath, roll my shoulders and resume tapping my own narrative.

One morning during Tim's visit I wake up with Mick Chase in mind. Forty years earlier I'd bolted from Madison to escape that toxic relationship. Seated in the rocker, I roll out the story over coffee as Tim sits at his computer. "I had $125 in my pocket, got on the Greyhound for Chicago and booked into the YMCA, $17 a night. I had to get a job, a place to live.... It was bleak."

Tim's eyes flicker at his laptop screen. "All these pictures of Haley. Don't know if I should delete 'em."

"Maybe not, just yet." Another memory flits overhead. "I once moved in with this guy Ian Burns in San Diego." I glance at Russ. "The guy who got weird and thought I was trying to poison him." I aim my voice back at Tim. "When we broke up he threw my stuff out on the yard, except he kept all the pictures of us. Wish I had a couple now. They were real photos back then." I draw a little square in the air.

"What did you tell me was wrong with that guy?" Russ asks from the recliner.

"Paranoia, I guess. He tried to make up, said he was seeing a shrink, but it was too late."

Tim flicks his eyes at me for a second. "Haley texted me yesterday. She wanted to know where I am." He pops off the couch, stretches, and rubs his stomach. "I weigh 107 now. I wanna put on some weight. People say I should be between 120 and 150."

"I don't know," I say, getting up. "Maybe not." I move toward the back door to check on our cat, who spent the night outside again. "A few more pounds wouldn't hurt, but you're different. Small-framed, from India."

"That's what I thought. I read that thing you wrote, about me being Davidian? From south India."

"*Dra*-vidian. Anyway, yeah, you seem pretty healthy."

Healthy like I was in my twenties, despite nearly-constant anxiety—like my son's, whose visit has drawn me back four decades. Times have changed, but I scrambled as hard as he is now for a place to land in life and be at peace. The trappings were different—in and out of the psych ward and men's beds for me, rehab and sober houses for him—but the distress was the same. I feel for him.

I leave the living room to stand on the back step and call for Metro. Our ten-year-old black cat—*Tim's* cat back in the day—has been acting strange.

She adjusted well to our move to town, soon venturing outdoors to lie in the sun in the fenced back yard, eventually parading outside the front gate for a minute, but returning to stick close to the house. She'd come in at dusk to spend the night, then complain for food in the morning as she always had. Now she doesn't want to be in the house—ducks in through a held-open door to eat, then wants out, howling bitterly until we let her go again.

I think it's the new cat next door that's got Metro fuddled. This other black cat sports white slippers and a little cravat, and she is bold, but not aggressive—unlike Angelo, the big gray marauder feline who scared Metro thirty feet up a ponderosa one evening soon after we moved in. I recently let a black cat in the front door, reached down to pet her, saw the white markings and realized my mistake—I put the audacious neighbor cat back outside.

Our cat spends her nights on a pillow in the back yard now, her eyes gazing at us if we call her, then at the house to the right, where lives the new tux-cat. It's cold out there, under 40 at night—but Metro won't budge. Tim's poor old cat seems as unsure of her place in the world as he is.

When Metro doesn't come, I rejoin Russ and Tim in the living room. "Brrr—cold out there." I rub my arms and sink back into the rocker.

Tim says the night he broke up with Haley he slept in his car. "I kept the engine running with the heater on all night."

"Whoa. Is that safe?" I ask.

"I'm alive." He's still on the couch hunched over his computer, working on an application for Goodwill. "I hate filling out apps," he says. "I'm just glad I was never arrested when I was drinking. Apps always ask." Then, "'Community involvement, contributions to businesses, service experience'.... Do I have any of those? I guess not." And in a moment, "Done. That was easy."

I say, "Tim, google *'safe to sleep in a car with the engine running?'....*" His fingers tap the keys in response.

He and Russ are going to our storage unit today for an extra sleeping bag Tim can use in his Honda. "Russ, can you help him fit stuff in his car? You're the Organizer. Maybe he can sleep on his clothes, throw a blanket over them. For insulation."

Tim's eyes bore into his Mac. "It's not recommended. Sleeping in a car with the engine running."

"Carbon monoxide," Russ says. "But it's not like you're in a closed garage."

"So at least crack some windows," I say. "What will you do during the days, when you're not working?"

"Go to the library, read, use my computer." Then, "Libby says to use Wet Wipes if I can't shower." He says he may book into a hostel for a warm night and a shower now and then.

At least he doesn't have to worry about hair. "Do you still have that fur-lined cap with the ear flaps?" I ask.

"When I tell people I'm gonna be living in my car they think I'm crazy. But I don't."

He's got this plan for makeshift shelter until he gets a new job and a place in Prescott, as he wildly schemes and hopes he will—but for now my son is homeless, like many people in his land of origin who have jobs driving taxis or fixing hair in salons, and choose to sleep on the sidewalks to avoid rent. But it's warm in Bombay....

As we hug goodbye I hold Tim tight. "Love you. Stay warm."

Predicted temperature in Flagstaff that night is twenty-eight degrees.

22

I've Just Unwrapped the Perfect Gift

THANKSGIVING APPROACHES AND Metro still won't come inside—though the neighbor cat with white markings has moved away. When temps dip into the teens at night I defy my cat's will and drag her wide-eyed, claws clinging, off her outdoor pillow and into the house, where she cowers in the guest room closet. If it's not the neighbor cat that's been upsetting her, then what? An adjustment problem with the new house, brought on by winter? If I believed in pet therapists I'd make her an appointment and get her on the couch.

Unlike his old cat, Tim isn't holding out in the cold. "Haley let me stay in the house a couple nights," he says, adding that he's thankful for the "good break-up." I say I'm grateful that his Honda is not his home. Now he's back in Prescott with his friends Cathy and Joe, sleeping on their couch. He has transferred to the Cracker Barrel here, and pinned down a little apartment near Joe and Cathy's. "I'll have the rent after I work for a couple weeks, but could you front me $500 for the deposit? They'll save the place if I pay it now."

I go with him to see the apartment. It has a cramped strip of kitchen and a dingy curtain strung over a plastered-in window in the tiny bedroom, but Tim is pleased. "The landlord Roger's a nice guy. He says he'll move in whatever furniture I want."

Right now it's bare bones—in the living room only an ungainly assemblage of dark wooden shelving, and a warped mattress in the bedroom—but a couple of moveable heaters do make the place toasty warm.

Russ sees the apartment the next day. "Nice tile in the shower."

We lend Tim the $500.

A week later, on Thanksgiving morning, comes the call: "I'm thinking of bailing from Crack-ass Barrel."

He may as well have hit me over the head with the phone. I set down my coffee. "Oh, Tim. *Why?*" He's scheduled to work 11:00 to 7:00 to help with pumpkin pie sales and turkey meal prep at the restaurant. We're reconciled to this and have been looking forward to his coming over in the evening after work.

"They said they'd give me more hours, too, but it's not happening."

I inhale deeply, then let breath out. "It's a job, Tim. They're not easy to come by these days." After the initial jolt, I'm calming. "Wouldn't it be better to hold on, at least until—"

"The manager's an ass. He makes me wear a hairnet even though I have no hair."

A pang jabs my gut. "Oh dear. Not fair." I draw in another stabilizing breath. "They need you today though, right? It's a busy day."

"Yeah...."

"I say stick with it till you get another job, or better hours...." I walk the phone from kitchen to living room. "Wanna talk to Dad, see what he says?" I raise my eyebrows as I pass the phone to Russ. Then, coffee cup in hand, I retreat to the bedroom where I can't hear words, only Russ's steady drone. When he comes in a few minutes later I peer at him. "So...?"

"He'll stay. He said you told him pretty much the same thing I did."

I exhale with relief. Thank God for Russ, my perfect partner in parenting.

After more coffee, Russ and I wrestle the old wooden leaves into the round table to extend it. We scrounge four chairs from other rooms and juggle them to fit with the set of four around the table. Then I wedge myself behind a chair to reach dishes in the breakfront. It's going to be snug, this first Thanksgiving in our little house. I throw on the big embroidered tablecloth from Madagascar, then arrange eight plates around the perimeter, relishing the heaviness of our white wedding stoneware. I lay cloth napkins and holiday silver, and on the plates, this year's place cards: rare, red maple leaves I've collected from our dog-walk street and personalized with a black Sharpie. I station myself at the head of the oval table; Russ will face me at the other end. Tim's red leaf goes near the silver candelabra in the center, for when he joins us after work.

Toward noon people arrive with food. Russ's divorced brother Roy has made sister Nancy's memorial tabouli with lots of parsley per my request. Nancy's widower-husband Ken and his brother Bernard from Florida have collaborated on a family sweet potato recipe. Sister Mary brings her usual quality pumpkin pies from Marie Callender's in Tempe, this year also a strawberry-rhubarb. Program friend Alice arrives last, offering chocolates and a blooming white gloxinia.

By 1:30 Russ's gravy is made, the free-range bird carved. Holly, up from Tucson, has helped set things on, and we pass turkey with the fixings.

People are eating and talking as I slip out to the kitchen to replenish the mashed potatoes. When I return, the front French doors open, and as if on marionette strings, my hands suspend the bowl of mashed potatoes in mid-air. Russ turns toward the doors, where Tim stares at us from under his black hood.

"You're done early!" My words release the marionette strings and I set down the mashed potatoes.

"I quit." He shrugs off his hood and moves toward Russ at the table. "They were short-handed. I had to do everything."

Russ hugs Tim. Ken stands to welcome him, then others scrape back chairs to do the same.

I become an automaton programmed to accommodate. I

motion for people to move closer around the table, then whisk a plate and silver onto the new place, fish Tim's maple leaf from the clutter and lay it on his plate.

It's Thanksgiving. *I shall not be moved from thankfulness.* I breathe deep, and in a rush of warmth I beckon Tim to his place next to me, hold him in a hug and whisper, "Too bad." I kiss the side of his bare head, then release him. "Sit."

He slides onto the kitchen stool Russ has brought.

That weekend, as I move through the French doors from the glassed-in front porch for coffee refills, the wall heater's blower comes on as usual, blaring like our old Hoover vacuum. Metro, eyes wide, shoots like an arrow from the living room back into the guest room. She has revealed the source of her trauma—and in venturing near the noisy heater, she's begun to face her demons. I detour into the guest room and bestow some congratulatory petting.

"I'm hanging out at Meg's a lot," Tim tells us a week later. "I really like her."

He worked with Meg for a short time seven years ago at a small natural foods store in town. He had her out to our big house a time or two. One day as I came home from school, I saw her Jeep with its bumper sticker from Mexico parked outside the garage. I didn't meet her—I left them to their privacy upstairs—but Tim said later they were just good friends. "She's seven years older, but we have a lot in common." He was nineteen at the time.

Back then Meg had a boyfriend, but Tim said the relationship was rocky. Sometime in the ensuing seven years—during Tim's plunge into alcohol, his recovery and his relationship with Haley in Flagstaff—Meg married the boyfriend and had a baby; now she is divorced. When Tim posted on Facebook that he was moving back to Prescott, she connected with him. "She just bought this house, and I'm helping her out a little. I did some yard work and made breakfast for her yesterday. But I still sleep at Joe's."

Without a job he has not been able to afford rent for the place he had his heart set on.

"Can you get the $500 back for the apartment?"

"I dunno. The bookkeeper is kind of a bitch."

We've trusted Tim to deal with this money, waited to see what would happen. He knows he owes it to us. It's been two weeks; maybe the management company has a legal right to it—they've been unable to rent the place to anyone else while they've waited on Tim—and I'm thinking we won't see our money again. We arrange for him to pay it back in weeks and months of manual labor. We'll whittle from his bill ten bucks per hour of work. He begins by helping us build a flagstone path beside the house.

After moving heavy flagstones one mild December day, Tim takes off his gloves and announces that the bookkeeper tore up the deposit check. "So would it be okay if I keep the loan amount?" He gulps water and sets the glass in the sink. "I have an interview at Goodwill this week, but I want to pay Joe some rent and buy food...."

I'm swept off my feet—so pleased he kept at the woman for the deposit money and wants to be responsible to Joe—and is so whole-heartedly committed to his new life, and is not drinking through all this—that I say, "Sure." I write him a check for $500.

"I thought we always made these decisions together," Russ says that night, though not before I've realized my mistake. He lets it go, but I hang on, berating myself for acting without Russ and falling back on the old habit of giving in to Tim—not taking time to think, as my Program exhorts....

But the Program sinks in before bedtime. The deed is done. I forgive myself, "let go and let the Universe."

♫

"Where will you be on Acker night?" Tim asks.

It's mid-December. He's got a job delivering pizza, has moved in with Meg and is paying rent toward the mortgage, which her dad has helped facilitate. Tim wants us to meet his girlfriend.

Each year a couple of weeks before Christmas, Prescott hosts the Acker Music Festival, and for ten years I've been the keyboardist for the Easy Street Jazz Band. We're seasoned musicians who gather once to practice, then play at the festival. Performing groups station themselves in buildings radiating from the Courthouse Square, and the public floods the streets, flowing down sidewalks and stopping in to listen, dance, and donate to the music scholarship fund. Between old tunes like "Puttin' on the Ritz" and "Stranger on the Shore," I chat from the keyboard with visiting friends, and during the middle set Russ brings me a hot toddy.

This year we're flanked by poinsettias in a bank in the Bulleri building just off the Square. From the piano around 8:00, I spot Tim in the crowd with a light-haired girl. Tim, who is about my height and maybe 110 pounds, is large beside her.

Russ returns and we finish the night with "Jingle Bell Rock." The crowd disperses as Tim moves forward with Meg. He introduces us. She looks me in the eye, smiles, and shakes my hand firmly.

Mike, our guitarist in from Portland, comes over, one of his little boys in tow, and greets Meg. "So I hear you have a baby now," he says.

"Bryson's almost three."

"Wait—you two know each other?" I say.

Mike looks at Meg. "Since Durango?"

"When we were both living there," she says. "Years ago."

Mike says, "Meg took some great photos of my band back in the day." His little boy clings to his leg; Mike pats his back.

Arms crossed, feet shuffling, Tim stands aside—like Metro, avoiding discomfort in the living room. I pull on my jacket, then turn to hold Tim in a goodbye hug. I stroke his back and say so only he can hear, "Congrats. I really like her too."

♫

Holly comes up from Tucson in time for the usual gift exchange on Christmas Eve. Tim spends the eve at Meg's with her folks, here from Colorado. Russ and I drop over the next day to deliver a bag of gift-wrapped, beribboned money and homemade cookies. I'm interested to see Meg's house, my son's new digs. Tim takes us to the kitchen, past a big trimmed Christmas tree at a front bay window. After the flurry of meeting Meg's family—her little boy, her parents, her twenty-something brother, her cat and dog—we stand around while Meg's mom, her Chihuahua in the crook of her arm, stirs chicken soup on the stove. "Nice tile design," I say, glancing at the floor, which is terra cotta with a large blue diamond pattern in the center.

Meg looks at me aslant. "Want to see the house?"

I trail her from room to room, *ooh*-ing and *ah*-ing over the commodious couch; the light, wood-accented bathroom where I glimpse Tim's shaver; the Spiderman-spread mattress on the floor in Bryson's room, overflowing with stuffed toys; the spacious bedroom next to the little boy's—but the bed in the big room is a single; Jess and he can't be sleeping there together, can they?

"Dad and I are getting a new mattress for Christmas," I tell Tim later. "Want our old one? It's a queen."

"That'd be great. We're pretty cramped in that small bed."

♫

Over Memorial Day weekend Meg's folks are down from Colorado again. "Come by if you can," Tim says. "There'll be tacos and stuff."

We sit out back in twilight with some neighbors, Meg's parents, and a couple our age she calls her "second family," who helped raise her in Durango. They became teachers at Prescott College and now live near us in one of our town's historic districts. Over tacos and drinks we talk easily and long. As we drive away Russ says Meg's dad has invited us to join them at a condo in Rocky Point, Mexico, in mid-October.

Tim comes by one day in June to get another piece of our excess furniture, the Coke bench he's always liked. As we're loading it into Meg's truck, he tells us her dad threw up after the taco party. "He's got these physical problems. Smokes a lot of pot on a medical prescription in Colorado, but he drinks a lot, too." I look at Russ and wonder if we'd be in for a Rocky Mountain High time in Rocky Point.

When the coke bench is in the truck, Tim slides into the driver's seat and says, "Oh yeah—I got a new job. At Panchito's. I start next week."

I gasp as if I've just unwrapped the perfect gift. He was drunk one time too many after three years on the job at Panchito's, back in the day; the owners, his old friend Libby's mom and dad, pulled him off the bathroom floor and fired him. "That's great, Tim!" I emit a little glee-filled sigh.

"They had a sign on the door. I took it down and crossed off Help 'Wanted' and wrote Help 'Hired.' Libby recommended me. It's full time, good pay. They gave me a key this time." He starts the truck and pulls away, the bench's white curlicue Coca-Cola letters glinting in the sun.

That night Russ raises his wine glass. "To Tim and his new job."

23

A Touch of Tropical Sprue

"Anybody home?"

Helen, the superintendent's wife and head of TASOK housing supplies, peered through the screen door of 98C. Before I could rise from the dining room table she opened the door, inserted her head and gawked at the papers strewn around the typewriter in front of me. "Working on your thesis, I see."

"Yep." I stood up and shuffled some pages together. "Finishing a revision to send out with Embassy mail tomorrow." I hoped to be done with it before Russ got home from school.

Helen stood inside now, smoothing her prim reddish hair. "I just came by to make sure you have everything you need. Now that you've been here a month, you know what you're missing. Men don't bother much with the kitchen."

"I think we've got everything we need. But thank you!"

"Maybe you'd like a bundt cake pan? They sell mixes at the Commissary now." She craned her neck toward the cupboards. "Maybe something else Russ didn't have?"

"Actually he spends more time in the kitchen than I do." He'd introduced me to the coffee grinder and the garlic press. Neither of us would miss a bundt pan. "We're pretty well set."

"Sheets? Towels?" She scanned the bedroom through its open

door, then aimed words back at me. "You know Mbange, up at the *atelier*, who works on the campus Toyotas?" Her tone went conspiratorial. "His son just died of AIDS...." She glanced out the screen door like some beady-eyed jungle rodent. "These people really should know better. I'd be careful who I shake hands with."

My heart lurched. I rapped the table with the edges of some pages, bent on collating. Helen's voice brightened in a last foray. "Maybe you need some fresh washcloths? Seems like Americans are the only people in the world who even use washcloths. We could teach these foreigners some things." She winked.

"We're fine. Really. Thanks." I sat down and stared at my papers.

"Well then, I'll let you get back to your work."

She left me with my thumping heart. I knew better than to worry about shaking hands with people. But I'd been back in Africa since January—a month, as Helen had reminded me—and symptoms of my honeymoon cold still plagued me; my head felt stuffed and achy and sometimes I'd wake up coughing. Could it be AIDS-related pneumonia?

Puss-Puss meowed from outside, and I popped up to get the door. He sauntered in and curled up on the couch. I heated a cup of coffee in the microwave and returned to sort out the story I was revising. Plunged back into its icy Wisconsin-winter setting, I relegated my fear to a back burner.

In Zaire in 1986, talk of AIDS could still blind-side me. Though I knew the disease was more rampant here than in the U.S., my fear had sat mostly dormant. President Mobutu, intent on preserving the god-like image of himself ascending into clouds on nightly local TV sign-offs, squelched all statistics that might shed bad light on his country's ills. And what actual news we saw or heard was in French or Lingala, which I didn't readily understand. Thus, spared the constant media drubbing I'd endured in California, I suffered fewer, shorter-lived episodes of panic.

In that thesis-focused semester, work toward my masters kept me occupied, as did friends, piano, local trips, and subbing at school in lieu of full-time teaching. My days were as full now as during my first stint in Zaire. And this time around, my new marriage enfolded me like a cozy shawl—until my husband fell victim to a menace swifter and stealthier than AIDS.

♫

"When it rains it pours." Dr. Darvish smiled as he shrugged off his wet jacket on the porch of our new, bigger place on Lower Campus. He drew a hand through his dark wet hair. It was a Sunday night in October, the rainy season in force, and the good doc had walked up the hill in a downpour from his stalled car outside the TASOK gates.

Having finished my thesis in California during the summer, I was well into the new school year, working full-time at TASOK, like Russ. But we'd both suddenly fallen sick.

I ushered the doctor into the living room, then lay back on the couch. Swept by tropic-defying chills, I pulled the quilt up over my shivering body as the doctor rummaged in his bag.

"We need to get Russ to the hospital. Tonight." Dr. Darvish pulled vials from his bag and began loading a syringe. "I'll give you both shots of Fansidar now, but Russ needs an intravenous drip." He motioned gently for me to lower my gym shorts and turn over. "These things hurt. Sorry." I felt so bad already that when he jabbed me in the butt I barely winced. I fumbled to pull up my shorts and lie back down as he went into our bedroom, where Russ slept.

I waited weak and helpless on the couch, my mind churning. Russ and I had figured this was probably a flu bug he'd caught from me; I'd had symptoms first. Or if not that, maybe we'd contracted something from eating the same bad food. It could be one of the myriad stomach maladies that plagued us *mundeles*—white foreigners who sojourned in Zaire. We often recovered without knowing what we'd had: Amoebic dysentery? Food poisoning from bad fondue meat at the *Plein Vent*? Maybe "a touch of tropical sprue," as the school counselor said.

Flushed with sudden fever, I peeled back the quilt and wiped my forehead with a hand.

We'd popped an over-the-counter antibiotic and figured this thing would pass. But before the weekend, I'd felt bad enough to take Thursday and Friday off from my new job teaching high school English. Russ was okay till Friday afternoon, when during his social studies class he suddenly felt so faint he had to hold onto a desk. When he got home to 52B he could hardly pull himself from the car to stagger inside.

Russ was in worse shape than I. Though headachy and nauseous myself the day before, I'd gotten out of bed to drive him to Mimosa, the compound ten minutes away where Dr. Darvish had an office in his house. The doc had taken blood samples from us both, then frowned. "It's the weekend, but I'll try to get you results by tomorrow."

We'd gone home and slept through Saturday and Sunday, our rest punctured by headaches, fever and chills. Dehydrated and thirsty, Russ retched as he struggled to drink water.

Now things seemed dire.

A stream of icy shivers coursed through me, and I burrowed back under the quilt. I looked toward the bedroom, where the doc still tended Russ—who was destined for the *hospital?* Not Mama Yemo, surely, the huge, poor public hospital filled with more sick Africans than it could begin to cure. Ngaliema would be better. A couple of teachers had given birth there; I'd visited. But even that smaller, newer clinic lacked up-to-date methods and supplies.

Dr. Darvish stood at the bedroom door. "We'll need to get him to Ngaliema." He glanced back at Russ, then asked, "Is there a friend or neighbor who could drive us? You're staying here and getting into bed."

I'd forgotten—the doc's car was *en panne* outside the gates. "Maybe Don Stafford, next door." There were no phones in TASOK teachers' houses in the '80's. I lifted my throbbing head and sat up. "I'll go see." As the doc reorganized his bag and pulled out bottles of pills, I slid into my flip-flops and dragged my leaden body out the door.

When I came back with Don, Dr. Darvish was sitting on the couch with my husband, whose heavy-lidded eyes, open mouth and labored breathing frightened me—it seemed he might pass out any moment. The doc drew a bottle of pills from his bag and handed it to me. "Chloroquine. Take one a day—a strong dose for a while. In a couple of weeks we'll go back to maintenance."

"So how long will Russ—"

"Can you drive to Ngaliema again in the morning?" Dr. Darvish said to Don, who nodded. The doc turned to me. "We'll see how he does."

Don and the doctor gathered Russ like a gunnysack half-full of grain, and with his arms hung slack around their shoulders, maneuvered him toward the door I held open. I touched Russ's back, then watched as the two men supported his body like dead weight and lugged him from the porch, down the gravel path through the dark wet night.

♫

The next morning, our driver/neighbor Don Stafford standing beside me, I sat feebly on the edge of my dozing husband's hospital bed. Avoiding the web of black vomit strung across the twisted sheet, I put my hand on his arm. "How are you doing, Russ?"

He stirred and gazed at me, then at the IV tube stuck in his forearm. "Better."

His voice was strained, but the message was clear. My head fell forward and touched his chest. Tears of relief seeped from my eyes.

As I raised my head, Russ pawed at the damp sheet near the vile vomit. "I threw up last night when they started the quinine." His words were soft but distinct. "No one came to clean it up."

I pushed what I thought must be a call button—it made no sound.

"There are no screens on these windows."

I followed Don's line of sight. Sure enough, mosquitoes floated in the humid air at the open windows—Anopheles or otherwise, all free to waft in as they pleased. If we hadn't already contracted malaria, we might have caught it in this hospital room.

No privacy curtain hid our view of a frail African man who lay in bed on the other side of the room. A woman in bright native dress sat on a mat on the floor beside him, stirring something in a wooden bowl. I touched Russ's arm again. "Did they give you anything to drink? Water? Are you thirsty?" He closed his eyes and shook his head.

Don looked into the bathroom, which had no door. "I don't see any towels." He stepped inside. "No toilet paper either." I heard a metal squeak. "No *water.*" He came out with a grimace.

Russ nudged the IV stand. "I had to drag this thing with me to the john. Nobody to help."

The IV sac was out of fluid. "Should this still be connected?" I looked at Don. "Couldn't he get air in his blood or something?" I pushed the call button again with no response. We'd seen no doctors or nurses or attendants as we'd come in—through outdoor corridors lit with glaring neon tubes.

Dr. Darvish had told Don he would come that morning, but it was only 8:00; it could be hours. I stood up, sure the doc would concur with what we were about to do. "Let's get him out of here."

We helped Russ sit up. He eased his legs off the side of the bed, his muscles working better than the night before. We got his shorts and deck shoes on. Still in the shred of hospital gown and holding onto the IV stand, he stood, then walked slowly between us, out of the room and into the hall. Surely we'd find someone on our way out who could help remove the IV.

A tall Belgian nun in a gray habit and wimple rushed up. *"Attendez! Vous ne pouvez pas partir!"* We couldn't leave—by order of *God?*

"Le doctor dit ca va," Don said, which was a lie; the doctor hadn't okayed this, but he would if he were here.

I touched the tube in Russ's arm and implored the nun—a nurse or doctor; her stethoscope rested on her huge white collar—*"S'il vous plait, nous aider?"* If she wouldn't help, I'd pull the IV out myself.

She raised her eyebrows, sighed, then deftly removed the tube and hooked it to the stand. We helped Russ into his T-shirt as the nun stood by, her hand on the IV apparatus. Then, behind her glasses, her blue eyes softened. *"Que vous allez avec Dieu,"* she said, blessing us on our way.

"I've never seen a sample so thick with malaria parasites,"

Dr. Darvish said of Russ's test when he'd delivered the diagnosis that rainy Sunday.

Timing had been right for incubation. It was two weeks since our camping trip to the river near the boulders—the place we called Crocodile Hollow—where the wicked Anopheles mosquitoes must have staged their attack. But I hadn't suspected malaria. Too much of a coincidence: only Russ and me, of the seven or eight who camped, came down with fever and chills. And we'd been on the prophylactic Dr. Darvish had prescribed.

Turned out that Daraprim, which we'd bought for years over the counter in Kinshasa, had lost its effectiveness as a malaria suppressant; hence the doc's heavy-duty dosing with the better Chloroquine—but not before the monstrous malady had reared up to strike us down. We needed two solid weeks of rest, off work, to recuperate.

The first daily naps we managed were rife with rich imaginings—were we even sleeping? Or delirious? The afternoon back from the hospital, as we lay in bed, Russ said groggily, "I just figured out all the causes of World War I and II in my head. In detail. Like it just happened...." He looked at the clock. "It's only been *two minutes*? Seems more like two hours...."

My speeding brain composed and reprised symphonic movements—or had Beethoven or Mozart already written them? I'd heard of cerebral malaria; could this be it? We were in a time warp, our minds racing.

But we steadily improved, until one day we sat out on the porch and gazed in wonder at the world we were still part of: My African violet on the cement ledge glowed an impossible iridescent purple in the hazy sunlight. The canopy of leafy, long-limbed campus trees formed an umbrella of blessed shade against the blue sky far above.

When we were well and back at school, I wrote a description of our illness. "Malaria Chronicle," I titled it, "a.k.a. We've Had Just About Anopheles"—the cheesy cleverness coming naturally. I cranked out purple mimeograph copies on the school's machine to send to family and friends back in the States. "I almost lost my hardly-had husband," I wrote. I said the quinine drip Russ received at that sad, unsanitary hospital saved his life.

At the end of the chronicle I wrote, "I've learned the miracle of life. It's that life's a miracle." It made my mother say that I'd found God.

Home from Africa for the summer of '87, we bought a rambling 1920's bungalow with dark woodwork, plate racks, and a built-in butler's pantry. Our new old house sat on a hill on Wood Street in Bloomington, Illinois. We would have a home base and be near family as Russ worked on his admin certificate at ISU during summers. We outfitted the downstairs with mostly used and gifted furniture, and rented out the smaller upstairs apartment to a woman who hauled in a big old upright piano. For many summers she would serenade us through the ceiling with "Onward, Christian Soldiers."

Russ set an old door on crates for an office desk in the cool brick basement. A sturdy sleeper sofa in our living room would accommodate visitors. We put a double bed in the front bedroom for ourselves, and a portable crib and dresser in the smaller back bedroom, which would be for Phillip Ashok, our adopted child from India.

Russ had gone along contentedly with my long-time desire to adopt. We'd done the footwork with a local social service place in Peoria during the previous summer, then begun working with an agency in Georgia, sending documentation from Kinshasa in the fall. "You can expect your baby within a year," the woman in Georgia told us brightly. In spring, teacher and embassy friends in Kinshasa staged a double baby shower for me and another prospective mother. Smiling for the camera beside the other woman, who was hugely pregnant, I held next to my belly the only photo Russ and I had received from India of our child-to-be.

We grew fond of the baby in the Polaroid photo on the fridge, our baby with his spiky black hair and dark "raccoon eyes," as we called them. We made official his new American first name, Phillip, using his given Indian name Ashok for a middle name. His rooms in Africa and Illinois were ready.

But by Thanksgiving of '87, when a month had passed without a progress report on the adoption, we called Georgia from the only phone on campus in 1988, at the superintendent's house. "I'm so sorry," the agency woman said through the muffled line. "The baby that was assigned to you at the orphanage in India has died. We've begun transferring your paperwork to another child."

"*Died?*" I gripped Russ's arm. This seemed unreal, like a malaria hallucination. "What did he die from?"

"We're told sometimes they just don't make it through the winter. I'm so sorry. You can choose a new name...."

We took the photo of our sweet, swaddled, raccoon-eyed baby Phillip Ashok off the fridge.

I'd sewn a quilt from Indian fabric, embroidering scenes of cats for our new baby; one square had a cat waving a flag that said "Go Phillip!" Before spring I pulled out the stitches and made them say "Go Timothy!"

Though malaria almost killed Russ, though we learned it might always be in our systems and could recur, I never worried much about it. Nor did I lose sleep over most other African bugs, some of which could be deadly: A TASOK teacher who'd gone on to teach in Egypt died of spinal meningitis. Yet my irrational fear of AIDS persisted.

In summer of 1988 our little Illinois TV screen filled with news of Ryan White, the brave kid dying of AIDS contracted through blood transfusions. His Indiana high school had expelled him, afraid others might catch it. I'd been in Zaire for years, for Godsake—certainly easier to contract it there, for someone with my history of sex and shots and acupuncture....

Like storms that upended shallow-rooted trees each year in Kinshasa, well-practiced panic swept back in to topple me.

But by mid-July I'd had enough. "What kind of mother will I make, thinking I might have AIDS?" I whined to Russ. Our adopted child was due from India within weeks.

Back then you had to wait days or weeks for AIDS test results. My parents happened to be visiting us in Bloomington on D-Day, the day of my appointment to learn the truth. I told Mom and Dad we were going out to pick up some food. Russ held my hand at the clinic as the white-coated technician told us the results.

We stopped at Lucca's for a drink to celebrate, then bought a bucket of chicken to take home.

I'd finally found the strength to slay my fear of AIDS—and our new son, Timothy Bunty, had survived the Indian winter. At the end of August, sweet and spindly and just over twelve months old, he was delivered to us off the plane in Chicago, and we held him in our arms.

I'd just cleared the TASOK jungle on a quick walk home to get something for school one day when I heard a pitiful cry. I stopped and listened. Sobs were issuing from nearby—from our own house. *Albertine?* I raced, heart pounding, across our back yard and through the screened porch; the door flapped in my wake. Our nanny/maid slumped in a chair in the dining room, heaving and wailing as if someone had died. "Albertine, *qu'est-ce qu'il y a?*"—what is it? I looked around, panic rising. "Where's Tim?"

She stood up. "*Non, non,* Madame—okay, Tim." She pulled a corner of her tie-dyed cotton *pagne* from around her waist, blotted her eyes and wagged a hand. "*Il dort.*"

I hurried down the short hallway and peeked in. Sure enough, Tim lay in his crib sound asleep, a little arm crooked, elbow at his side, as usual. I returned to the stricken nanny. "What's wrong, Albertine?"

Now straight-backed, head held high, she looked me in the eye and said in English, "It's nothing, Madame."

Nothing? I'd never heard anyone cry like that.

"*C'est vrai,* Madame, it's nothing," she insisted, smiling from behind puffy eyes. "Just a little problem in my village, with my family. *Mais ça va!*" She whisked her dust cloth from the coffee table, turned her back, and began assiduously dusting the filigreed edges of the buffet—my cue to pry no further.

We'd had part-time domestics in Kinshasa before: strong, dark-skinned men in white shirts and shorts who worked part-time for two or three of us, cleaning our little apartments and washing our clothes in the shared machines out back. I could not bring myself to say "houseboy," the traditional term; I called personable, six-foot-tall Mikina our "houseworker" instead. These guys, whom many singles employed, worked for a couple of hours then left, and though we appreciated them and gave them extra money now and then, we didn't know them well—unlike Albertine, who came to feel like family.

Ample-bodied and immensely capable, thirty-something Albertine was a TASOK institution. She'd been employed by school families with young kids for years, and we were fortunate to get her. During Tim's first year with us she plumped him up on bananas mixed with formula from the Commissary, and occasional *saka-saka* and *fufu* on picnics with other tots and their nannies in our adjoining back yards. Always in good spirits, Albertine carried Tim snug on her back wrapped in her *pagne* as she cleaned and cooked and washed our dishes.

We paid her well—albeit on the local scale, which meant very little compared to Stateside wages. We gave her money to help build her house *en ville*, as other of her TASOK employers had before us. She once went with us out for dinner at the Mandarin, a favorite restaurant on the Boulevard. We threw a birthday party for her on our screened porch; in the video she's holding Tim on her lap, beaming as she opens gifts and cuts the cake I made.

Albertine put on a good show. From a village a grueling lorry ride away in matriarchal Bas-Zaire, she was the breadwinner for a sprawling family, an uncle in charge of her two little children as she worked. The Kinshasa house we helped her build was a one-room, tin-roofed shack. We saw it once, in its dun-colored, straggle-treed neighborhood laced with dirt paths leading to a communal faucet. Compared to others in her family Albertine was well-off, with a house and a good job, but like so many Zairians, she was impoverished—and still responsible for her extended family in the village. Being weak was not an option.

That's how it was, employing help in countries where we lived and taught. We were privileged, we rich foreigners, programmed to take advantage of the wage disparity, paying salaries that were a pittance on our own countries' scales. It was our role, to my mind a duty, to hire the locals, giving them a decent income. Jobs with Americans were prized. We paid better than other foreigners, and we were inclined to kindness.

But in Zaire, average citizens were stripped of rights and dignity, not to mention anything like living wages. According to statistics, the most corrupt officials in the world ran the country, from President-dictator Mobutu down to his minions, all renowned for skimming money from the country's coffers and demanding pay-offs, obedience, and accolades from their underlings. Destitute Zairians had little recourse. They learned to ask more of foreigners. "*Patron,*" they would say, hands out and open, "*donnez-moi un matabiche*"—give me a tip, a bribe, never mind what for; you owe me. That's how I took it, as *noblesse oblige* and beyond.

Albertine had asked humbly for the *matabiche* to roof her house, and over the year we gave her a couple of hundred dollars, freely and with gratitude; we did owe her. But we would never give her enough to wipe the overwhelming hardship from her life.

Tim with Albertine in our TASOK kitchen

Kinshasa, Zaire

24

Afire with Guilt

After Zaire, Russ was hired as director of the little American school in Madagascar, his heightened position hurtling us upscale from our TASOK lifestyle. We lived in the immense, director-designated house near the American School in Ivandry, a ritzy section of the capital, Antananarivo—Tana, for short. We rambled in our mansion with its maze of parquet-floored rooms, grand staircase, two-level fireplace, and sunken living room. Rangy red poinsettias disguised high concrete walls surrounding the premises, glass shards embedded in the tops of the walls to deter thieves. A Malagasy guard was on duty 24/7.

We became close to our workers: Berthe, a live-in nanny/maid; Louise, a cook; and the three alternating guards. Armand, Olivier, and Pradier spent their night shifts wrapped in plaid wool blankets in a little room at the back of our garage—it was cold there in the highlands.

We tended to our employees' emergency needs—money for doctors and meds for them and their families—and when we traveled home to the U.S. we brought back requested clothes and electronics. We took food and coffee out to the guards, gave them warm sweatshirts bearing U.S. logos, and, though they were paid by the school, occasional gifts of money. We were grateful for their

Johnny-on-the-spot opening of the heavy metal gates as we drove out, and when we honked the horn on our return. We appreciated their faithful attentions, especially to Tim, whom they'd give piggy-back rides and push up and down the pebbled drive on his plastic trike.

In our second year, soulful-eyed Pradier, the senior of the guards, honored us with a printed invitation to his daughter's wedding. On the Saturday of the event—Russ in white shirt and tie and I in my best dress and highest heels—we clambered after our wise old cook, Louise. Wearing a floral-print dress and silky shawl, she led us off the road and down a steep, rock-strewn dirt path to the wedding site. In a worn but well-pressed suit, Pradier greeted us, the only *vazahas*—white people—with a shy smile and a hearty handshake. He ushered us to rickety chairs at a table clad in a clean white cloth beneath a makeshift shelter of plastic sheeting propped up by stripped tree branches. We settled in next to Louise to enjoy a close-up view of the ceremony.

The bride, in long, snow-white lace, and her tall, dark-suited groom stood solemnly before a striking cliff of rocky reddish dirt—*Madagascar* being Malagasy for "big red island," named so for good reason. The couple repeated vows which we didn't understand, but whose strong and loving sentiment was clear. Then tin plates of *ro*—rice with chicken and *brede*, the tangy local greens—were placed before us. Pradier handed Louise two metal tablespoons, which she held out to us with a deferential smile. The bridal party and all other guests ate rice with their fingers; we gratefully used our spoons.

♫

One day after emptying baskets of fresh fruits and vegetables from the market onto the kitchen table, Louise turned to me with sad eyes. *"La fille de Pradier est morte."*

I gasped. *"Pas vrai!"* How could the lovely young bride be *dead*, two months after her marriage?

When he introduced us at the wedding, Pradier had spoken proudly of his daughter's profession as a policewoman. Soon afterward she had accepted a position in Mahajunga, a warm city on the far north coast; she and her new husband moved there to launch their married life.

Police work may have been risky business in Madagascar. But it was not the job that killed this bright young woman. When we offered Pradier our sympathy along with some money in a card, he shrugged and repeated Louise's scant explanation: *"Elle est tombée malade."*

She simply fell sick—and died. Of *what*? He didn't know. No doubt some tropical malady—malaria?—for which we *vazahas*, with our boundless resources, would have been afforded a sure cure.

Often on Fridays in Madagascar, we strapped Tim into his car seat in the back of our small red Jeep-like Suzuki, gear packed around him, and navigated the potted, winding, asphalt road through the countryside to Mantasoa.

We felt fortunate to share with an Embassy friend the lease of a quaint, stone and wood-lined cabin in this forested fingerlakes region three hours from Tana. On weekends in Mantasoa we hiked through pine woods, lazed in a hammock strung between trees by the lake, and paddled near the shore in a leaky wooden boat. In the evenings we played games on the round stone table by the fireplace, burning logs gathered for a few coins by a Malagasy man who lived in a shack nearby. Russ made pancakes for breakfast in the crisp, sun-drenched mornings.

It was still daylight with clear skies one Friday on our way to Mantasoa, when half-way there, we came upon a dozen school kids in blue uniforms traipsing home along a path beside the road. Russ slowed to a crawl as one girl skipped across the road in front of us. Accelerating, he didn't see the other girl dash out from behind a parked car. He braked and veered, but couldn't prevent the sickening *thump*. The Suzuki stopped. I yelped, then flew around to check three-year-old Tim in his car seat; he sat uncomprehending—had he seen? I turned toward Russ, who slumped over the wheel. A vice closed over my gut, forcing out raw sobs. Russ straightened at my weeping and backed the car slowly from the road, letting it idle.

Two children scurried shouting outside my partially-open window; through a blur of tears I watched them rush ahead and off the road. I rolled up the window. I couldn't see the girl we'd hit, and didn't want to—though my eyes flicked compulsively through the glass in search of her. Suddenly the face of a strong-jawed, frowning man was inches from my own. He pointed a menacing finger and spat Malagasy words through the window. My heart thundered.

During orientation in Zaire, the American Embassy had instructed us to flee the scene of any Third-World accident. "If you injure someone from a tribe or village, don't stick around and try to help," an official told us, adjusting his tie. "Foreigners have been stoned to death."

I grabbed Russ's arm. "We can't stay here." I'd flashed on our music-teacher friend's accident at the wheel of a TASOK Toyota Corolla. She'd hit a pedestrian on Matadi Road, and—over a stiff drink afterwards—told us, "I saw him fly off the road, and I drove off." She shook and gulped more vodka.

As the Suzuki pulled onto the road, sobs poured from the reservoir of grief and fear inside me. Russ squeezed my quivering knee; then, both hands on the wheel, he headed toward Mantasoa.

A few steady miles down the road, back at our normal cruising speed of 90 kilometers per hour, 55 mph, Russ squinted into the rearview mirror. "What's this?"

I rubbed a hand over my teary eyes. A white pickup passed us, and then a second; two yellow-clad men in the bed of the last truck waved their arms—gesturing us to stop? Suddenly we were in a movie. Russ sped up and tried to pass. The trucks slowed, weaving back and forth across the road in front of us until we pulled off and stopped. I whimpered as the two characters in yellow jackets clambered from the truck bed. The driver emerged from the cab and strode toward us with the other two, as did someone in the other truck. We sat panicked, engine running, as they surrounded us and gawked through the windows.

I glanced back at Tim, whose eyes were wide with fear. As if someone had flipped a switch, I stopped sniveling, undid my seatbelt and rolled down the window. *"Excusez-moi,"* I said, opening the passenger door. Russ shut off the engine and reached to hold me back, but I made my way out, cocked the seat forward and hauled my son from the back. Heart fluttering, I braced myself against the car door and held Tim wrapped in my arms, as if these men might rip him away. The nearest one, gray-haired and light-skinned, looked on with something like sympathy in his almond-shaped eyes. I pulled Tim tighter and fell into rhythmic whimpering against his little shoulder.

Out of the car, Russ, his back to me, spoke to the men. Then one came with him around to my side. "They're police. They want us to follow them to the station for a report. They have my Malagasy license."

Heart thumping, I shifted Tim to my other side. "What about the girl? Is she alive?"

"They said she went to the hospital."

As we trailed the pickups onto a bumpy dirt road I sat trembling, clutching Tim on my lap in the passenger seat. These men were not outwardly threatening, but what amends might they exact for hitting the little girl—for perhaps killing her? I stroked Tim's silky hair.

Fifteen minutes later we stopped in front of a plain block building flanked by tall grasses; green terraces of rice stretched out behind, no town in sight. Inside the building, a smallish, caramel-colored man in a dark blue uniform leaned back in a wooden chair at a desk with an old typewriter, a clunky phone and some folders. Seeing the yellow jackets enter he rose to attention. Low-toned words filled the space. The desk man handed a paper to the apparent chief of police, who beckoned Russ into a small side room to file the report.

Left in the large-windowed outer waiting area, Tim and I drew onlookers like a freak circus attraction. My stomach fluttered as people appeared from nowhere—a woman with two barefoot kids, some men in straw hats and work clothes, a teenage boy in a frayed shirt—joining the policemen to watch the show. I joggled Tim and wagged my head, blubbering in French—*"Quel désastre!"* (cry and rub eyes). *"Je suis très, très désolée!"* (cry some more). I staged a confused and desperate drama until Russ came out, the chief stern beside him.

"They want us to go to the hospital," Russ said. "The mother's there."

My heart flopped. I stared at the chief and shook my head. *"Non—je ne peux pas! Pas avec mon fils!"* I could not go to the hospital and face that mother with my own child safe in my arms, didn't he see? *"La Maman....c'est terrible!"* I gripped Tim tighter, shook my head and dissolved in tears again—but then caught myself, straightened, and scanned the onlookers, who pressed closer. Somebody had to understand. An old woman in a faded dress peered quizzically at me. How could she make sense of my antics? They made no sense, even to me. I only knew I could not face the mother of the little girl.

Through tears, I glared at Russ. "We're not going to the hospital. We can't take Tim there!" I glanced at the faded woman, drew Tim's head to my shoulder and whined piteously, a mother *vazaha* off her rocker—more acting, more show—for effect? Or was I purely wracked with pain for the poor mother and her child? Real and unreal mushed together in a muddled mélange.

We were getting nowhere. I yanked myself out of my blinding, ineffectual hysteria and spoke over Tim's head. "So is the girl alive? Do they want money?"

"I think that's why they want us at the hospital—to pay the medical bill. Maybe she's alive." How could Russ be so ludicrously calm? "Do you want to wait here, and I'll go?"

"Leave us here, without you?" Tim was becoming fretful and wiggly in my arms. I set him on his feet and grabbed his hand. "Let's just give them what we can and get out of here...."

Which is what we did—what you always do in a Third-World mess like this, assuming you know the ropes. Russ drew out his billfold.

We arrived late in Mantasoa, anxious and exhausted. As we pulled up to the cabin, Tim awoke in his car seat. He stretched and looked out. "Dark a'ready!" he said, and rubbed his eyes. My dear little son, safe and sound.

At school in Tana on Monday I poured out the story of the

accident to Madeleine, our kindergarten-teacher friend, a well-to-do Malagasy with a masters from New Jersey. "*Pff!*" She flicked her hand as if banishing a pesky fly. "These country people act like they own the road. That girl should have watched where she was going." She reached for my hand and pressed it. "This sort of thing happens often. It's not your fault."

Within a couple of weeks we received through local mail a typed, legal-looking notice about the accident. Madeleine read it, then waved it in the air. "This has been made up for *vazahas*. Don't worry."

No word of the girl's condition, but we sent the small amount of money requested in the notice. Madeleine said, "I'm sure the girl's just fine."

But hitting that little girl had set me afire with guilt, and I did not see entirely eye to eye with my friend. Those country people did own the road, or should have. As we say of Native Americans, they were there first—the village Malagasies who labored in the rice fields and practiced their deep, rich culture: their east-west taboos, the burying of their dead in sturdy tombs and unburying them for visits with the ancestors during *Famadihana*, the Turning of the Bones, in All Souls season. They were the real owners of this Big Red Island, the ones who named it. It was we interlopers, we foreigners—the French first, in Madagascar—who should have had no right of way, who barged in and jammed tall buildings into cities. We lined the soft green hills with asphalt that would ferry us from exploitative businesses to plush vacation sites, ripping the land from beneath the Real People, speeding past and over them as they hung on—still hang on, for dear life—to dirt trails on the sidelines.

My overworked conscience came by way of my mother—she, who spent her life chasing after goodness like a heat-seeking missile targets aircraft. I'd watched her hone in on troubles and turpitude with conscientious, worried efforts—bent on securing peace and prosperity. For years she taught school full-time, a prize-winning teacher investing heart and soul and most of the weekday hours in her students. With a larger income than my farming father's, she paid the bills and managed household finances. She planted and harvested huge gardens, canning full years' supplies of fruits and vegetables. She gutted, cut up and canned the chickens Dad butchered each fall. She washed clothes in a wringer washer, made hot cereal every weekday, cooked big pots of beans, and baked loaf upon loaf of our daily bread on Saturdays.

Through it all Mom policed her three daughters, chastising us for chores not well-enough done, for lapses in goodness—or so I felt, as I struggled not to disappoint her. My father, hard-working and sensitive, had his tent in Mom's camp—with occasional desertions. Once as Mom was doing schoolwork, my sisters and I wouldn't stop bickering. "Spank them!" Mom exhorted Dad. But he said, "They're good kids, Ma," and she dropped her appeal.

Back then contentment eluded my poor mother, and I must have sucked up her proclivity for unrest along with her self-admittedly scanty breast milk. As the oldest, I often felt to blame for her distress. Later, as an adult and then a mother, I'd find serenity fleeting. I wasn't good enough to warrant it for long.

During my time in the Third World, to soothe my anxious soul, I found meager ways to give: kindness to local employees, staging and support for charitable causes. But years in, still that farmer's daughter yearning for approval and devoid of a spiritual foundation, I'd done little besides stockpile hopelessness and shame. I was the well-to-do foreigner, unable or unwilling to give enough, to help the natives enough....

And on the way to Mantasoa, in an ironic twist of fate, we left that little native girl by the side of the road, fleeing the scene to save ourselves.

I would one day shed guilt like a snake shedding skin—but not for decades. Meanwhile, Zaire and Madagascar had made me sick to death of poverty. I found myself at the unbridgeable chasm between *them* and *me*—and it seemed that any minute I might plummet from my high, sunny cliff of privilege into the abyss.

In our last spring in Madagascar, when Tim was five, we adopted our second child, coffee-colored Holly Misa, a strong and spunky three-year-old. Three days after my March birthday we moved her from the cot she shared with a caregiver in a small house full of poor people, into her own soft twin bed in Tim's cavernous bedroom with its shelves of toys and books and a jungle gym in the middle. We taught her to enjoy cartoon movies at the push of a button on the big TV upstairs. I showed her how to use one of our flushing porcelain toilets instead of squatting outdoors in the dirt.

During Illinois summers, in stores and parks and at the library, people would see me and Russ with our adorable brown cherubs, and they would smile and sometimes comment on how wonderful it was, what a good thing we had done. I smiled, but cringed inside. They had no clue how self-serving my adoptions were. I had done it to feel good— saved these little urchins from the life we witnessed on the streets of their home countries, mixed brown with white to form my family in a naïve attempt to further world racial integration. I'd scooped up these waifs like puppies from the pound, cute little beings whom I could love, who would love me in return—and render me deserving of my privilege in this world.

Not that adopting needy children isn't a good, kind thing. For years I'd considered mothering poor kids who needed homes on this over-populated planet, instead of birthing unneeded babies; hence, my attraction to Val Heinrich for his Zero Population Growth bumper sticker, back in the day. And in adopting Tim and Holly, I was doing good—ergo, I *was* good.

Of course, there was more to my adoptions. I'd wanted to be a mother, finally, and my children made one of me, bless them; with Russ and assorted cats and dogs, we were a real family. When the children arrived I loved them at first sight, Tim wrapped in his Lufthansa blanket off the plane from India, and Holly barefoot with a ribbon in her hair in her little foster home in Tana.

But our adoptions had not proved salve enough to soothe my

conscience. Finding myself up-close and personal with crushing poverty in those low-income countries had undone me.

In our mid-forties, Russ and I were hooked on practicing our professions overseas. The schools were wonderful for us and our own kids; we made good money and fast friends. The lifestyle was adventurous, affording wide, interesting, low-cost travels. People we knew switched countries every few years for new, exotic experiences, and we followed suit.

Russ was director of our little school in Madagascar, and I taught English, math and science to 5th through 8th graders, and art and music to 3rd through 8th—whatever was needed. As fine an experience as it was, after four years, I wanted a change. It was *my* turn next, time for *my* choices to take priority: fewer grades and courses to prep for, please!

At the hiring fair in Iowa, Russ was offered a school directorship in Bolivia, under a superintendent, in a town called Cochabamba; I would be the 5th and 6th grade teacher for the combined class of a dozen kids.

Pictures of the city and country were gorgeous, the geography, history and culture intriguing—like those of all the countries we had known. But sources proclaimed Bolivia the poorest country in South America. Families of six lived in one-room shacks; they lacked education, health care, and clean water. Could those picturesque peaks ringing the Cochabamba Valley, the nearby Mayan ruins, and llamas in green highlands ward off the thunderhead of poverty that threatened to crash over my head?

New Family of four in Bloomington, IL

25

More Humbling Circumstances

Bolivia is a relief, I wrote family and friends as we settled in Cochabamba. *It feels more like the Second World.*

Maybe it was their diet of 200-some varieties of potatoes, but the indigenous Quechua Indian women, on the lowest rung of society, in their bowler hats and full, colorful skirts, looked sturdy and happy. And Bolivians seemed more self-assured with foreigners than the natives we'd known in Africa and Madagascar. Our first Bolivian maid, short-haired, pants-wearing Regina, earned far more than we'd paid any houseworker, and she soon demanded a change of hours that we couldn't make work for us. When she would not compromise, I gave her two weeks' notice. She asked for severance pay of two months' wages, and I gave it to her.

Regina was my equal as no previous household employee had been. Also my equals were the many well-dressed, restaurant-attending, movie-going, market-patronizing Bolivians we encountered each day in the city.

Unlike at jobs in previous foreign countries, we were responsible for our own housing in Bolivia. For a few hundred bucks a month we rented a modest, glass-front A-frame on a dirt road outside town, where we had 360-degree views of the

Andes Mountains that ringed the Cochabamba Valley. Like the residences of all middle class Bolivians, ours had walls. The guards were a sturdy Quechua couple: Jose, quick, wiry and grinning as he swung open the gates; and his plump, wide-skirted wife Bianca, who tended the roses smiling broadly around the gap in her front teeth. These two came with the place and were included in the rent; they had their own small house on the property.

Cochabamba, Bolivia's Garden City, has balmy, spring-like temperatures year-round and rich soil that nourished the landlady's dozens of thriving rose varieties in our garden. But valley winds hurled smothering waves of dust across the yard, and plastic bags—virtually nonexistent in Africa and Madagascar during our time—blew helter-skelter, settling in tattered colonies against hedges, walls and fences. Mongrel dog packs roamed the gritty, gravel streets; when I ran in the dusky mornings before school, I carried a rock in each hand to ward off attacks. Because city plumbing was unreliable—commodes couldn't be trusted not to overflow—we dutifully deposited our soiled toilet paper in the trash instead of flushing it. We shared this custom with everyone except the very well-to-do—like the family of the Bolivian beer tycoon who'd financed our new school.

With these more humbling living circumstances, and in the company of so many better-off citizens than in Africa and Madagascar, I lost sight of the unsettling gap between myself and *them*, the natives of countries in which my foreign wealth had clung to me like body odor.

Our family flourished at AISB, the spiffy new American International School of Bolivia. I felt immediate fondness for my twelve expressive, energetic 5th and 6th graders, mostly Bolivians. They inspired me to create engaging cross-curricular units. During our study of Ancient China in social studies and the Periodic Table in science, my students made and exploded gunpowder in the high school chemistry lab. We read the African folktale "Anansi the Spider" for language arts in conjunction with the study of arachnids, and for math we strung a giant spider web from a corner over a school stair landing—a feat requiring *diameter* and *radius* and *pi*. With the art teacher, a flamboyant young Bolivian woman, I organized a unit around Incan history which included a field trip to a local museum and the making of Inca-style pots in art class.

Four-year-old Holly loved her warm, motherly preschool teacher and her cozy classroom, where she learned the alphabet and made bright finger-paint designs. With his caring first grade teacher's "whole-language," reading-for-meaning approach, Tim decoded pages of favorite books like *Go, Dog, Go*.

As director, Russ facilitated daily operations and problem-solved for the PK-12 school, and during the superintendent's frequent absences he was in charge. Teachers and parents came to him for advice, trusting his cooperative, hard-working style. One period a day he escaped the office and taught high school geography, a favorite subject.

♫

One day in early March I was alone in my classroom after school when Russ made a surprise appearance—usually I collected Tim and Holly, then had to pry Russ from his downstairs office to head home. Now he stood grim beside my door. "Doug just fired me. We have two weeks to leave."

An hour earlier, on the very day Doug, the superintendent, returned from his month-long teacher-recruiting trip in the U.S., he had accused Russ of overstepping his authority—of making some decision with the PTA which Doug didn't like. "You purposely got parents and teachers in your camp," the super had said.

Russ slumped against my classroom wall. "I feel like a piano dropped on me."

Just three-quarters of one sweet school year spent—and we had to leave? I'd hoped to stay for years! Parents and teachers rallied in our support, holding meetings and dinners to sort things out and restore Russ to his position. But Doug, whom at first I'd liked and trusted as one of the most humane and affable administrators I'd met, would not relent.

Over Bolivian beers early on, Doug had told stories of being sabotaged on a high-powered job in California. Now he was the saboteur. He had convinced the Bolivian beer baron, his school co-founder and long-time buddy, that Russ had gravely, unforgivably erred.

During our eight months in Bolivia we'd experienced a whirlwind of adventures. We made good friends, adopted cat Willie and dog Lobo, and improved our Spanish. We dined often at La Estancia and other great restaurants, bought carved wood bunk beds and wool weavings and bubbled green glassware at the huge local market, went to festivals and concerts and parades. A quaint little town called Tiquipaia was a half-hour drive away, a frequent day trip with friends on weekends, as were drives out of the valley to gaze at llamas like white cotton puffs on the green velvet flanks of the Altiplano. We traversed the damp cloud forest to camp in the tropical Chapare, and dipped ourselves in a cool, clear tributary of the Amazon.

We promised the kids our next place would be just as nice.

♫

"What could be so bad about living in Paradise?" Russ emerged beaming from the butler's pantry of our Bloomington, Illinois, house. The phone still in his hand at the end of its stretched-out cord, he announced we had new jobs.

When we'd left Bolivia we had stopped to visit Cat and Ray, friends from TASOK days now on St. Croix in the U.S. Virgin Islands. They'd learned of jobs available on St. John, an island-hop away, and recommended us.

The phone interview had yielded the offer, and Russ was channeling Tevye from *Fiddler on the Roof*. What could be so bad, indeed? Russ would be director of Pine Peace School—*Pine* for *pineapple*, *Peace* a play on *piece of land*. I would teach 5th and 6th grades combined; Tim and Holly would attend another fine school, tuition-free.

But salaries were low, and this time we'd get no plane flights, no travel or shipping allowance, no money for housing—no benefits at all, except health insurance. They could book a small condo for us for $1500 a month, which seemed a fortune....

And we'd soon learn that most basic commodities were flown from the U.S. mainland to St. Thomas, then ferried across Pillsbury Sound to St. John, causing exorbitant prices on the tiny island: A half-gallon of milk, standard fare for our growing kids, cost $2.95.

We bought a used, beat-up Rocky Daihatsu at a premium, and once a month on a Saturday we sprang for the $50 car ferry to St. Thomas, where we stocked up on food and housing supplies at Cost-U-Less, the giant warehouse store—"Cost-U-More," locals dubbed it. The milk might be sour, a loaf of bread moldy or a head of lettuce rotten inside, but there was no taking it back.

We rarely ate out; restaurant prices were prohibitive—except for those at Skinny Legs across the island at a fuel-oil-smelling, small-boat dock on Coral Bay, where we could get good, simple burgers for $5.

For most of our time on St. John we had no washer or dryer, so once a week I bundled laundry to the expensive, crowded public laundromat in downtown Cruz Bay. I took along bread, cheese, and an apple, and ate it engrossed in a book as clothes spun in clanking machines around me.

Our pay was lower than Stateside educators'. And unlike at our other jobs abroad, we owed taxes, to the U.S. and the Virgin Islands. We traveled little; we saved nothing.

But Paradise was worth every pinched penny. From the moment we slipped into the warm, silken waters of the Caribbean, we knew we were in heaven. We gazed at the dazzling sea from our balcony and drove past spectacular views of its pristine beaches on our way to school or town; we lazed on its fine, champagne-colored sand as we read and napped and talked and partied—all birthdays were staged on the beach. We swam, sailed, and snorkeled in the water's gentle waves.

On the eight-by-five mile, roller-coaster piece of earth that was St. John, the sea was the best thing. Home and school and town, inland, were humid, and spiked with rocks and scrub. There was little call for the kids to play outside for long, and inside space was limited, Tim and Holly in a tiny room with bunk beds. On weekends, with hours free, we packed food and floaties and snorkel gear into the Rocky and spent the better parts of Saturday and Sunday at the beach. The kids were at home in the water, swimming far from shore with classmates, snorkeling in ten-foot deep water over coral reefs with brilliant fish, and plunging like experts to see starfish on the bottom. I'd float on the surface, marveling through my goggles at my colorful kids among the flashing schools of fish. On a sailing trip with friends, five-year-old Holly dove from the top of the mast straight into deep water two dozen feet below. At the end of the Reef Bay Trail hike, Tim swam far from the shore over stingrays to meet the Sadie Sea, the boat that would take us back to town.

St. John's Pine Peace School, belying its name, proved as prickly as the monkey no-climb trees in the stream bed—called the *gut* by locals—of the stony land on which it sat. I had only nine 5th and 6th graders, but most were restive. Possessed of parents who seemed abusive, neglectful, or over-indulgent, these kids couldn't help but act out. Most had been in their little private enclave since kindergarten, honing individual and group dysfunctions for years. Behaviors such as blurting out and wandering at will around the classroom worsened with the onset of adolescence. I wasn't good at keeping kids involved in classroom studies for long.

One day in October, thirteen-year-old Grace suddenly turned her dark glare on timid Jeannie and bellowed, "I *heard* that, slut." Grace bolted from her chair and loomed over her victim.

I was interpreting a math problem for fourteen-year-old West-Indian Benjamin, who couldn't read. I left him to insert myself between the girls. "Grace! Let it go." I guided her back to her desk and peered at her math paper. "Look—you got this hard one right! I bet you can do the next."

"*Dumb*-y, *dumb*-y, can't *read*, can't *read*...," big 6th-grade Allan droned, head-down, voice aimed through his armpit toward Benjamin, two crooked rows behind him.

"Allan! 'No personal insults,' remember?" We'd made the classroom rules together—for naught, it seemed.

As I hurried to help Allan, Benjamin bolted from his desk and leveled stormy eyes at his nemesis. "Faggot pimp!" He hurled a pencil; it ricocheted off Allan's arm. Allan yelped, dove below my knees for the pencil and reached around me to wing it back. It bounced off the wall next to the wheezing air conditioner's moldy stain. Classmates guffawed.

"Let's sit down, Benjamin, okay?" I clung to my calm, gentle manner like an octopus to its rock.

Then Dustin erupted: Turned toward the fracas from his desk at the front, the shrimp-sized 5th grader cackled hysterically.

"Stop!" I snapped. Shepherding Benjamin back to his seat, I shot peeved words at Dustin. "Why isn't your book open yet? I know you can do that geometry. You're so smart!" At his parents' insistence I had him working in a 7th-grade book.

"Whatever." Dustin flapped the book's cover open. Closed. Open. Closed....

We're all here because we're not all there, proclaimed someone's bumper sticker in the school's parking strip. It fit my St. John students and their parents—and me, too, I was beginning to think.

Among those "not all there," Benjamin and his family stood out. Benjamin's mother, Miss Marceline, was a tall, proud, proper-mannered, white-gloves-wearing West Indian from down-island in Grenada. She worked as a maid at the ritzy Westin Hotel. In a conference, she defended her son's belligerence. "He's a *good* boy, Miss. He just needs special *attention*."

More attention than I could give him.

Benjamin was the oldest, longest-attending West Indian student at Pine Peace, there since kindergarten. He'd hung on despite failing two grades. The school catered to their few West Indians, offering scholarships and creating special programs; they'd cosseted Benjamin for years, hoping to claim him as their first West Indian "graduate."

In his early school years Benjamin had been simply nonachieving and mischievous. But adolescence hit him like the soccer ball he slammed into the wall at recess, and defiance streaked through his strong, maturing body to decimate the class. He launched verbal or physical attacks on classmates whenever I left his side.

I dumped my predicament on Russ, who tried valiantly to help. He learned Benjamin's parents lived apart, in different buildings on their few acres of property tucked behind a locked fence far from the sea in distant Coral Bay. Miss Marceline pampered her boy, and Mortimer, a muscled native construction foreman, beat him. One day Russ was startled to watch Mortimer pull a switch off a campus bush and whip his boy in the parking lot for misbehaving in class. Russ intervened, suggesting less-hurtful discipline like grounding or time-outs—but Mortimer glowered. Continentals did not mess with Island ways.

Then one day in the office Mortimer told Russ, "My boy is being denied his Civil Rights in dis school."

Benjamin was the only black kid in 5th and 6th grade, other than Grace and Raquel, who were mixed-race. Mortimer now claimed that his son was being discriminated against by white classmates and teachers at Pine Peace—including me. He began calling Russ at home late at night, rambling for an hour about Martin Luther King, Jr., and what he died for. "My boy needs freedom to be his *self*, suh, and your school does *not allow it*. Your school did not teach him to read, and den dey held him back. Because he is *Black*. Because of our *race*, which Martin Luther King died to save. Suh, dis is not *right*."

Mortimer had a point; centuries-long derailment of race relations had undoubtedly fed into this train wreck. But now it was a case of strained teacher-student relations. By Thanksgiving I knew I had no chance of taming the beast inside poor, troubled Benjamin. I felt helpless. Russ's hands were tied as well. Stress had spilled into our home in the form of bad tempers all around.

The Sunday after Thanksgiving, as I lay on the smooth sand of Francis Bay, my stomach roiled in dread of returning to school the next day. I turned to Russ, beside me. "Would we go broke if I quit my job?"

He slipped a hand into his Tom Clancy book and looked at me. "We'd manage."

I stayed till Christmas break, when Benjamin presented me with a parting gift—a little wooden table he'd made himself.

Tim and Holly in our front yard

Cochabamba, Bolivia

26

Pi in the Refrigerator

SECOND SEMESTER ON St. John, free from regular teaching, I formed an after-school singing group of Pine Peace girls, charging singers $3 for each Tuesday and Thursday session. I brought my electric piano, cradling it in my arms as I walked the mile from home in shorts and a tank top, up and down the sunny hills of Gifft Hill Road to school. The little group delighted in singing for school programs. For "Yellow Submarine," we cut out and painted a long cardboard sub with portholes that the girls looked through as they sang and swayed beneath blue cardboard waves.

Holly, mature at five and a good singer, was the youngest in my group. Seven-year-old Tim played in the *gut* with his friend Zeus until my singing class was over; then we all rode home in the Rocky with the piano in the back.

I began giving weekly piano lessons at my house. One student I took on was Jasmine, a sprightly 6th grader from my former class. As she came for her lesson after school one Wednesday, Jasmine plunked down her books, scaled the sofa and began walking across its top edge as if it were a balance beam. *How glad I am not to be teaching that class of hers,* I thought.

Rhonda, a Continental, long-time island inhabitant and new friend—who would years later visit us in India as she adopted her own child there—offered me $10 an hour, any hours I chose, to clean and paint the trim on her luxurious rental houses. I walked the hills to work and back, and loved laboring on Rhonda's decks, stopping to gaze at the turquoise sea as I gulped water and mopped sweat with my bandana.

Those days I felt strong and relaxed and tan—and rich enough.

♫

As we cruised happily into our second school year on St. John, I began a correspondence course in advanced fiction writing with the University of Iowa. I also continued my paid activities—the singing group, piano lessons, and painting for Rhonda.

One afternoon in mid-September I looked up from cleaning paint brushes on the deck at Sundance, one of Rhonda's houses that overlooked the snorkeling bay of Chocolate Hole. The sky seemed strangely colorless. Suddenly the dreadlocked plumber from Dominica walked into the living room behind me and announced, "We be fucked, mon."

"What?" Rhonda came from installing a pot rack in the kitchen.

"Hurricane Marilyn be hittin' here for sure. Tomorrow. Just heard on de radio." He pointed at the big glass windows. "Better get dose boarded up."

Hurricane Luis had blown through just a week before with little damage, though St. Croix had seen more. On the phone, our friend Cat told us she and Ray had stood in the silent, eerie eye of the hurricane sipping cocktails; luckily, their house and school were spared—unlike many other buildings on St. Croix.

"Can you help close this place up?" Rhonda said to everyone—the two maids, the plumber, and me—as she flew into action herself, closing shutters.

The Islands knew how to deal with hurricanes, and we'd learned the basics from friends. The storm was due the next night, Friday, as close as anyone could tell, so Friday morning we went to work in the lower-down, less-expensive house we'd moved into the previous spring. We put huge duct-tape *X*-es on our glass doors and windows, and stowed loose, vulnerable belongings in drawers and cupboards and the oven, taping them shut; we put furniture up on blocks against flooding. Russ drove down to the Marina Market and bought more candles, extra batteries and canned beans.

School let out early Friday. Our island friends Corinne and Rafe convinced us to spend the night with them, their two kids, and their dog Hanna in the bunker-like Pine Peace bathrooms downstairs, below the great room, across the hall from my old classroom. They'd moved into the girls' bathroom; we dragged sleeping bags, snacks and bottles of water into the boys'.

Strong winds came and went for hours. We couldn't sleep. Electricity went out; we lit candles and used flashlights. Corinne's short-wave radio issued crackling coverage of the storm as she tracked its progress on a map.

About 10:00 a friendly West Indian named Credence blew in on clouds of marijuana, his long dreads dangling. He offered hits on his pipe, then set up camp in the hallway outside the bathrooms.

When the gusts became even stronger—over 120 miles per hour, almost category 3, we would learn later—Marilyn roared like a train hell-bent to leave the tracks. Atmospheric pressure must have wreaked havoc in my abdomen, for I felt cramps like I hadn't had since pre-menopause days. "You stay here," I told the kids, holding my belly as I pulled myself from between them. I stepped into the hallway to see and *feel* the two huge plate-glass doors to the outside bowing inward as one, expanding where they joined at the metal-lined crack, straining against the lock—the massive span of glass breathing in and out like the lungs of a giant killer whale. How could this raging gale force not break the feeble lock, rush in and wipe us out?

I fled back to the restroom. "Russ, I'm scared."

He rose on an elbow from where he lay atop his sleeping bag. "I just heard Corinne talking to Credence. The radio's full of static, but she thinks she heard this thing is on its way out."

As the wind howled we drifted in and out of fitful, soggy sleep. We awoke when a West Indian man and woman entered through the plate glass doors, letting in a massive *whoosh* which they pushed back and out, wrestling the doors closed behind them.

They lived just up the hill; they'd panicked when a heavy plank shot through the wall into their stereo. "I was right *dere*," the wife said, pointing with a trembling hand. "It barely missed my head."

The next morning we emerged from our bathroom bunker into a pale, dead stillness. The island seemed naked, her trees stripped of leaves and branches, houses downed and broken. Portions of the school's roof had caved in over a couple of classrooms, destroying books and carpets. A huge piece of sheet-metal roofing lay bent over a seesaw on the playground; the nearby picnic table was upended against the fence.

Up on the road, the canvas roof of our convertible Rocky Daihatsu was gone—no great loss; we preferred it down anyway, even in the rain. Our house was fine, a little water leaked in under doors. Other folks had fared much worse. For months we would see my old student Allan's big house tilted from its place on a bald hillside, unlivable. Holly's dance teacher's house was ripped off its moorings and destroyed, her family's sodden belongings plastered to a hillside. They found their old dog Pi trapped in the refrigerator outside, gaunt and quivering. Driving into town for ice in the coming weeks, we would pass what was left of a little West Indian house on a corner, two sides gone; shirts and dresses gripped their hangers in an open closet, vulnerable as the occupants who'd left them there.

FEMA gave us lanterns and camp stoves. We hauled drinking water in gallon jugs from Cruz Bay, stringing the jugs out of the way on a rope attached to the ceiling, taking them down to use and refill as needed. Ice from Ben & Jerry's ice cream freezer cooled food in the fridge. We took sponge baths, hauling water up in a bucket from the cistern beneath the floor. Before, we'd watched TV sometimes—"Bill Nye, the Science Guy," and "Wishbone," the story-telling dog—but Marilyn had wiped out cable; now we played games and read books by lantern light.

We'd hoped to splurge on an inflatable dinghy that year, to take us out to tiny nearby islands—but Marilyn blew that plan out of the water. Its after-effects dragged on so long that we sprang for a generator from Cost-U-Less instead. We would not have power back for three months; phone service took five, and TV longer yet.

After the storm the island was plagued by armies of mosquitoes, carriers of agonizing dengue fever—"break-bone" fever, the locals called it. Our house had no screens or glass windows, only shutters. Writing at my computer beneath an open window, I felt the wispy-legged pests light on my bare calves and arms. Repellant didn't cut it—or I didn't use enough. I spent Thanksgiving in bed, wracked by waves of fever, severe headache and aching bones.

All of us came down with dengue. Poor Holly threw up seventeen times in a twenty-four hour span—I was well then and could empty her bucket and cool her forehead.

Russ's mom and sisters flew down from the States for Christmas, too late to change plans; one after the other, they succumbed to dengue too. After the holidays we packed sister Mary, weak and feverish, onto the ferry to start her trip back to Arizona; Russ's mom developed symptoms back in Illinois.

Through it all I never worried—though there was no known cure, and a couple of people died. Unless you needed intravenous drip for hydration, as our national park ranger friend Julie did, there was nothing to do but take painkillers and let the fever run its course. I was buoyed by the fact that so many people came down with dengue; it was a well-known island curse, taken for granted and dealt with. Afterwards, people reappeared in public gaunt and worn, and you knew where they'd been. I lost ten pounds myself.

For our tenth anniversary three days after Christmas, everyone well at the moment, Russ and I left the kids in the care of his mom and sisters and went out to celebrate. From the balcony at Asolare, an upscale restaurant on the North Shore, we sat gazing at sparkling lights over the sea, relishing mixologist Corinne's complimentary drinks and our seafood dinners. After a bite of succulent lobster drenched with drawn butter, I said, "I need to teach full-time again."

Russ agreed. We were going in the hole financially on St. John, using up our savings. We could not spend another school year like this.

In February I stayed home on the island with Tim and Holly while Russ flew off to the International School Services recruiting fair in Philadelphia. On the phone from his hotel, he said, "How does Bombay sound?" We'd have free housing again, and our flights paid. I twiddled the cord. "They'll provide you a full-size piano at home, and they're giving us our own driver. I guess traffic is pretty crazy."

I would teach middle school—6th through 8th grade social studies. Russ would earn his biggest salary yet as an assistant to the superintendent. And we would get to experience Tim's homeland.

But India was rife with the three *P*'s I'd come to fear—population, pollution, and worst of all, poverty.

Fifteen hundred miles away, Russ waited for my answer. I squeezed the cord. "Okay then. Sounds like we're off to Bombay."

27

I Know I Had It All Together

In mid-June of 2013, we've staged a road trip get-away from the messy remodel of our little Arizona house. We are in Littleton, Colorado, with my sisters on a Tuesday when my right thumb starts to hurt. Russ inspects. "I think you got a sliver when we moved those boards in the garage."

An expert sliver extractor, he begins to probe, but I draw back. If it is a sliver, it's far under the nail. Poking around in there will hurt like blazes. "Just let it be," I say. "It'll probably fester out."

Russ leaves to visit friends in Fort Collins on Wednesday, and I go on a six-mile hike with my sisters and the dogs. As I walk, the pain in my thumb intensifies. Carol says, "Maybe soaking in salt water." That night at her house she fixes me a dish of warm solution, but afterwards my thumb has a pulse like tribal drumming.

The next day I stand with Carol in a tattoo parlor as our younger sister Chrissie sits on a cot having a delicate cricket design inked onto the inside of her foot. It doesn't hurt, "just stings a little bit," she says, grinning. I'm encouraged to dare a peace sign on my arm—but at the moment, painful rhythmic beating in my thumb squelches all thoughts of peace. My nail seems to be separating from the flesh beneath, the thumb tip turning red. As we go to lunch I pop another Advil. That night I take three.

The following day the thrumming drives a regular bass beat toward my wrist, but we're scheduled to go to an annual antiques and collectibles fair in a park. I gobble Advil, and for an hour I guard my aching hand close to my abdomen as we traipse around admiring old furniture and knickknacks and linens. I stray from my sisters to inspect a washstand that looks like ones we had growing up. When I turn to leave it, my thumb bumps the edge, and I yelp in pain. I hold my hand and cry softly—but there's nothing to be done. I heed my Program's advice to accept the things I cannot change. I don't want to be a wimp with my sisters; they've got to remember my old hypochondriac tendencies. They're acting like this thumb thing is nothing, and they're probably right. I ask the Universe for patience.

Russ comes back from Fort Collins late the next afternoon, and as I pour out the saga of my suffering, he frowns. "Those are your piano hands." He holds the wounded one, inspecting the thumb. "We need to do something." I lean my head on his shoulder.

We drive to a pharmacy in town, thinking to buy drawing salve, but when the pharmacist sees my thumb, he says, "That's infected. It needs to be lanced."

At urgent care a doctor gives me Vicodin and lays me on a gurney. Russ holds my good hand as she numbs my thumb with three separate injections to the tip.

The painful shots seem to have no effect. I turn my contorting face away as the doc cuts and scrapes and presses the pus from my thumb. I hold it steady, but the rest of me tightens and twists in pain. Tears trail down my face, and Russ strokes my quivering legs on the bed. The doc apologizes. She cuts and scrapes some more as I writhe and whimper. Finally, she says, "Done."

As we drive to the pharmacy for antibiotics, my head floats on my shoulders like a smiley-faced helium balloon.

Back at Carol's by 7:30 for a barbecue that night, our last in Colorado, I'm still floating. I drink no alcohol; I've taken another Vicodin. I happily recount the adventure.

I learn later that my infection is MRSA—*methicillin-resistant staphylococcus aureus*. Pre-Program, I would have panicked; in rare circumstances, MRSA can be deadly; they'd made a big to-do about it in the high school where I taught a few years before. Now I'm simply grateful for modern medicine, and for that kind Colorado doctor on duty on a Friday night.

♫

That same summer, after a women's vacation-retreat with old friends in New Mexico, I'm steering home toward Arizona under blue skies when I hear the news on NPR: nineteen Prescott hotshot firefighters killed in the Yarnell fire. *Nineteen?* I turn up the radio.

Over the following week, the Granite Mountain Hotshots' memorial in front of the fire station on 6th Street swells with flowers and messages and crosses and firefighter T-shirts from around the country. Sets of nineteen proliferate: teddy bears, candles, flags; nineteen full bottles of water. A fire-quenching rain, the first of the season, pours down the day after the tragedy and continues for days. The memorabilia have become a sad, soggy mess.

"Crazy," both Tim and Holly say. Most of the nineteen dead were in their twenties, like my kids. Several went to their high school. Everyone is connected to someone who knew a hotshot or two. Prescott feels smaller now, as if we 40,000 inhabitants have shrunk together and cling tighter, like the warp and woof of boiled wool. "Everybody's Hometown" has slipped its footings.

♫

A week after the fire, Russ and I stand in our back yard on Garden Street in Prescott, staring at our house. A tear trickles down my cheek. "It's ruined." I look sideways and brush off my face so Quinn, who's young enough to be my son, won't see I'm crying. Russ squeezes my hand.

Our little hundred-year-old house is in the middle of major surgery for expansion. Under the saws and hammers of contractors Quinn and Riley, the backside has been ripped off, exposing painted fir floorboards, ragged remnants of a half-dozen styles of old wallpaper, and a 1917 calendar from the Central Kansas

Mining Company. An entire glass window, slathered white and trapped between walls by a 1920-ish addition, has come to light and now stands propped against a fence.

The house lost its balance when they sliced off the back, and the old kitchen we hoped to preserve sank toward the gaping wound. The granite counters split at the seams, and the cupboards below them pulled apart, leaving gaps now filled with construction debris. Drawers won't open. And worst—the guys had not thrown a tarp over the roof before the sudden dump of heavy rain a week ago, so the kitchen ceiling sags with pockets of water that burst, spattering appliances and sending grimy, snail-like trails down walls and cupboard doors.

I turn back to Quinn. "I need you to tell me it's going to be okay...."

"Don't worry," he says. "We'll fix it. And when it's done it will be beautiful."

Beautiful, he says, and my despair drains away like Arizona rain running off this hard ground. I touch Quinn's back in gratitude.

♫

In early August, Tim calls. "I have bad news, I guess."

My grip tightens on the phone. What now? Out of a job again? He hasn't been back at Panchito's for a year yet.

"Meg and I broke up."

"Awww. That's too bad." She's become my Facebook friend during the scant year they've been together. "I'll miss her."

Losing his job would have been worse.

I glance out the window, phone to my ear, and resume bustling around this little furnished cottage we're renting downtown during our remodel. It's a Sunday morning, rainy and dreary, as it has been for days. I'm trying to find my piano music for today's Unitarian service—which starts in an hour, I realize, glancing at the watch on my wrist, the watch that was missing for days but appeared in the nightstand drawer yesterday.

"It was my decision to leave." Tim does sound calm, more grounded this time than when he and Haley split. I suddenly remember he's not working today; he's off Sundays. I look at my watch again: 9:10. I should leave by 9:30. I'm not finished dressing. I haven't had any breakfast, and I still can't find my music. "But she agrees," Tim says into my ear. "It's better for both of us."

"What happened?" I flip through the pile of stuff near Russ's computer. No music books there.

"Nothing, really. She just started being annoyed with me all the time. And she didn't let me discipline Bryson at all." I remember how she doted on that little boy of hers. "He bit me once and I didn't dare say anything."

"Oh, Tim, I'm sorry. That's hard." I search a stack of books on the shelf under the TV and mumble into the phone, "I must've left my music at the other house. Dammit. I know I had it all together...." Unlike at our previous home-away-from-home this summer, there's no piano at this cottage; I've been practicing on the congregation's baby grand, or wrestling the tarp off my own old upright at Garden Street. God knows where I left this music.

"Well, I'll talk to you later. I just wanted you guys to know."

"Wait—where are you now?"

"At Joe's, till I find an apartment. I want to get my own place for real this time. There's this girl at work who really wants to date, but I told her not till I finish *Grand Theft Auto 5*, and anyway, I don't want to live with anybody for a while."

I remember he's been dying for this video game to come out. Probably still addicted to gaming, but that's his business. "Thanks for letting us know, Tim. Hang in there. You'll have to come over sometime and see this place. We're here for a month yet."

In the living room Russ motions for the phone and takes over the conversation with Tim. I go into the bedroom, slide my earrings from the little dish on the dresser, and rack my brain for where else my music could be. As I walk around searching again, I twiddle the tiny posts into my ears, three in each, without looking in a mirror—always multi-tasking lately, it seems. Mindless.

Just as I think I'll have to drive to Garden Street the music appears on a chair under the table by the door. I eat some yogurt and an apple. In the bathroom I sweep the brush through my long gray hair, catching a glint of my silver earrings in the mirror. Russ calls, "We better go."

Settling into the car, I take a deep breath. "I seem rattled by everything under the sun these days...."

Russ puts on the windshield wipers to clear off the night's rain. I click my seat belt into place and lean back, my music in my lap.

"...but I just realized I haven't lost a single earring or contact lens since we left Garden Street."

"That's good." He always has to help me search when one of those goes missing.

"Better yet, Tim didn't lose his job, thank God, and it didn't even occur to me his bad news could've been another relapse."

Bits of gratitude appear in the midst of our disruption, like the sunlight that pokes through gray sky as we drive.

♫

I message Meg on Facebook: "Still friends." I add a heart and a smiley face.

"I hope so!" she replies. "I'm sad. I didn't want Tim to leave, but I understand. I love him."

I write back, "'Friends' is good."

It's a wonder to me, the way my kids handle romance. Holly has been with Rick for over two years in what seems a loving, grounded relationship; they spend nights together at his place or hers. I recently asked Holly, "Do you think about living together? It would save you time and money."

"We've talked about it," she said. "But things are good the way they are." They're twenty-three.

And at twenty-six Tim seems to want to *find himself,* as we used to call it back in the '60's, when I was fumbling, trying to locate and reassemble parts of my own discombobulated young-adult self. Tim's last two long-term loves have been women seven years his senior with young children; I can't help thinking that his shrugging off their control of his life is a good move. "I'd like to join a yoga group," he said recently. And, "When I'm settled again I'll get back to playing guitar more, maybe get a drummer." At the moment, he seems in no hurry for another relationship.

My kids seem so unlike me when I was their age, charging in and out of love affairs in search of the perfect mate, like a mouse scrabbling for cheese in a maze. I'm pretty sure Holly's had sex with just one person, Tim with maybe four or five. By Tim's age I'd slept with dozens.

Well, times have changed. Unlike Tim and Holly's youths, mine coursed through an era when "penicillin was a cure-all for any misjudgments," as a writer-friend said. With more harmful sexually-transmitted diseases afoot, my children know to be more cautious. Still, when I think of the sheer number of my young "misjudgments," I admire my kids for making fewer.

♫

Tim fidgets in the wicker chair on the covered porch. "I messed up." He turns away and gulps coffee.

"Oh? What'd you do?" Russ asks. We're sitting outside our rented cottage. It's another drizzly morning, September now.

"I went over to Meg's yesterday to pick up some stuff, and she asked if we could 'try again.' I spent the night, but I shouldn't have." He shakes his head. "We got into this big fight. She was yelling and crying."

"Sounds like a break-up relapse," I say. "Reminds me of when I split with my first boyfriend, Andy. He kept coming over, trying to be 'friends,' but I just felt sorry for him. I finally told him we couldn't see each other, period."

"Well it's *over*-over now. I won't see her any more. Unless it's by accident."

"And then you'd cope."

We sit in silence on the porch. The gray of the sky matches the two rental cottages on this property, ours in back, off the alley, and the one in front which we can see through the bedraggled, ivy-covered arbor.

Tim stirs his sugar-laced coffee, takes a sip and sets it down. "Things aren't great at Joe's right now. Ryan's been getting drunk and obnoxious every night."

Their old buddy Ryan was Tim's first apartment mate back in his drinking days, the one who drove him out by selling marijuana from their place. Ryan has been paying rent for a back bedroom at Joe and Cathy's, where Tim's flopping rent-free on the living room couch.

"Cathy wants Joe to throw him out, but he doesn't have the heart to."

Russ says, "I'm sorry to hear Ryan's having such a tough time." Ryan was once Russ's student.

"Sounds like all the more reason for you to have your own place," I say.

Tim stands up and stretches, ready to leave. "I'm looking almost every day now."

Next day I read a message he's posted on Facebook: "I'm so happy I don't drink anymore. Watching a friend struggle with it sucks but reminds me why I don't."

28

Heaven to Be Home

Guilt sits in the shadows of my consciousness again. It stalks me as we choose brushed-nickel bathroom fixtures and order sleek new fans; it assails me as we deliberate between paint colors with treacly names like "Scandinavian sky" and "sprig of ivy." Guilt, because we have the time and money to indulge our every wish for this new house, while some folks after the Yarnell fire have no houses, and no insurance on the ones they had. Not to mention our contractor Riley with his wife Claire and four little kids and another on the way across the street in a house that lacks space and decent heat—as he labors to install our superfluous upstairs powder room with its skylight. "Wanna trade?" Claire said one day as she delivered lunch for Riley.

Mixing guilt with dread of the daunting clean-up and move-in task ahead, I have created a mountain of gloom as massive as the thirty-ton load of topsoil we've ordered for our new yard.

At our bi-weekly meeting I tell my sponsor, Carla, "I can't help feeling guilty over being so fortunate. I thought I was over this. But I feel the same as I did over poverty in Africa and Madagascar."

"So, you've been dealt a good hand, and you're squandering it with guilt," she says. "That's no help to you or anyone."

"I've been trying to let it go. It's just—why shouldn't others be as lucky as I am? I should do more to even it out."

"People feel guilty when they've done something wrong. You've done nothing wrong."

"But I don't deserve so much—"

"You do. You and Russ have worked hard as educators. I know you give, and you serve. You deserve a comfortable, happy life."

Carla sits back in her chair and lays one hand into the other, Buddha-like. "I think guilt is related to shame. It comes from feeling unworthy, not good enough. I've had to let go of a heap of shame myself. It can be a real affliction for us folks from the Midwest, with our moralistic Protestant upbringing. Maybe those cold winters froze it into our souls." She winks, and her calm brown eyes look into mine. "It takes energy to keep manufacturing reasons for deserving to be in the Universe, doesn't it."

I'm feeling teary now.

"Indulging in guilt or shame is like acting on an addiction. It's a harmful habit. When you tire of the self-flagellation, you'll get help. Ask for divine grace, and watch for it. When it comes, abandon yourself to it."

I take a deep breath. "Wish I had a tape recorder. Your words are so soothing." I wipe my eyes and look at the clock above Carla's head. It's been over an hour. I get up and pet her old dog on the floor beside my chair.

As I leave her peaceful, book-lined house, my eyes are drawn to the pine-strewn boulders just behind it, the backdrop of intense blue sky, and I think of "divine grace." I may get it from views like this, when I take time to notice. I think I've just received it, with Carla. I think I receive it often—I just haven't named it.

Abandoning myself to divine grace? Not sure what that means. But recognizing it is a start—like recognizing gifts, and being grateful. I do that more now. I can get this.

♫

"Ryan pours beers into an empty gallon milk jug and drinks it all at once. Two six-packs' worth sometimes. A couple nights ago he threw a jug against the wall and passed out in the living room.

I've gotta get out of here."

The ongoing drama of Tim's life spills from the phone into my ear. I feel for him, poor guy. He does need to get out.

"I'm keeping track of apartments to check on. I like that old Prescott Inn downtown. It has rooms with bathrooms and kitchenettes, and I can afford 'em, but the only thing available right now is a room with a shared bath. They said keep calling back, people are always moving."

"Well, that sounds good."

"I was wondering, could I stay with you guys in the meantime? I'd pay rent, fifty bucks a paycheck. I just have to get out of here."

Generosity rushes in as quickly as hot water to our new brushed-nickel bathroom taps. "Sure, Tim. I'll just make sure with Dad. You could try out the futon in the new upstairs. And use the bathroom up there."

After countless hours of cleaning and moving roomsful of possessions, we've spent two nights back home on Garden Street. Tim helped us bring in the heavy oak platform bed yesterday, and last night we slept in our new bedroom. Workers still trail through the house to install doorknobs and banisters and touch up walls and floors, and we have more arranging to do—but it's heaven to be home. How could we not share our new space with our son, who is in such straits? Offering him a place makes me feel more deserving of our luxury.

One night a week later, Russ and I are crawling into our soft bed when I let out a sigh. "I'm feeling weird with Tim here. He seems to just hang around and do nothing but play video games. He's been here over a week, and I don't see him looking very hard for his own place. Do you?"

Russ takes my hand.

"I know he gets stoned sometimes when he goes out walking. I don't care, except he comes back and tries to talk to me when I'm busy. He's not himself, and I just don't want him around, and I hate that that's true...."

Russ clears his throat. "It's true for me too. It's hard to know what to do." He lets go of my hand and turns off the light. "Maybe we just wait."

But my serenity's shot through again, and my thoughts ramble as I lie awake. Tim's paying rent, being solicitous and helpful, cleaning up after himself, eating more often at work than with us; on what grounds would we throw him out? Still, we've got to do something, because my serenity's under seige. I breathe deep and ask the Universe for clarity.

Next morning an idea comes with the light Russ lets in through the blinds. Over coffee I suggest to Tim that he could take the place with the shared bath at the Prescott Inn, and move when a better room opens up.

He's seized with it, as if he thought of it himself. That day before work he checks into the Inn, and the next day we help him move his gaming gear and big TV, the Picachu nightstand I painted for him back in the day, his bags and baskets of clothes.

I like the Prescott Inn. It has historic photos in the spacious lobby, and grand staircases and wide hallways, all lined with the original dark wood. Tim's room has tall windows with shades and filmy curtains, and he's near a public balcony. We help arrange the stuffed wingback chair to face his TV, and put the single bed against a wall.

Tim's been at the Inn for a week when he calls. "Can I stay with you guys again?" He has itchy bites all over his back—his room has bedbugs. And though Joe and Cathy have finally tossed Ryan out, they won't take Tim in. "I don't blame 'em," he says. "They're renting the place and don't wanna take a chance on bedbugs."

He's talked to people and researched bedbugs. He comes over with unwieldy black garbage bags full of clothes to wash and dry in our new laundry room. He's got a lot of clothes, many more than I. Another addiction? Not my business. We wash batches of clothes in hot water.

On the internet I've tracked down a product rated highly effective: "JT Eaton Kills Bed Bugs." It's toxic to pets, but I'll be sure Metro and Iris don't get near. I find a bottle at the nearby

True Value Hardware. I give Tim rubber gloves and a face mask and have him spray his car trunk, backpack, and the shoes lined up outside.

He's at work at Panchito's when his clothes are finally dry. I carry them in warm armloads to his room, where I sit on the floor and fold T-shirt after T-shirt, most emblazoned with heavy-metal band names and dark slogans—I can't tell which. I caress the soft cloth as I smooth each shirt, turn back its sleeves and sides, and lap the back-bottom up to form a neat rectangle. I place the shirts in multi-colored piles, make separate stacks of jeans and boxer shorts.

♫

Tim's mastered *Grand Theft Auto 5* and he's dating Renee, the young woman at work who was attracted to him. She lives with a roommate out in Prescott Valley, twenty miles away. Tim doesn't want to move in with her, but he spends occasional nights there.

His presence in our house wears on me again. He's got his gaming TV set up and is now sleeping in the new "guest room," our old bedroom, using my old bath. I want to organize and decorate for actual guests, but I can't.

Worse, his pot habit has become increasingly annoying. After a week, I bring it up over morning coffee on the front porch with him and Russ. "I have to tell you, Tim, I don't like being around you when you're stoned. You turn into a zombie."

He nods knowingly. "That's just what Renee says. *Zombie*. Meg used to say that, too."

"Grass seems a lot stronger than it was in my day." It's easy to tell when he's stoned. And I think he binges when he has some on hand. It's his business if he spends his bucks on dope instead of saving up to rent a new place—but all the more reason for him to leave. I don't want to judge his habits.

"I'm gonna keep doing pot though." He's adamant. "It helps me not crave alcohol."

And his guitar, and a yoga practice, and a place of his own—things he's professed to want—I think, but do not say. If he's not languishing in my house, I won't have to think about it.

I take a deep breath and plunge on. "You know we love you, Tim. We appreciate your paying rent and being helpful around here. But it's probably better for us all if you leave after this week." I feel a tug in my upper right gut—my liver? This seems to be where sadness hits me lately.

Tim nods, then stretches out his arms and upper body, like he did when he was a baby in his crib. I want to cry.

"You know I'll be happy to look at places with you, Tim," Russ says.

Tim reaches to scratch a spot on his back, though he's said the bug bites don't bother him much any more. "I can stay at Joe's for a while now, no problem." No bedbugs have taken up residence in our new house; Joe knows it's safe to let Tim stay.

Tim goes to work that day, then comes home and packs before leaving to spend the night at Renee's. I look in his room and see his folded clothes assembled in organized sections on the bed and floor, some in an open suitcase; two black bags hold folded clothes as well. I reach down to the suitcase and brush a hand over his Opeth T-shirt, smoothing it.

The next day Tim calls from work to ask if he can leave some things in our garage—including the bags of clothes; he has too much to take to Joe's.

Both Russ and I have meetings that afternoon. When we get home, Tim's things are gone. His room feels empty, like my heart. I take a deep breath and pull the sheets from the bed.

29

Fish in Water

TIM STOOD BESIDE our bed in the dark, poking me awake. "My bed's wet."

I sighed and hauled myself from the sheets, letting Russ sleep. In my nightshirt and bare feet I followed Tim across the hall to the big bedroom he shared with Holly. A stand of shelves divided the room; on the other side of it my daughter slept, city light filtering in through curtains beyond her. I pulled clean pj's from Tim's dresser.

All was quiet in our eleventh-floor Bombay apartment on this school night, except for the burble of the aquarium that formed part of the tall divider in the kids' room. Angelfish and little silvertip sharks drifted in the glimmer from the desk lamp on Tim's side. He shucked off his wet Batman pj bottoms and took the dry ones I held out. I readied a clean bottom sheet as he pulled the wet one from the plastic liner.

My fourth-grade son's occasional bedwetting was not a physical issue, our pediatrician in the U.S. assured us, and parenting books urged patience. I tried to keep in mind Tim's first chaotic year of life: abandoned by his birth mother, handed off to a poor orphanage, relegated to the hospital with malnutrition and pneumonia when he hit U.S. shores. The bedwetting was surely caused by residual stress, the sign of a need for love and attention lacking in his past. I did my best to compensate. But the previous summer in our Illinois house, my patience as thin as the sopped sheet, I'd asked Tim if he could tell when he had to pee during the night. He murmured, "Yeah...."

"So why don't you get up and use the bathroom?"

"I feel lazy."

I dug my nails into my hands.

A book I'd consulted said that bedwetting was "almost never due to laziness".... But the book's suggestion to make an older bedwetter help clean up his own mess had seemed mean—until Tim's admission.

"Here you go, Timmy." I handed him the fresh sheet and left the room.

♫

Tim had often pushed my buttons. He flitted about me sometimes like a gnat I wanted to brush away.

When he first came to us feeble and sick, he'd been clingy, and his neediness persisted when he got healthy. On the two-hour drive home alone with him from a visit to Russ's family one night in Illinois, my toddler son wouldn't stop crying. He'd eaten before we left; he wasn't hungry. I pulled off the deserted farm road in the dark, got out and checked him in his carseat in back; he wasn't wet. I kissed him, stroked his head, handed him some animal crackers and a Hot Wheels toy, got in, turned on the ignition—and his crying escalated. Driving, I soothed, I sang, I ignored. As his sobs continued, I implored, I howled, I cried. It was a stand-off. Hell-bent to get home I drove on, wallowing in an un-motherly muddle of resentment, guilt, and confusion.

Early in the school year, Tim's 2nd grade teacher in St. John had suggested sending him back to 1st because he wouldn't buckle down and read; he couldn't stay in his seat. I told her he was like that at home, too. But I knew boys developed later, began reading later. Tim's tough first year of life had certainly delayed him; he would catch up. I asked, "Can we give him time?" He stayed at grade level throughout his school career—but not without struggle on all sides.

When my mother took my young kids to a Wisconsin fair one summer, Tim wouldn't stop handling candy for sale at a booth. "He wouldn't mind me," Mom said. "I had to pull his hair to make him stop."

I understood. But instead of physical discipline, we tried positive reinforcement: "Finish your homework and earn an hour of TV." But Tim's homework would be dashed-off and shoddy, and I'd resort to nagging reprimands—and let him watch TV anyway, to keep him occupied, to keep the peace. Meanwhile I was able to ignore Holly, my easier child, whose behavior rarely ruffled me—my strong, analytical daughter, who would grow up to tell us she had learned how *not* to be from her brother.

I wish I'd had more patience and attentiveness for both my children. But I used these up on other people's kids in my classrooms, where I was admired and paid for it.

When we'd told the kids we were moving to India, Tim shrank against our little St. John balcony. "You'll lose me."

"No, we *won't!*" I said. "Don't worry, we'll guard you with our lives!"

When we first hit the teeming sidewalks of Bandra, our Bombay neighborhood, Tim strode ahead of us as if he owned the place. Not for an instant did he fear that we would lose him in the hordes who looked like him. Dropped into his homeland he was a fish in water, confident he could keep easy track of us.

That first year we traveled widely on the subcontinent. On winter break we took an overnight train north to the Golden Triangle, including Delhi and the Taj Mahal. As we assembled for a family photo in front of the Palace of the Winds in Jaipur, an Indian onlooker took Tim's arm to pull him from us—as if he were some local waif. "He's ours," I said. "Our son!" As I drew him close, Tim frowned.

We'd made sure to slate our son's southern birth town for a tour that year. In lush, coastal Kerala, the state where he was born and lived his first year, we removed our shoes to enter an ornate Hindu temple. When a smiling turbaned man *namaste*'d us and dabbed our foreheads with ceremonial bindi's, Tim rubbed his off and sulked his way through the temple, shrugging my arm from his shoulders.

But he loved our visit to his orphanage in the city of Cochin—now Kochi.

The director grasped our hands and wagged his head, delighted to lead us on a tour. The orphanage was enjoying better days than when Tim had lived there, underfed and under-attended, nine years earlier. The current babies, a dozen in cozy cribs, some older ones toddling around in a playroom full of toys, looked well-fed. One round, light-haired little girl fondling a teddy bear was destined for parents in Minnesota.

Introduced to us in thc playroom, a childcare attendant with white streaks in her long black hair was startled to recognize Tim from the baby photos we'd brought; her kiss coerced an impish grin from him.

Back in the office the director said, "Can I serve you in any way? Tell me." I showed him Tim's early documents and photos and asked if there might be any record of his birth parents. The director's eyebrows rose. "We can see." Then he planned our afternoon. Taking Tim and Holly's hands, he told them they could have lunch, watch TV cartoons, and play with the babies—"whatever you like." We said goodbye to our kids, and they were whisked away by a smiling woman in a yellow sari. Then Russ and I were sent off with our driver and tour guide to orphanage gardens in green countryside an hour away. On arriving at the farm we were greeted in song by older children in blue uniforms, and led through rows of thriving fruits and vegetables.

Returning to the orphanage before sunset, we learned no trace of Tim's birth parents could be found. I'd had little hope. When the director asked what improvements we thought the orphanage might make, I suggested keeping records of birth parents, if possible.

We joined our kids in the playroom, where Tim happily pedaled among the babies on a plastic trike too small for him and

Holly played with the tot headed for Minnesota. We staged photos of our young kids each carefully cradling a baby. We gave a gift of money, then said farewells. In the car Tim glowed. "We got to watch *Aladdin* again."

As we walked to a restaurant in Cochin that evening, a man said something to Tim in Malayalam. Tim shrank away.

This had happened before, and would again—someone expecting Tim to understand Hindi or Marathi in Bombay, Malayalam there in Kerala. It embarrassed and confused him. He would never be at home in his homeland.

Of course none of us were at home, really; we were foreigners. But I felt as at home in India as anywhere I'd been. My worries about pollution and poverty soon evaporated in the golden Bombay air, and I felt a peacefulness I'd never known.

It must have been some quality of the light—our being in the Torrid Zone on a spit between Mahim Bay and the Arabian Sea—that lent the city its golden hue. The streets were filled with shiny Tata busses, bumblebee-colored taxis and rickshaws, and meandering blonde cows; tall alabaster buildings rose on either side. Orange marigolds draped temples, stalls and statues. Perhaps the colors' reflection off the air's water molecules—air suffused with dried cow dung and burnt-umber vehicle exhaust—enhanced the curry-colored atmosphere.

Bombay's air was the foulest we'd encountered. But I didn't sweat the pollution each weekday as our driver, Nissar, drove us the hour to school and the hour back through exhaust haze. These were chunks of free time in my weekdays, nothing to do but ride—sometimes with windows closed and air conditioning on, but sometimes windows open. And I relished our Saturday open-rickshaw trips to Pali Hill Market for groceries—never mind the amber glow of the sky ahead. I'd wear a long swathe of tie-dyed cotton around my shoulders; when I encountered putrid air I held the cotton over my nose as locals did.

Our fifteen-story, humidity-streaked apartment building was

surrounded by an asphalt parking lot. The only outdoor amenities were a rusted swing set in some weeds and a grassy oval yard the size of a tennis court. In the early mornings I trotted down the stairs from our eleventh-floor apartment, jogged alone a few times around the yard, and puffed my way back up the dim stairway to the eleventh floor—my exercise routine during the school week.

On our second Sunday in India, I announced that I was going out for a walk. Russ glanced up from the kids' video. "On your own?"

"Yeah." I hurried out, descended in the elevator, then took the tree-lined, patchy asphalt connector to Bullock Road, where people strolled around the Bandstand at the Mahim Bay seafront. Small kids rode a rusty mechanical ferris wheel, their parents smiling nearby as if there were no danger of the rickety contraption's collapsing and killing their offspring.

Much of Bombay seemed in similar peril of buckling, perched as it is on land reclaimed from the sea, susceptible to cyclones and earthquakes. First to go might be apartments like ours, many stories high, ungoverned by U.S.-type building codes, load-bearing walls sometimes ripped out in remodeling. A multi-story building we passed on the way to school would crumble in the spring, killing a few hundred people; for weeks, we saw emergency workers combing the rubble for bodies. But taking my cue from the many Bombayites who nonchalantly lived and worked in high-rise buildings, I spent no time worrying about such disaster.

That balmy Sunday I turned right on Bullock Road, passed the Bandstand, turned right again, and was swept into a flow of people. They poured off sidewalks and along the street from all directions, old and young and middle-aged, couples and families in brilliant saris and crisp kurtas—a contrast to my jeans and long-sleeved shirt.

Most people wore shoes or sandals—and the gorgeously-bright saris, whether cotton or silk, disguised any impoverishment. I felt comfortable in the closeness of the crowd. We glided along, fabric swishing as we made room for each other, swirling together like the sky in Van Gogh's *Starry Night*. No one gaped at me, the rare white person among them. Lilting conversations floated on air fragrant with oils and spice.

Like a gentle tide, the crowd took me to the shores of a church, tall and white-spired, gleaming in the sun. Along the sidewalk were stalls decked with miniature white-wax body parts—arms, legs, hands, feet—propped carefully, or hanging on string lines. I had seen such devotional items before, at a church in Mexico. The wax figures represent afflicted body parts that had been—or would hopefully be?—healed; offered at the altar, they are testimonials of faith. Other stalls sold candies, fruits, and gilded pictures of Jesus and the Virgin Mary. Portuguese Catholics had settled Bandra; its past must have evolved into this Sunday fare for Catholic Indians.

At school on Monday, Nipa, our gracious, grandmotherly librarian, smiled. "You happened on the Mount Mary fair. It's been going for 300 years, every September. I hope you tried the *chikki*—kind of like your peanut brittle."

Nipa is Hindu. Her response gave me my first awareness of the respect Indians seemed to pay each other's religions. During our time in India I would find that everyone honored Diwali, Christmas, Eid Al-Fitr, and dozens of other religious holidays. I loved our low-key Christmas in Bombay—decorating the palm tree in our living room, the kids and I making Christmas cookies and sharing them with Hindu and Muslim friends, seeing colored lights appear in department store windows near school.

That Sunday it was as if I had offered a wax heart and asked for healing of all my fears at the altar at Mount Mary Church, for I felt blessed with a rare sense of serenity.

♫

In India, the gap between our prosperity and the masses' poverty was the widest we would ever know. Our apartment, which took up the entire eleventh floor, cost the school $5,000 a month to rent. It had three large bedrooms, four baths, a spacious living room with glass doors opening onto a balcony that overlooked the bay, a dining room with windows from which we watched green parrots alight on power lines, and a maid's quarters behind the granite-countered kitchen. As promised, a full-size electric piano awaited my fingers when I arrived. We bought Indian-made textiles, had furniture built, and hung lace curtains at the wall of windows facing the bay—all at no personal expense. Our maid and nanny, Dolly, treated us like royalty; our kind chauffeur, Nissar, drove us to school and wherever else we wanted to go. On low-traffic Sundays we drove ourselves in the Consulate car to the Breach Candy Club with its opulent salt-water swimming pool.

In contrast to our way of life, rows of tin-roofed shacks huddled along narrow streets to form the view below our balcony. At night, festive lights shone from the shantytown; we sometimes closed the plate-glass doors on the twangy Indian music that blared up. At stoplights as we drove through town, our car was besieged by beggars—often ragged children, some of them missing fingers or whole hands. They peered in, curious, hoping for a gift but expecting nothing—or so it seemed, because they smiled even if we left them with nothing. "Don't give them money," warned Nipa, who was well-heeled herself and gave to charities. "They'll likely drink it up. Better to give bread, if you want." Which we did. And we did favors for our servants, bought them U.S. clothes and gadgets, as we had in other countries—though they seemed grateful for their jobs alone, and asked for little in addition.

My Embassy friend from Madagascar had been right when she'd said the poverty wouldn't bother me in India, that "India has *everything*." Everything being multitudes of poor and rich and in-between, the boundaries hazy. Many wealthy Indians lived in Bombay, the financial capital of India. Several Indian colleagues at the American School of Bombay—ASB—were well-off; a flutter of servants once served us tea at high school teacher Azmina's mansion near school on a quiet, leafy street. Some street dwellers with good jobs chose not to pay for housing; they formed communities on sidewalks. Our plucky, *paan*-chewing masseuse lived in a cardboard shack on the rocky beach by Mahim Bay. We were amused that she insisted Russ pay more for his weekly massage because he was bigger than I—but together, our massages cost less than seven U.S. bucks. She grinned each time we paid her, adding a big tip.

We were surrounded by and interacted with Indians of all

income levels. And all classes wore bright, intricately-patterned saris, salwar kameezes and lungis; wagged their heads in that agreeable, equivocating way; and appreciated our presence. We were All One, it seemed to me, no one begrudging or assuming, no one better than another.

Of course, for centuries Indians were cemented by the caste system into rigid feudal roles. Over time the effects of caste have lessened, boundaries blurred. There's much easy intermarriage now, and discrimination based on caste has long been illegal; an "untouchable" became president of India while we were there. But remnants of caste linger. It's perhaps still deep in lower-class Indians' nature to "know their place," however wretched, and to accept it. Hence the happy face of India I perceived—and lack of the guilt I'd felt over poverty in Africa and Madagascar.

It did not escape me that India's impoverished are serene in part because of their dismal, accustomed place. The irony hovered like the flesh-eating vultures over Bombay's Parsi Towers of Silence—but it did not alight to consume the ease of my experience on the subcontinent. I remain grateful for the sense of peace that filled me there, the peace that would come back and back to lead me to name India the spiritual navel of the Universe—to feel that if I should die there, it was meant to be.

Our family fit in easily at the American School of Bombay. The kids made friends and liked their new teachers. Wispy, ash-blonde Mrs. Saito—her husband Japanese-American—dealt gently with Tim and his rambunctious but good-natured cohorts. And Tim liked speaking French with Madame Hoa for a period each day. Ever entranced with creating sounds, he rattled off French words to us, one day chanting, "Moon-Hee-Hur,...Moon-Hee-Hur,"... which turned out to be not French, but the name of a female classmate from South Korea whose sister I had in middle school.

Holly's young British teacher, Mrs. Hazelhurst, sold on the whole-language approach, encouraged her first graders to write words the way they heard them. We squinted at the letter Holly wrote to us for the October parents' night, full of words with *j*'s, *k*'s, and *z*'s and almost no vowels—it was incomprehensible. But Holly read it without faltering, describing what she liked about school and things she did in class. In a month or so, to our relief, her writing would contain words we recognized.

As assistant to the superintendent, and overseeing the ambitious new-school building project, Russ savored working with Indian architects, businessmen and city officials. Also wearing the hat of middle school principal, he got help from Nipa—who was his admin assistant as well as our middle school librarian.

I fell in love with teaching at ASB and tripping daily up the winding wooden stairs to my tiny third-floor classroom in the old apartment building that housed the middle and high schools. My little white wood desk faced an open window that looked through the tops of neem and peepal trees onto Desai Road below, bustling with vendors. A sliding door in my classroom opened to a small space with a copy machine, school supplies, and a teapot. Deepak, our middle school aide, kept hot tea, steamed milk and sugar ready; I ducked out of class for frequent refills.

I taught 6th, 7th, and 8th grade social studies, five classes, each with a dozen students from across the globe—Europe, Asia, the Americas. Kids coexisted in close clusters of three or four at locally-built wooden desks.

A paper Great Wall of China, to scale, soon graced the hallway near the middle school lockers, courtesy of my 6th grade ancient history students. When we reached World War II in 7th grade, I moderated a lively debate over use of the atom bomb. American history came alive as 8th graders read from slim fact-filled storybooks by a native of Bombay; the dusty set I'd discovered on a shelf proved more interesting than the thick, wordy American texts, which became supplemental.

As student council sponsor I organized after-school trips across town to an Indian school, where ASB middle schoolers worked with preschoolers bussed in by an Indian education charity from the sprawling Dharavi slum—destined to be the site of the movie *Slumdog Millionaire*. These urchins were as enthralled with us as we were with them, their voices erupting in delight at stories, games, and songs.

In the spring we middle school teachers accompanied our fifty students on a field trip to Mahabaleshwar, one of the hill stations used by British colonials as a get-away from Bombay's crowds and heat. We stayed in a rambling old compound and led class activities in a spacious hall. One morning, pine-fragrant air wafting in through tall open windows, I guided students to draw carrots and strawberries from the local market—looking more closely at the objects than at their paper—then shading with colored pencils. Back home I posted the realistic renderings in the middle school hallway.

So it was at ASB that my teaching merged with a blessed sense of leisure and well-being, as if India had bottled a new elixir for my professional life—I had only to uncork the bottle and tip a little into each school day to reap the benefits. My enthusiasm for study topics came naturally. Class discussions sparked and glowed; all students were involved. Reason and kindness squelched the behavior of a couple of rowdy boys inclined to blurt out; discipline was easy. I loved being with and guiding my students, and they caught the spirit—or was it that I caught it from them? A rare equanimity prevailed, as if the honeyed ways of the Indian culture had filtered through the classroom walls.

At Tim's orphanage

Cochin, India

30

No One Could Fix This

"ARE YOU SITTING DOWN?" My sister Chrissie had called Bombay from Wisconsin one morning in October. "Mom has lung cancer. The doctor says stage 4."

On the far side of the world, I sank into a chair beside the phone. Mom had never smoked—no one at home had. How could this be?

After Mom had retired from teaching, she and Dad moved from the farm into the little town of Barron nearby. She became a prize-winning golfer, ran museum tours for kids, was active in her church, birded and gardened, and traveled her continent, poking into Canada and Mexico. She was fit and healthy—still had naturally dark-brown hair at seventy-five. During my acne-plagued teens she'd said, "Some day you'll be glad your skin's oily like mine. It'll stay young longer." Hers had.

I spilled news of Mom's cancer to my teacher-friend Azmina. "That's not a death sentence these days," she said, "especially for someone like your mom." I happened on a book at the Crossword Bookstore on Desai Road: *50 Things to Do When the Doctor Says It's Cancer*. The American author had survived stage 4 lung cancer by practicing the fifty things—things my mother could do. I shared some of them with her in letters: exercising, drinking lots of water, practicing hobbies; she wrote that she was already doing them. Her letters were upbeat; she was doing well. She'd be fine!

Word of Mom's cancer had knocked me off my pins for a moment. But India caught my fall, and all was again—still—amazingly, wonderfully well for me on the subcontinent.

Until our second year.

On the first day of school I pulled open the front door and almost dropped my bags. Mr. Borg, the superintendent, stood like the grim reaper near the bottom of the middle school stairs. Tightening my grip, I pressed on.

"What are you doing here?" The super's question whizzed past me like a warning shot.

I whirled to face him, ready for a shoot-out. "I have students to teach." Heart pounding, I rushed up the steps to my classroom.

As I launched into my second year's first period with new sixth graders, Mr. Borg slipped in and stood by the copy room door. I carried on, as teachers do when administrators observe classes—though I could feel my voice pitch rise with anxiety.

After introductions I passed out blank sheets of paper and instructed kids to draw a map of the world. They sat stunned, as if I'd told them to copy dictionary pages—as a grade-school teacher of mine had once done to punish us for throwing snowballs. "That's impossible," someone said.

"Start with stuff you know," I chirped. "Anyone?"

A girl raised her hand. "Continents?"

"Oceans," said another.

"Sure! Put in some *continents* and *oceans*. And *countries*. Maybe some *cities*, if you can." I waved a hand like a magician, willing each item to appear—willing the super to disappear.

I'd used this activity before to kick off year-long studies of world history and geography. Most kids drew blobs of continents in odd locations, misplacing oceans and countries—as they were doing now. "Don't worry, this won't be graded. We'll keep your map, and you'll be amazed when you compare it to the one you draw in May."

Would I be around in May? I glanced at Mr. Borg, bent against the copy room doorframe, arms crossed, staring out my window.

When the bell rang, he motioned me into the copy room and said, "I'm coming to your apartment this evening. We'll sort things out then."

I propelled myself through the day. A smile pasted on my face, I chatted blithely with Nipa and others over lunch. Between classes I fled to the copy room and poured tea with unsteady hands.

On the way home after school, my 5th grader Tim and 2nd grader Holly prattled about their day from the back seat, excited about the school year ahead.

I dreaded what the evening would bring.

♫

"I'm sorry. It was the Board's decision." Across from me in our living room, Mr. Borg fiddled with his tie, a red one with Bugs Bunny on it.

"But why *now?*" I said. "This is so unfair!"

"I'm sorry."

I'd dismissed Russ's apprehension the day before, on Sunday, when he'd been called to meet the super. "It's probably something about the new-school project," I said. But Russ came home slumped and shaken. On the day before school was to start, his job was gone. We'd get a whopping severance—but we had two weeks to pack up and leave.

We'd returned to Bombay the week before. After two summer months in our Illinois bungalow, our family had luxuriated in a business-class trip back to India, stopping in Singapore to visit the zoo, with its sun bears and free-range orangutans. Now we were all to leave Bombay—and go where?

From the couch I glared at Borg. "Our own kids just started school! They need to go to school." I drew in a sharp breath, turned away and reached for the Zairian stone figure beside me on a table. I exhaled and turned the little statue of a man over and over in both hands, seething like a volcano ready to explode. "What about *my* job? They didn't fire me, did they?"

"Well, you're a package deal...." Borg raised his eyebrows at me and flipped the end of his Bugs Bunny tie.

"*No!* That's wrong. I'm *not giving up my job.*" I set the stone man smartly on the table, making Russ jump. I bolted from my chair and flew down the hall to the kids' room—they weren't there; Dolly had taken them to play with neighbors downstairs. My heart beating hard, I flopped on Tim's bed and stared at the fish drifting in the cloudy water. The tank needed cleaning. What would we do with these fish?

When the heavy apartment door clanged shut, I popped up. Borg was gone. I found Russ at the kitchen counter pouring whiskey into a glass of ice. "Sorry," I said.

"I don't blame you." He got another glass.

Borg would talk to the Board, Russ said; we could probably stay on for a while. The super hadn't expected me to put up a fight about my job. Russ looked at me through teary blue eyes and handed me my drink. "That's what he said, 'Put up a fight'."

We had no answer as to why this had happened on the day before school started—why it had happened at all; there must be more to it than money. Russ's salary was nothing, compared to the millions the new school was costing.

We sipped whiskey on the balcony as tinny music rose from the shantytown and murky dark enshrouded us. We batted around suppositions like ping pong balls, and roared and cried about the injustice, until we had to go downstairs and get the kids for bed.

♫

The super handed down the Board's verdict in his office the next day: I could keep my job all year, if I wanted; our kids could go to school; we could stay in our apartment. "Russ can be a house husband. Maybe take a class or something. Whatever he wants." The super rubbed his hands together as if washing them of the whole affair, like Pontius Pilate.

Our meager relief was soon sucked under by a riptide of reactions. Middle school staff and students, bereft of Russ's presence, wanted to know *why*. Tim's and Holly's teachers were perplexed.

I said all I knew—that Russ's job had been eliminated. But that made no more sense to other staff members than it did to us. Middle school might manage with Borg's distant direction, if Nipa took on lots more work. But Russ had gotten the new-school project underway, attended the groundbreaking ceremony with dignitaries; now that the construction was launched, he'd been expecting to do oversight.

Russ had asked if he'd made some mistake with the money, if they thought he might be stealing—but Borg assured him that wasn't it. So *what*, then? All of us, staff and parents, even servants, wondered. "Sir is a good man," Nissar, behind the wheel, affirmed, a wrinkle in his brow.

Stress over the not knowing coursed through my school days like sewage-tainted water through Dharavi Slum pipes, stripping me of the health and wholeness I'd come to enjoy in my little classroom. The subject of Mr. Erickson's leaving kept popping up through lulls in classes until finally, in a September student council meeting, I allowed students—or did I guide them?—to draft a letter to the Board. The letter's last line made it a petition: "We want Mr. Erickson back." Students signed, and Sandra, the student council president, delivered it.

But no one could fix this.

One day in class while facing the chalkboard, I felt so dizzy I thought I might collapse. When the bell rang I fled to nurse Fran's cubby-hole office across the hall and poured out pent-up fear. "Something's wrong. I felt like I was going to faint in front of the kids!"

Fran, an ethnic Indian raised in England and the mother of Sandra, my student council president, took my vitals. I should be checked for diabetes, she said, but anxiety was probably causing my dizziness. She massaged Tiger Balm into my temples, and as I left for class, she said, "Come in here any time."

My blood test for diabetes was negative.

When I had another dizzy spell in class, I took refuge in Fran's room.

Our lack of understanding of Russ's firing lingered like the haze over Mahim Bay—always there. Late in September, toward the end of the monsoon, the Board deigned to talk with upset teachers on a Monday night. Not invited, Russ didn't attend the meeting. I rode to ASB with Tim's French teacher, Hoa, who lived nearby. Nissar drove us through rain that poured down and rushed along the curb. In the library Mr. Borg and six grim Board members sat behind long tables, their arms crossed. We teachers sat on folding chairs facing the men; behind them, against the walls, colorful, dripping umbrellas fanned out like an outrageous floral backdrop.

The discussion unleashed, faculty members demanded answers. "Russ Erickson has always been fair and supportive. What has he done wrong?" said Nipa. "It's our right to know."

"We're not at liberty to say," the Board president said.

"Why not? Who's stopping you?"

The president sat poker-faced.

"How can you fire someone without reason?" implored Tim's 5th grade teacher.

"There is reason; we just cannot explain."

Prodding continued. "Is it about money? Someone bribing you?" This from the high school math teacher from New Orleans.

The president kept mum. A couple of other Board members shook their heads.

Teachers pressed on for an hour, rehashing thoughts, seeking truth, to no avail: The Board stonewalled us.

On the ride home, plowing through water up to the hubcaps, we strove to gain inches as the thick traffic crawled and stopped, crawled and stopped. My hand clasped the lowered window, and I felt the rain still pelting down. I stared into the wet darkness and began to cry. Eyes filled with tears, I turned to Hoa. "This is all so *wrong*, and there's nothing I can do!" I cried louder and began to shake my head from side to side.

The car stalled again, and Nissar glanced back at me, his brow pinched.

Hoa, once a Buddhist nun, took my hands in hers. "Lena. You're here. Right now. Nothing needs to be done. Everything is okay."

I paused for a couple of quivery breaths, then pulled my hands from Hoa's and shook my head. "No. Nothing is okay! I can't stand not knowing why this is happening. It's so wrong!"

On the two-hour ride through the deluge, Hoa kept trying to calm me. But I fought her off as if possessed, like one of those crazy patients in my psych ward days, releasing a month's—or a lifetime's—worth of distress.

We dropped Hoa off, and through bleary eyes I watched her walk away, her mango-colored umbrella a bright spot in the dismal night.

♫

Though Russ recalls this as a "dark time," he bore up well, making good on his role as house husband. He tended the kids and saw to meals. He took to eating only papaya for lunch and walking for hours on the streets of Bandra—doing penance for an unimaginable, imagined crime. He became healthier, lost weight. He may have had bone-deep anxiety, but it didn't show. He seemed to take this catastrophic monkey wrench in our affairs with much more equanimity than I—and that, along with a couple of Kingfisher beers each evening, kept me acting normal for some weeks.

But I remained on high alert for a way to fix things, to reclaim Russ's job, and with it, our contented lives in Bombay. At school, Laura, the sympathetic middle school English teacher, spoke to me of a "mole" in the office: Gayle Giamatti, Russ's secretary, who now worked with Borg, had her eyes and ears open for info, Laura said. Rumors flew. Someone told me that a Board member who'd been in London at the time of Russ's dismissal had called the move "draconian." If true, I thought, he might be in our camp, able to rectify the situation, maybe make it go away.... Some days, hopes soared as high as the bright green parrots outside our eleventh-floor dining room window.

One week American friends sent bright news from Bangalore,

where they'd just moved from Bombay: The principal had left the Canadian school their kids attended in the southern city; there was an admin opening. Russ hastily got papers in order and called. The position had been filled.

On a Sunday in October I pulled myself out of the Breach Candy pool, drew my long blue ASB T-shirt on over my wet bathing suit, glanced at the lawn and did a double-take: The thin, light-haired guy strolling with a drink was the Board member who had called Russ's firing "draconian"—he was back from London. I slid into my flip-flops, hurried to the café and bought myself a gin and tonic. Then I made a beeline for the man, forced a smile and asked if I could talk to him. We sat with our drinks on the grassy bank beside the pool, and I calmly asked him why the Board had let Russ go. He stared into his glass and shook his head. "It's too bad. I'm sorry."

"So...?"

"I may not agree with the decision, but there's nothing I can do."

"You *may* not agree? Do you or don't you?"

He shook his head again. "It doesn't matter."

"Dammit, it does matter! This is wrong. Can't you do something?"

"I'm sorry." Holding his drink aside, he got to his feet.

My eyes burned as I turned away. He'd been my last hope, and he was in league with the rest of them.

Back in the classroom I struggled to keep my chin up. Though Fran and supportive teacher friends kept me dog-paddling most days, spells of light-headedness still pulled me under.

On a Saturday at home, Tim and Holly out with friends, I sat grading a quiz for my 8th grade U.S. history class. I'd asked students to list items on the Bill of Rights. Halfway through the papers, one of Ranita Singh's answers stopped me short. "The right to have bare arms," she had written. I stared at the words. Ranita had no clue what *bearing arms* meant—but she knew something more important: In America, women didn't have to follow the Indian custom of covering their arms.

My tears blurred Ranita's silly, poignant words. Teaching American history to a class of mostly non-American kids in India was absurd—as my smart British student Sandra had once ventured. I was failing my students. I could do nothing right. My life was an unfixable mess.

I threw aside Ranita's paper, slumped back in my chair, and bawled and moaned until Russ came in. Unable to calm me, he called Hoa over. As I lay racked by panic on the guest room floor, she quieted me with meditative words.

Late that Sunday night I bolted awake in bed and shouted into the dark, my heart racing.

"Lena!" Russ's hand was on my arm. "What's wrong?"

"There was this big red fireball.... Like a *bomb* inside me. I felt like I was exploding!" I clutched my chest. "I think I'm having a heart attack."

Russ turned on the lamp. "You just had a bad dream." He put an arm around me and took my wrist.

This was not the first or last time I would trust skills Russ had picked up from his nurse-trained mother. As he settled two fingers on a spot on my left wrist and checked his watch, my panic ebbed.

In the morning, exhausted and jittery, I called in sick, then phoned Nurse Fran, who sent a doctor over.

I told tall, gray-haired Dr. Patel about my heart explosion the previous night, and my frequent dizziness. I sat on my bed as he checked my eyes and ears, my throat, my heart and lungs. He had me extend each arm and leg; he tested my reflexes.

Shoving instruments back into his bag, the doctor asked, "What reason might you have for such anxiety just now?"

"Well...," and then it spilled out. "The American School fired my husband, and we don't know why, and I'm still working for those jerks."

The doc pulled a comb from his shirt pocket and stooped to peer into my vanity mirror. "What do you think you could do about this problem?" He drew the comb through his steely, pomaded hair and patted the just-combed sections. Then he straightened and slipped the comb back into his pocket, prescribed over-the-counter valium, and picked up his bag. He was gone before I realized his nonchalance had birthed, *in toto,* my solution.

The next day at school I spoke with ASB's business administrator, an American woman I hardly knew, who listened patiently as I rattled off reasons for my resignation. "I'm stressed, but I can make it to Diwali break." The Hindu Festival of Lights began in three weeks, on Monday, November 17th, that year. If I quit on Friday of the previous week, we'd have time to pack up and be in Wisconsin for Thanksgiving on the 27th.

The woman shook her head. "It's too bad. I've heard good things about you. Your husband, too." She drew a paper from a file. "I'd say this is circumstances beyond your control. We'll pay you through the end of the semester."

We planned to go back to the States, bide our time and gear up to attend international hiring conferences in February.

♫

Perhaps the stars over the subcontinent had aligned perfectly that November of 1997, for we were destined to stay in India.

The American middle school English teacher at ASB, our friend Laura, had grown up as a child of missionaries in northern India and attended Woodstock—the oldest international school in the world, renowned for its music program. In the hill station of Mussoorie, in the foothills of the Himalayas, Woodstock was founded in 1854 as a Christian school. Laura said, "I know you and Russ aren't strictly 'Christian' and you'd have to go as volunteers, but Woodstock is always looking for good people."

Laura's husband Ben was an American who'd grown up with her at Woodstock School; now an Indian citizen and a Bollywood actor who'd had a small part in the movie *Gandhi,* he lived and worked part-time at Woodstock. On a visit down to Bombay in early November, Ben seconded his wife's suggestion. "Woodstock always wants good people."

For the interview, we took a train to New Delhi and a car the rest of the way, up treacherous mountain switchbacks to what would be our new school. We were accepted on the spot as volunteers for the spring semester—one semester only. We'd have basic room and board. Russ would be a curriculum consultant for the accreditation process Woodstock had begun; I would teach 7th grade music class, lab piano, and a writing class or two. Tim and Holly would attend school tuition-free.

We staged a joint goodbye party at the Breach Candy pool for Tim and Holly who, with friends, spent an afternoon swimming and diving, writing on T-shirts and eating burgers. Staff friends gave us autographed photo books of India which would sit on coffee tables in every house we would live in from then on.

After lunch on my last day of school, I walked into my strangely dim classroom. Candles flickered at the front; soft music played. The next-door classroom's corrugated divider was open—and the entire middle school sat silent in desks and chairs and on the floor along walls. The student council president, Sandra, and another 8th grader, a non-resident Indian girl from Australia, ushered me to a chair in front. Then kids read poems and offered flattering and funny tributes. And as I dabbed my eyes, thinking it was over, they handed me some lyrics and played Mariah Carey singing "Hero."

Rows of somber kids of sundry nationalities, shoulder to shoulder, rocked to the reassuring song. Undemonstrative South Koreans wiped their eyes. My Italian 7th grader had his arm around a Canadian 8th grader. British Sandra wept along with me, and others joined. That Indian sweetness, now laced with melancholy, had infused the place one more time.

Lights came on; there were photos and hugs and farewells. I gathered bags and left the little classroom and the students I would always love, then walked down the winding wooden staircase and out to Desai Road.

Russ's birthday in our Bombay dining room

31

Genetic and Pre-existing

FULL GROCERY BAGS in hand, Russ and I enter the back door of our newly-remodeled Garden Street house and are brought up short at the scene: Tim and Renee, his girlfriend of three months, stand at the kitchen counter. Tim waves a sheet of paper like a flag; Renee smiles brightly. "I wrote you a note," Tim states. "Our roommate is throwing us out."

We put bags down on the hallway bench. "You just moved in," Russ says. Tim has been living with Renee and her friend Stacy for less than a month.

Tim's leading lady speaks in a breathy rush. "Stacy and I were good friends! She was happy to have Tim move in. It lowered the rent! But then she started locking us out, and suddenly she doesn't want Penny there"—Renee's gentle pitbull mix. Renee raises an eyebrow over her big square glasses. "We've been nothing but nice to Stacy."

"It's just weird." Tim flicks at his phone.

"She even took down the shower curtain because it was hers." Renee rolls her eyes toward Tim, who glances up from his phone; they share a look.

I scan Tim's note as the two ramble on:

Sorry we missed you.... ....roommate has decided to hate us....

....apartment-searching.... ....super tight for money....
We would both be responsible for paying you back. Renee is really good at managing money (she has stellar credit)....
Love
Tim & Renee
P.S. Left some chips and salsa

"Such drama," I say, removing the salsa lid and dipping a chip. I pass Tim's note to Russ.

"A place in P.V."—Prescott Valley, ten miles away—"looks really promising, $550 a month," Tim says. "We know they'll take Penny."

Renee nods. "We're looking at it tomorrow."

"We've gotta move, like, *now,* and we just don't have enough for the deposit and first month's rent." Tim casts sheepish eyes at Russ. "I know this is the millionth time I've asked for help. But we *will* pay you back."

Renee nods vigorously, her heart-shaped face smiling from behind her scholarly glasses.

Unlike with his last two mates, Tim and Renee seem equal: mid-twenties birds of a feather, caught in a whirlwind. Now both scan their electronic devices. Renee holds up her tablet, showing us pictures of the P.V. apartment.

Russ and I glance at each other in agreement. Russ says, "We can probably help you out, if it's not too much."

The young couple's flightiness glides into breathless thanks. They stow their devices in pocket and purse, we hug, and the two soar off stage-left, out the front door.

♫

Soon after he'd moved in with Renee and her roommate, Tim dropped by after work and dug bills from his pocket.

"Here's the loan payment. I got a $2-an-hour raise last week." He paced the kitchen, fiddling with his phone and talking rapid-fire. "These days are killing me. I have to drive Renee way the hell to Chili's in P.V. and then get back here for my job, then pick Renee up after work, sometimes late. And Panchito's has been slammed." His phone growls. Poking at it, he says to me, "I feel anxious all the time. Maybe I should see a doctor."

"Do you exercise? That's good for stress. You once mentioned yoga...?" I really thought a never-ending twelve-step program like mine would be the best bet to relieve his anxiety, but I wouldn't say that again.

"I'm always walking at work."

A week later he came over with a load of wash. He talked with Russ outside for a while, then strode around the kitchen as I poured us drinks. While his clothes washed, Tim flicked at his phone and chatted with me. "You're welcome to sit, Tim."

He took a sip of apple juice. "I can't sit. Renee says I never sit down, even when we watch TV. I'm too anxious. It drives her crazy. Maybe I could get a prescription from a doc."

He looked wan and thin. His fingernails were down to the quick again. "I have some left-over valium from that tough year I was teaching...." I gave him a back rub, then drew a few Valium from my bottle and cut one down the middle. "See how you feel with half. It was enough for me. Your constitution's like mine."

He downed it dry, shoved the others in his pocket, threw his damp clothes in a basket and was gone.

I'd just read a thick, scholarly book linking addictiveness to anxiety. Mothers who give up babies for adoption are stressed, the doctor-author says; they pass anxiety on to their infants in the womb, and beyond. Early anxiety can lead to addiction in a predisposed individual.

Holly gets anxious too. Early in college, she had a bout with eczema. The campus medical center told her stress may have brought it on. She recently emailed me for help with her resume and said she was nervous about an upcoming job fair; I suggested deep breathing. Holly's also afraid of bugs. But she's not as perennially high-strung as her brother—and she's not substance-addictive. Her pre-adoption life hadn't been as rough as Tim's. She was well-fed and cared for by a poor but loving foster mother for three years; then we'd taken her home and hired the foster mom as her nanny for our last months in Madagascar. Whereas

Tim was handed as a baby to an impoverished Indian orphanage where they couldn't feed him well enough his first year—then he was whisked far away and adopted by an anxious mother....

Not that I caused my kids' problems; my Program has helped me dispel that notion. But many times I've wished I could raise them again. I'd spend more time with them, be more relaxed.

Tim was working so hard to get life right. I wished I could cure his anxiety, but I knew I could only give love and support—and I loved him so.

I poured his unfinished apple juice back into the bottle.

Next day we were gratified by a note on Facebook: *"I love my parents so much. They are the most loving and supportive parents that I could ever ask for."*

Tim told me later that the Valium didn't help.

♫

The apartment in P.V. falls through, but Tim and Renee find a little ramshackle two-bedroom house down a bank on busy Sheldon Street. It's noisy and dusty and not a great place for their dog Penny—and soon, two cats. But rent is inexpensive at $500 month-to-month, and it's a nice little square house, over 100 years old, like ours, with ancient doors and wainscoting. We give them money for the deposit, which brings Tim's loan to $1500.

Renee has been working full-time at Chili's in Prescott Valley, with good wages, tips and benefits. But Tim still drives her to work. One day he pops in to tell me he's been having stomachaches. I give him a shot of Mylanta and put some in a small bottle to take home. As he rushes out, Tim says Renee's grandparents have a car she can use. "She's taking her driver's test this Friday."

But she can't get the car on Friday, so she doesn't take the test.

♫

Tim is in the emergency room.

It's 9:00 pm on a Sunday night two weeks after he and Renee have moved to Sheldon Street, and Renee has just called. "They think he has something genetic and pre-existing," she tells Russ.

"I wonder how they could make that diagnosis so fast," I say. Worry clings as Russ and I dress quickly for the hospital.

On a bed behind the curtain, our twenty-six-year-old son is hooked to a tangle of tubes and tape; one leg is bent, revealing a skinny, vulnerable thigh. Sitting close to him, Renee holds his hand. She turns grave eyes on us. "Thanks for coming. He was in such pain. It could've been heart-related, so they took him right in."

Tim grunts and presses fingers to his sternum. "It felt like a knife in here."

In Oscar-worthy performances, Renee gazes at him and he grips her hand.

Tim points through an opening in the curtain. A screen behind the nurses' desk shows his heartbeat veering wildly, from 105 to 76. We don't know what it means, but hospital staff seem unconcerned.

"So what's this about 'genetic and pre-existing'?" Russ asks.

"That's what they said." Renee's eyes are wide.

A doctor enters. "Are you still in pain?" When Tim nods, the doc says, "It could be inflammation. We'll put an anti-inflammatory in the IV." A nurse comes in to make the IV adjustment. "This should act pretty quickly," she says.

Within minutes Tim peers wild-eyed around the room and back at us. "Whoa. Weird. You look more 3-D than normal. Like somebody cranked up the contrast."

We sit waiting. Finally the doc comes back and tells Tim he can leave when he's ready.

"But what's wrong?" I ask. "We heard something about a 'genetic and pre-existing' condition...?"

"No." The doc flashes a benign grin. "I said we had to do some tests to make sure it *wasn't* anything genetic or pre-existing. He's young and strong. His heart's fine. It could be a bruising of the sternum, something like that."

I ask, "Could it be stress-related? He's had a lot to deal with lately."

The doc's reply is a definitive No. But I suspect he's wrong.

We'll find out later that with the high-deductible insurance we carry for Tim, the total bill for his emergency visit is $1700. More cause for stress for the young couple.

Back at home two days after the hospital, Tim and Renee decide his malady is in fact anxiety-related. "Renee researched it on the internet," Tim says on the phone. "We think it's a peptic ulcer."

"Maybe. Or acid reflux, like mine." Though we're not a genetic match, I keep coming up with uncanny similarities between me and my son. "When the doc gave me Valium during that bad teaching year, he told me he thought stress was trying to tear a hole in my gut." I recommend probiotics, baking soda and Mylanta.

Two weeks later, Tim comes by. "I quit Panchito's." His eyes dart at me for a reaction.

Damn, I think. *Out of work again.* "Oh?" Eyebrows high, I force a look of interest.

"Renee supports my decision." He pulls a folded piece of paper from his pocket. "Can you help with my resume?"

We update it and print copies. Tim is grateful. "I'm checking out some places this afternoon."

He says Renee has a part-time job at Bean's Coffee House in Prescott. She's expecting to get more hours; then they'll make her assistant manager and she'll quit Chili's.

Renee gets her driver's license and the use of her grandparents' old white Lexus. Tim interviews at the new-and-bigger Bean's, a bistro near the mall. "My manager's the same as Renee's. He's a recovered alcoholic, same amount of time as me," Tim says. Soon comes a Facebook announcement: *"Officially hired at Bean's Bistro. I'll learn to cook fancy food that requires skill. I welcome the challenge."*

I dub Tim and Renee the King and Queen of Bean's.

But Renee's additional hours and better position don't materialize. She quits Bean's—and soon, Tim does too. He stays long enough to train his replacement, but returns part-time to Panchito's. Renee finds a lucrative once-a-month overnight job as a nanny, and her mom pays her for doing odd jobs—but it's not much money, overall.

By now it's mid-July. I catch Tim's latest Facebook entry: *"Working 2 jobs for next 2 weeks. Going back to Panchito's cuz it's a better fit. Now I just need to tackle my near life-crippling anxiety disorder. I'm extremely thankful to have such a loving and patient fiancé who supports me through everything. She truly is my rock."*

Yes, they're engaged.

It caught me off guard when Tim told me shyly over the kitchen counter the week before that they were talking about marriage. They'd been together what—four months? "So you think this thing will last?" I dumbly asked.

He buys Renee a diamond ring on sale, financed by her grandpa to be paid back when possible. The couple have official engagement photos taken. They owe a lot of money. Renee's grandparents offer them a better house in a nicer area for less rent. They talk of having a family.

Yikes. I'm a bit player who can't keep up with the plot.

32

Frozen

"I'm cold." Ten-year-old Tim rubbed his arms through his damp sweatshirt. "When are they coming?"

"Soon, I hope." I pulled my bedraggled kids closer, brushed a strand of wet hair from my face and turned to Russ. "Do you think they're still on their way? Maybe we should try to find the coats in the luggage."

Russ squinted through the haze toward the rocky roadway beyond us. "The admin guy said they'd be here. It can't be much longer...."

Half an hour earlier, the driver of the black Ambassador taxi had dropped the four of us and our bags next to a stone wall in front of Woodstock School. Ten yards behind us at the top of some steps stood a large-windowed building, but no soul in sight. Where were the guys who were supposed to take us to our house? We waited wet and shivering under the biting February sleet like displaced creatures from the tropics.

The endless flights from Illinois to New Delhi had been followed by a rumbling six-hour train ride north to the town of Dehradun in the temperate Doon Valley. Then the taxi driver met us for the last leg of the journey. As he stowed our bags in the trunk, he beamed. "I am happy to be taking you to the queen of hill stations."

Mussoorie, perched at 6,000 feet, was a one-and-a-half hour trip up a narrow, winding mountain road. About mid-way the driver announced, "Soon you will see snow on the Himalayas."

But we never did. The weather had steadily worsened on our ascent until the road was slick, the sky fogged-in, and sleet pelted the car. I'd begged the driver to slow down, fearing any moment we might tumble to our deaths over the sheer, unguarded edge. Finally the road widened for our passage through the town of Mussoorie, and then we were at Woodstock. We unloaded, and the taxi vanished into the fog.

"Here they are." Russ motioned to three Indian men walking out of the mist. They greeted us and swung our biggest bags to their shoulders. Russ and I gripped carry-ons, Tim and Holly hefted their sagging backpacks, and we traipsed after the bearers up the steps, around the tall building, and along a forest path to our new home.

When we'd left the U.S. that bleak February, I had accepted a sad fact: Though she'd fought valiantly for a year and a half, Mom's cancer was making steady progress on its march to claim her life.

As we were hauling bags out of her house, she stood in the kitchen, one hand on the counter for support. When she reached for medications in the cabinet overhead, a pill bottle slipped from her fingers and hit the floor. She bent over and began to cry, driving a stake through my heart. I dropped my bag and went to her, but she picked up the bottle and shook her head. "I'm okay." I stood helpless as she popped pills into her mouth and washed them down with water.

Mom was still teary as, wrapped in winter coats, we hugged goodbye. With Tim and Holly strapped in the van and Russ about to turn the key in the ignition, I sat in the passenger seat holding the door open, blinking back tears.

Russ turned the key. My parents waved, went in and quickly closed the door against the winter chill. But as if frozen, my right arm held the van's door ajar. "What can I do? I can't stay here. We have to go back to India!" I started to cry softly.

Russ put his hand on my knee. "Your mom's strong. She'll be okay."

She wouldn't be okay. But I knew what he meant. Mom would handle this, as she had everything else.

If Russ's firing in Bombay had held a silver lining, it was that we'd been able to spend time with Mom during her cancer months. Through the holidays and after, her attitude had been good, her sense of humor intact. She'd worn on her bald head the turquoise cap I'd bought her, with its white splotches labeled as different species of birds' shit. Lounging on the couch, she visited with ease. "Dad's been a rock through this," she said, her eyes gleaming. And she'd sympathized with us over losing our jobs in Bombay.

I wiped my eyes and closed the van's door.

Our Woodstock house was part of a hundred-year-old duplex tucked on a hillside among tall trees. It trapped the damp winter cold in its thick concrete walls and held us prisoner to bone-chilling temperatures that persisted for weeks. One morning before Russ lit the fire, the Fahrenheit kitchen thermometer read 43 degrees.

The wood stove was the focal point of the house. A square wooden dining table and chairs stood nearby, and a dark-blue couch stretched along an adjacent wall. The stove warmed us if we kept it fed and sat right next to it, but spending hours away at school, we often had to douse the fire and return to a cold house.

We slept cocooned in flannel sheets inside zipped-up sleeping bags under thick, kapok-filled cotton covers, but we still needed hot-water bottles to make nights bearable. We boiled water on the gas hotplate, filled five floppy rubber bottles, wrapped them with towels, and cuddled them in bed like warm puppies—two-dog nights for me, one dog enough for each of the others. It still took a half-hour for me to defrost enough to let sleep happen.

Thank God for the electric heater in the tiny bathroom, and hot water in the shower. I'd heat the room before entering, quickly undress inside, then stand soaking in the streaming, steamy balm, warding off for as long as possible the frigid air that lay in wait. Afterwards I'd resume playing the victim, pulling within myself like a resentful bear in hibernation, performing only subsistence childcare and household tasks.

One day as I lay reading under a blanket on the couch near the stove, Holly's face appeared over the top of my book. "Mom, look." She dangled a shredded shoelace near my eyes and held her wounded shoe aloft in the other hand. "My shoelace broke."

I brushed away the taunting lace. "I can't help it. You'll have to get along till we go to the market."

"But *Mom*...."

I raised my book and shut her out.

At night I'd hurry the kids to bed, hot water bottles set to tuck into their layers of bedding, so I could get ready for the daunting night myself.

"What about our story?" a kid would plead.

"Ask Dad." I was pulling sweatpants on over my long underwear.

Russ read the bedtime stories and did most other child-related duties during those first Woodstock weeks. Did I even kiss the kids goodnight? I showed Russ little affection. I let my family fend for themselves and felt too beleaguered by the cold to give a damn.

As the season dragged on, my impatience grew. One day I yelled at Tim and stopped just short of swatting him for leaving clothes on the floor. Awareness of my poor behavior hit me, and guilt compounded my woe. I should have been mature enough to deal with a little chilly weather; my kids and Russ stood it with good enough cheer. But I continued to grouse and moan, trapped in ice with my bad attitude.

♫

I was long gone from India when I realized the Woodstock winter had been my scapegoat for a load of squelched emotions. Anxiety brought on by our untimely job loss had turned to frenetic energy—for in short order we'd had to get rid of excess stuff, inform and pay workers, say sad goodbyes, pack up and move out of school and home, flying from our dream life in Bombay. We took our two Indian cats, Walter and Little Puss a.k.a. L.P., with their pricey feline photo passports and health papers. The sight of lithe, Abyssinian L.P. fresh off the plane in Illinois, his nose and lips raw from gnawing at his crate through the long flights, had made me cry.

We'd poured the cats and kids into our summer/default home in Bloomington; unpacked, reorganized and stashed in the basement our mammoth shipment of dishes, foreign décor, furniture and linens; then we'd careened through the holidays.

Arriving just before Thanksgiving, we fell in with the customary family mob at my sister Chrissie's in Wisconsin. Over turkey, her husband called us "charity cases"; I felt the part, even laughed about it. Through Christmas and New Years I plastered on a smile and injected fake cheer into my demeanor—especially for Mom, who was soldiering through her cancer, finding joy in decorating the tree and stuffing handmade socks with gifts. Within a month I would leave for northern India; my mother should see me as composed as I was seeing her, despite my tamped-down anxiousness—we still didn't know why Russ had been fired in Bombay.

We convinced Russ's sister Nancy to safeguard Walter and L.P., having the cats' front claws removed to protect her Illinois furniture. In February we said goodbyes all 'round again and closed our Bloomington bungalow and hurtled on to our fall-back gig in the icy hinterlands of Asia....

And I was abandoning my dying mother.

No wonder my spirit froze along with the rest of me.

♫

During those polar Woodstock weeks I channeled any positive energy I could muster into teaching. Dressed in long underwear, bluejeans, and a knee-length wool salwar-kameez over a long-sleeve shirt, I led middle school writing classes, 7th grade music, and my favorite—a piano lab class for elementary kids. The well-equipped piano lab made me the improbable Queen of Music Tech.

From my teacher's piano at the front, I faced a dozen beginner students each at an electric keyboard. I wore headphones through which I could listen to a single student, or all students at once; a microphone allowed me to talk to individuals through their own headphones. I'd have the class play a song together from their classroom books—"Twinkle, Twinkle, Little Star" or "Bingo"—and accompany with rhythmic chords. I loved watching dark-haired kids from the subcontinent and other Asian countries, a few Anglo blondes and brunettes among them, bent over the keys.

For weeks upon cold weeks, schoolrooms full of bustling bodies felt warmer than home. With its constantly-stoked stove, the library was especially cozy, so I lingered there after classes to check papers and do lesson plans. Then I trudged the dirt path home to meet Russ and the kids, and we all walked back to the lunchroom to take advantage of our "board"—endless meals of curry with rice and bland veggies, bread, tea with hot milk, and cakes or puddings for dessert. I sat glum over the carb-filled fare.

Undaunted by the cold, Russ reveled in our new spartan life. He made sure we had hot water, ample wood and coal and a blazing fire. Relieved to be back at meaningful work, he fell into a comfortable role helping teachers with Woodstock's accreditation process.

Tim and Holly flexed their social muscles again, soon liking their new teachers, making friends and fitting in. Many of their classmates were boarders, living in dorms, their parents sprinkled around the globe. Outside of school, our kids' close friends were children of staff members like us. Tim played with tow-headed pal Sam, the son of an Australian elementary teacher, in his house up the hill from us; Holly and Tim both shot hoops on the cement pad outside with Anika, the daughter of Indian teachers who lived next-door in our duplex.

Though undeterred by the frigid temps, our children cringed at the palm-size, albeit harmless, spiders that sometimes trundled across our floors. When a child implored, I'd toss a dishtowel over a hapless arachnid and release it outside.

Our kids also feared the long-tailed, gangly langur monkeys that made themselves at home in the trees near our houses. Due to schedule differences, we often sent Tim and Holly to school on their own; other children joined them on the five-minute walk. Langurs would descend to the wooded path, frightening the kids. "Anika told me a monkey grabbed a girl's backpack once," Holly said. "They're bigger than I am. *Scary.*"

The langurs did hang boldly close. We watched them cavort in the trees outside our living room window, and we'd hear them thump across our corrugated-metal roof. In the spring, if we left the windows open, we might have to shoo marauders out. One morning we found a T-shirt of Tim's in shreds, ravaged by the monkeys but still clipped to the clothesline—luckily not a favorite, and one less article of clothing for the *dhobi* to wash.

Once a week, for a few rupees, our *dhobi*, a cheery, hazel-eyed Indian mute, worked the magic of creating immaculately-folded clean clothes from the soiled ones he'd whisked away. Seated cross-legged on the floor, he pulled one pristine piece at a time from a basket and silently presented it, laid across his palms—each spotless shirt, each tidy pair of pants, each neat set of underwear a gift.

Our *dhobi* joined others washing clothes communally in the river far below, then stringing the separate pieces across the plush green valley to dry. In spring, from a high hiking trail, we could see the line of Woodstock laundry fluttering in the breeze like the Tibetan prayer flags in Mussoorie doorways.

Small, sporadic comforts like clean clothes and hot showers barely lightened my winter gloom. And as if my war with the cold did not cause sufficient grief, I suffered from diarrhea, gas, and stomach cramps, soon diagnosed by the campus nurse as *giardia*. Though we boiled drinking water, disinfected vegetables and never ate common carriers of giardia like strawberries and lettuce, this fecal-borne infection was common at Woodstock, and its consequences seemed worse than the amoeba we'd fancied we had in Zaire. Giardia came to rival malaria for Most Abominable Third-World Illness, because with me it was chronic, persisting for weeks. Twice I took the recommended medical cure, a heavy-duty, several-day course of Flagyl, to no avail.

During my third severe round of pain and diarrhea, an Indian high school teacher told me to try garlic, a natural antibiotic. Chopped into bits and swallowed with water it wouldn't taint the breath, she said.

Near Easter, around my fifty-first birthday, miracles happened. Not only had the garlic cured me, but spring arrived with divine warmth that thawed my frozen spirit. Wild purple irises bloomed—descendants sprung from century-old missionary gardens. Thousands of the renegades peppered pathways and cascaded down green hillsides at Woodstock and beyond. Bright purple blooms graced walks to school, neighbors' yards, and our mountain hikes. They blessed my birthday season. I picked some and brought them inside. With colored pencils on a square of watercolor paper, I sketched and shaded one delicate iris face and sent it to my mother.

In the couple of letters I received from her at Woodstock, Mom's handwriting was wiggly, but her words glowed with a peace that passed my understanding. "Methinks I did too much," she wrote, newly aware of how hard she'd worked: how she'd labored to provide for, control and perfect herself and the lives of all those near and dear to her, it seemed. Now she was giving up that practice; she had learned to simply *be*—a skill I would begin to learn myself, years later. She'd been kneeling in her garden, weeding and tending spring flowers. "The peonies are up already," she wrote. "They should be good this year."

After the hellish Indian winter, Woodstock spring was heavenly. The four of us took hikes along steep green trails to Prakash's market, where we bought fresh bread and chunks of fresh cheddar cheese, then picnicked with a panoramic view of snowy Himalayan peaks. Sometimes we walked to town for dinner at an upstairs Chinese restaurant. Russ and I were invited to teas, dinners, and one wild party at a Tibetan friend's house where we drank beer and danced to rock music in dim rooms open to the cool, moonlit outdoors.

Our family took a long road trip down to Rishikesh, where back in the day the Beatles had consorted with the Maharishi

Mahesh Yogi. In air fragrant with incense and marijuana, we walked across a long, swaying bridge among a throng of Indians wrapped in saffron-tinted fabric. On the other side, descending steps to wade in the clear, cool Ganges, I collected a film canister of water—my only souvenir of Rishikesh.

Woodstock school days flowed through the rest of the semester as easily as the Ganges through the subcontinent. On our morning walk to classes, the pristine mountain air resounded with flutes, violins and sitars as students practiced outside. I relaxed into enjoying my small classes, my volunteer status and sparse schedule keeping me from working too hard. In May I played piano for a choir concert held outdoors in the brick-lined quad, where we sent a ripping chorus of "New York, New York" into the star-spangled Indian night.

Dressed up in Mussoorie, India

33

A Snag in the Smooth Fabric

One day Holly came home frowning. "Mrs. Chavan asked if I was a Christian, and I didn't know what to say."

Mr. and Mrs. Chavan, Anika's parents and our next-door neighbors, were evangelical Christian Indians, Mr. Chavan a Baptist minister. "What did you tell her?"

"I said I didn't know."

Here was a snag in the smooth fabric of my days.

Christian principles were posited and paramount at Woodstock; we'd understood this when we signed on. Our skills and experience as educators would be appreciated, we were told, and we'd be accepted as the agnostics we were—but only for a short time. "You are most welcome here...for this semester," Mr. Randall had said pointedly before he shook our hands.

Most Woodstock staff were staunch, traditional Protestants—Lutheran, Methodist, Presbyterian—and an air of Christianity hung about us, though lightly. People prayed "in Jesus' name" before meals, and school meetings began with Christ-filled prayers.

At least we were not required to attend Christian chapel services each morning as permanent staff did. Even Hindu, Muslim, and Buddhist students had to go to chapel, but Mr.

Randall had exempted us. Russ and I made friends with the few staff members who understood and perhaps even shared our lack of belief in Father, Son and Holy Ghost, but still got along with everyone, as we did.

I longed to alleviate Holly's discomfort over Mrs. Chavan's question. "Next time maybe you could say you come from the Christian *tradition*. We believe in a lot of Christian ideas, you know, like people should be kind and not hurt others. So you're Christian in *some* ways."

Probably not helpful, poor child. And Mrs. Chavan's question had brought up issues as prickly as the bed of thistles outside the cafeteria. I wanted to tell her to mind her own business. Instead, I harbored resentment toward her for dragging back shreds of religious guilt I still hadn't banished: guilt over ousting the conventions of organized religion from my life, then fearing people's opinion of me; guilt over having no confidence in my own belief system; and now, guilt over failing my kids in the religious education department. But knowing we wouldn't be staying for long, I smiled at Mrs. Chavan and skirted the thistles.

Then Tim ran me into a thorn bush. He'd picked up a classmate's rupees on the classroom floor and was caught pocketing them. His teacher made Tim return the money and reported the incident to the principal.

Our eleven-year-old son, a thief. What had we done wrong?

That afternoon, Russ, Tim and I met with Mr. Randall in his office, where he gently recounted the incident. "Is that what happened, Tim?"

Tim nodded, hangdog.

"It's easy to be tempted, isn't it? I don't blame you for picking up Sajid's money. Do you think it was right to keep it?"

Tim shot a sidelong glance at the principal and shook his head.

"Would you be willing to write a short note apologizing to Sajid?"

My son was absolved of his misdemeanor in a trice, and with no hint of retribution.

As with Mrs. Chavan's question, I felt a twinge of guilt. I'd never been the best parent. I should have been more patient, more confident and understanding. Like Mr. Randall.

Email made it to our school in the foothills of the Himalayas in that spring of '98. Rare messages were printed and conveyed by a technician from the school's lab computers; we went to the lab to send replies.

One day in June Russ came home with two emails bearing the same message—the word *urgent* glaring in each like a cop's red light in the rear view mirror. *Come home*, my sisters wrote. Mom was in the hospital.

I would have to leave Woodstock early, alone, before school was out for the summer. A travel agent on campus made the plans. On my last day at school, Chuck Samuels, a popular, devoutly-Christian music teacher, beckoned me into the music room and stood close. "May I pray with you?"

The wooden blinds were open, the space filled with light. Chuck spoke quiet words. "Watch over Lena and Russ and Tim and Holly, we pray you, Jesus," he said, and "O Lord and Savior we beseech you, in your precious name," and more—the sort of throwback religious words I'd long found distasteful. But I stood patient and breathed and let it all wash over me, comforted by the pause in my hurried leaving, and by Chuck's lulling tone, and by his caring.

I would see Russ and Tim and Holly in a week, but as I hugged them goodbye, that seemed like forever. I was soon away and down the hill, the driver bearing me to an office in Dehradun where, just before they closed at 5:00 p.m., I received the ticket for the first leg of my trip. We drove four more hours to the outskirts of New Delhi, where in a dark basement in the dead of night, as prearranged by the Woodstock travel agent-magician, the driver awakened a guard who rose from his cot and handed me the rest of my ticket. The car sped on to the Delhi airport, where I caught my plane to Amsterdam—the layover there long enough for me to take a sauna and a shower and to buy an overflowing cone of pale pink tulips for my mom.

The tulips rested in an overhead bin as the plane soared west through darkness over the ocean to Boston, then Minneapolis. From Minneapolis, in daylight, I caught a bus to Menominee, Wisconsin, where my sister Chrissie picked me up; we drove the hour home to Barron.

In her hospital bed, Mom was hooked to machines. Her eyes were closed, her breaths short; she looked thin and frail. Her hair had grown back in a short, gray shock; before the chemo, a year earlier, it had still been dark brown.

I took a breath and rustled the cone of tulips. Mom's eyes opened, and she smiled.

At peace in her private, dark-green room, my mother put me to shame. Here in the valley of the shadow of death she felt no fear, while I, strong and healthy, lived in habitual apprehension of the days ahead.

During her last week Mom had many visitors in the hospital. She would motion toward the pale pink tulips that "Eileen brought home from Holland." They would stay fresh to grace the room for the rest of her life.

In a week, Russ and Tim and Holly arrived to see her, and in a few days more, my mother died.

My family was away that day, Russ on a job interview in Arizona, Tim and Holly with friends in Illinois. My dad and I were at his house, still asleep that early morning when the phone rang.

In the hospital an hour later, I held Mom's hand and phoned my sisters. "She's sleeping forever," I told them.

♫

Years later, I would grasp that Mom's brand of faith—her Methodist church, service projects, and prayer—had often soothed her worried soul. *The Upper Room* sat on her bed stand; for years she read the Christian booklet's daily devotional messages—which I dismissed as pap back in the day, but which, I would come to realize, embraced spiritual principles much like those of the meditation books I began reading later. It would take my son's alcoholism to lead me to those books—to the Program that would teach me to surrender to some Greater Power, as Mom had.

Until I'd found peace for myself, it had been hard to recognize it in my mother.

34

Don't Let It Happen Again

Mom left me too soon—and too soon, I'd been pulled from India. But before we departed, India had thrown my family a lifeline to our future. One of the rare emails we'd received at Woodstock had come from Russ's sister Mary in Arizona, alerting us to an admin job at a school called Boulder Pass. "They don't give much information, but their office is in PRESCOTT."

Three years earlier, remembering fondly my time in Arizona in the '70's, I'd suggested a summer tour. A couple of hours northwest of Mary's, we'd discovered Prescott with its tall pines, creeks and boulders, and an appealing town square. We bought a piece of land ten miles from town.

With Russ's recent job dismissal in India, finding overseas positions might have been difficult. And Tim and Holly were approaching middle-school age. We were ready to settle in the U.S.—but we needed jobs.

Boulder Pass had sounded good in the interviews, claiming to be a superior alternative to middle schools and high schools in big public districts. With a dozen students working at their own pace in small classrooms, the school would accommodate individual needs. High school students with jobs could work toward graduation in any of the four-hour, independent-study sessions, morning, afternoon, or evening.

We had hearts for the concept, and the jobs paid well enough. The only positions available were at the Cottonwood branch, a little over an hour from Prescott, and we leapt at them. Russ was hired as site supervisor and middle school teacher; I would run one of the two morning high school sessions and the single afternoon one.

We did not see the storm clouds gathering in sunny Arizona skies.

"I wish we had a maid." Holly pouted as she gathered clothes and toys up from her floor.

I felt sympathy for my eight-year-old daughter, spoiled by life overseas with servants. "It won't take long to finish picking up and vacuum. Then you'll be done."

She glowered at me and went back to work.

Holly's little pink room was one of three bedrooms in our small rented ranch-style house in Cottonwood. Across mountains from Prescott, this town was smaller, hotter, and 2000 feet lower—but we didn't plan a long stay. Prescott was our final destination.

The house's marine-blue carpet showed every bit of dirt and debris dragged in off the dusty, gritty yard by four people and two cats; vacuuming was never done. And we needed to wash clothes and dust furniture and scrub bathrooms and water the landlady's roses in the bone-dry backyard.

I was as spoiled as Holly. No more cooks setting meals on the table, as we'd enjoyed in Madagascar and India, and we had less money for eating out. Despite our two jobs, I felt strapped. Teaching didn't pay as well here as it had overseas, and our move with Allied Van Lines had cost a fortune. We hadn't yet sold our Illinois house. And we were paying income tax again.

Compared to life abroad, existence in the U.S. was tough. The kids cleaned their own rooms, and each prepared dinner one night a week. Tim's Tuesday standard was tacos from a box, with added ground beef, fresh shredded cheese, tomato, lettuce and onion; on Wednesdays Holly made spaghetti with Ragu sauce, and a green veggie on the side. When Tim cooked Holly washed dishes, and vice versa. Russ and I covered Mondays and Thursdays, and Friday was pizza night. We ate all our meals together, as we'd always done. We even continued "Best Thing."

As we began eating, someone would call out "Best Thing," and each person said the best thing that had happened that day. You could have two or three—but at least one best thing was required, even if it was "School finally got out," or "I don't have to wash dishes tonight." The tradition of Best Thing continued at our dinner table until the kids left home.

It wasn't until Cottonwood—Tim's looming adolescence and our difficult jobs—that "Worst Thing" slipped in at the table.

Within the first week of my job at Adobe, I discovered that teaching there, in any normal sense, was impossible. The curriculum consisted of a thick text for each high school subject—English, history, algebra, chemistry, economics—and a set of mastery tests kids were to pass to complete each required course.

Most students didn't want to be there but were required by parents or probation officers. The few with any real desire to graduate dabbled in various texts and made desultory attempts to pass the required tests, but most kids just fooled around. I could not run classes in any one subject for all; freshman-through-senior students were at different places in different courses—and I wasn't qualified to teach math, science, or economics.

One day a brash girl with piercings in her tongue and elsewhere looked up from rifling pages of a chemistry test. "God dammit, Lena! You need to be more like Patti."

I'd never met Patti, my predecessor, who had "taught" one semester at Boulder Pass, then moved to Colorado. "What do you mean?"

"She helped us with the tests."

"You know I'll help, if I can...."

"No—*really* help." She slapped the test down on the table and glared at classmates for corroboration.

Turned out Patti had given students answer sheets, and they'd passed tests—even graduated—by cheating.

"What? I can't do that. How would you learn anything?"

"Fuck learning!" Jeb, a wise-ass senior, shot out of his chair. "We need help to succeed in life—that's why we're here." He pointed to the poster on the back wall that said, *Failure is not an option.* "It's your job to help us pass." He flopped back onto his chair.

I felt more like a security guard than a teacher. Many students were district school dropouts who couldn't get with the system—about equal numbers of whites, Hispanics, and Native Americans; some had been expelled for truancy, drugs, or violent behavior. Many were from homes with alcoholic, disabled, and/or jobless parents. They came to classes irregularly and after little sleep. Some were probably stoned. At school they dozed over closed books or talked loudly about work and drugs and sex. "Just wait." A sixteen-year-old blonde girl jabbed at her very pregnant belly and spoke to the Apache girl next to her. "This'll happen to you, too."

I felt sorry for these kids. But I was their teacher, not their social worker. Most couldn't pass the tests without answer sheets—even open-book, which I encouraged. The only shot I had at educating them was to first accept them as they were, then guide them to be good and strong in any way I could.

I was so disheartened by the curse words fouling the classroom air that I went home one day and crafted a lesson. The teens who drifted in the next morning found the whiteboard filled with words in columns, in my own bold handwriting: *motherfucker, bastard, cunt, cocksucker*—a dozen or more bad words I'd heard reverberating off the walls.

"*What—?*" Pierced Girl was shocked. A couple of boys sniggered. The Apache girl said, "Lena! Teachers don't use words like that!"

"Teachers? What about students? You people talk like this every day. *You're* offended? How do you think *I* feel? I've never been in a school that allows this kind of language. But if you can use it, why can't I?"

If my impulsive lesson cut down on the profanity, it wasn't

for long.

Russ's middle schoolers were no better. One day he and students seated in the classroom heard a kid in the tiny corner bathroom yell out to a buddy: "Justin! Come in here and help me hold this wild thing."

Was there an institutional discipline code? Certainly not enforceable. Cops could be called and kids thrown out for drugs or violence or sexual assault. All else was allowed.

The Monday after Thanksgiving I arrived to find a new student sitting in my classroom. He'd been enrolled by Tess, the office aide—a tough, older woman who'd worked at Boulder Pass since its creation.

The morning high school class upstairs, taught by a long-time friend of Tess's, had several fewer kids than mine—and this new kid in my class proved himself a troublemaker right away.

I fumed all morning, and at lunchtime I confronted Tess over the office counter. "Now I've got sixteen students and Ashley has thirteen. I'm willing to keep this new guy, if you put a couple of mine upstairs."

"Ashley'll quit if I give her any more kids."

"What about me? This isn't fair. Do I have to talk to John?"

She glared at me. "Go ahead."

I knew Tess would talk the director into siding with her. "This is bullshit!" I grabbed my lunch sack from the counter, banged out the door, strode across the street, and slammed my right foot hard into the boulder at the entrance to the park. "*Fuck!*" I sank to the grass, holding my foot and sobbing.

My right big toe swelled up, and I eventually lost the nail. But the incident had set me on a new path. I gave my two-weeks' notice the next day.

In January, as Russ resumed his daily grind at Boulder Pass, I began subbing in the Cottonwood-Oak Creek District. After

Boulder Pass, subbing brought fresh air and a brighter view of life. I especially liked going to the two middle schools, being in the company of contented teachers and inquisitive, disciplined students; if we'd stayed, I could have snagged a permanent position in one of the two—Tim's school, or the one in nearby Cornville.

But the best thing that happened in January would take us away from the Verde Valley and its schools: Our Illinois house sold, paving our way to a longed-for home in Prescott. We set off on weekend planning trips, driving up through the tiny old mining town of Jerome, then across Mingus Mountain to our mile-high hometown-to-be. We found a builder and an architect in Prescott, and by March we'd broken ground.

Russ and I had designed our new Arizona house while we lived in the Himalayan foothills. It wouldn't be big, but we'd have an upstairs with two bedrooms, a bath, and a living area for the kids. There'd be a fireplace downstairs. We'd have a back patio, an upstairs balcony, and a front porch with a swing where we could sit and gaze at Granite Mountain in the distance.

That spring, sailing through sub days, dreaming of our new house was my Best Thing.

"Worst Thing." Tim trailed a fork through his spaghetti one Wednesday night. "I got arrested."

A couple of hours earlier, we'd opened the door to find a tall policeman holding our frowning son by the shoulder. "Does this boy belong to you?"

The officer had spotted Tim and his ne'er-do-well pals walking on the red metal rooftops of Mingus Union High School, just up the street from us. The cop yelled them down, scaring the daylights out of them, then drove them home.

In our doorway, the officer was sympathetic. Tim and his buddies could have been hurt, he said. Before he turned to leave, he pointed a finger at Tim. "Don't let it happen again, son."

At the table we reinforced the lesson. "You don't want the cops talking to you again, do you, Tim," Russ said.

But I was mildly amused. "Mingus calls itself the 'Proud Home of the Marauders.' What's a little marauding from outside?" I patted Tim's hand. "Your crime wasn't that bad."

Russ gave me the evil eye, then looked at Tim. "Just don't do it again."

A year later, I was reading student essays at the kitchen table in our new house in Prescott when the police called. "We have your son at Hastings. He stole a CD."

Russ wasn't home yet, and I couldn't reach him. Head spinning, I drove the fifteen minutes to the media-and-book store's parking lot in Prescott, where Tim and the cop stood beside the police car. I pulled up and got out, greeted the officer, then leveled my eyes at Tim. "What happened?"

What I meant was, *What in hell made you put that CD in your backpack? Didn't you learn not to steal back at Woodstock?*

Tim looked away.

The officer was stern. "He's thirteen, 7th grade. Hastings isn't going to press charges, but Timothy can't go into the store for a year." He held out his clipboard. "I have to file this report with the juvenile justice department." I signed the report.

I drove Tim home in stone-cold, fuming silence, turned him over to Russ to talk things out, and went back to my schoolwork.

The next day Russ and I sat across a desk from a juvenile detention officer named Jaime who said he could set Tim up with some community service, if we agreed. Russ raised questioning brows at me. "Throw the book at him," I said.

Tim spent a Saturday afternoon pulling weeds in a parking lot with a half-dozen foul-mouthed, tattooed older teens—like my kids back at Boulder Pass. He came home beat in his grimy black hoodie. "That was horrible."

On a Friday afternoon, across the coffee table from Holly and me, Tim pranced like the cock of the roost. "She skipped school!

You have to punish her!"

For once, his sister was in trouble. She glared at him through tears.

"Stop, Tim." Beside my daughter on the couch, I stroked her back. "She couldn't help it."

I'd received the call from her 4th grade teacher in my middle school classroom that morning. "I'm just checking to make sure Holly's okay. No one phoned in her absence, and no one answers at home."

I sped the twenty-some minutes home to find my daughter in bed upstairs, covers pulled around her head. "I didn't get on the bus," she whimpered. "I hid behind the bushes till you and Dad were gone."

As I sat beside her on her bed, I learned what had caused my daughter's Friday to take a tragic turn.

Her semi-annual appointment for professional hair re-braiding near Phoenix was set for the next day, Saturday. On Thursday night I had begun the laborious, several-hour job of extracting her tight-kinked hair from its dozens of tiny, intricate braids, and loosening their synthetic extensions, so she'd be ready for the weekend re-do.

The job took two sittings of a good three hours each, with breaks—and abundant strength and patience from us both. As Holly held her head erect and watched TV, shifting position for me as needed, I concentrated on fine comb and finger work, trying not to hurt her or break off too much hair.

By bedtime Thursday night I'd taken out half the braids; we could do the rest Friday after school as Russ drove the two hours south. We'd finish at Russ's sister Mary's, where we would spend the night before the early Saturday appointment nearby.

We'd been using Coco, a glamorous African-American hair stylist, for three years. She had always accommodated us with Sunday all-day appointments so we could take out all the fraying braids in leisurely sittings on Saturday. Unfortunately, this Sunday Coco was busy. This was our first Saturday appointment—and it would be our last.

On Friday morning before school, I tamed Holly's freshlyunbraided chunks of wayward hair the best I could, corralling them in rubber-band holders and barrettes. Not a professional hair-do by any stretch, but not bad. "You look nice." I smoothed sections and adjusted holders as Holly grimaced at the mirror. "Anyway, your gorgeous face makes up for one day's undone hair." I smooched her cheek.

At nine years old Holly was already developing curves, growing up; meanwhile, she was coping with yet another new neighborhood and school and set of classmates, trying to fit in and do well and be liked. The only black student in her class, she was, as always, different and singled out. This wasn't all bad; her friends admired her exotic braids, her dark, foreign beauty and her poise. But like all adolescents, she just wanted to be like everybody else.

Worst Thing: This very bad hair day had brought my poor girl down.

On the rocks in Oak Creek Canyon, Arizona

35

I'm Sorry I Can't Help You

THE COUPLE WERE seated behind china and silver at a white-clothed table, and as we walked in they rose to meet us. Holly's birth mother wore a dark jacket that hung loose from her shoulders, her father a suit jacket with frayed lapels over a T-shirt. In their mid-forties, the two looked worn and tired, as if they might buckle like old cardboard—but smiles lit their faces.

I wanted my kids to connect with their roots, and if possible, with their birth parents. We'd taken Tim at age eleven as far back as we could, to visit his orphanage in India. Holly's turn came the summer of her eleventh year. She knew her story, given up as a baby and fostered for three years before we adopted her. She was a little scared, but eager for the trip.

Relying on the magic of email between that far-off corner of the world and ours in the American Southwest, I'd arranged the visit with her birth parents in Antananarivo, Madagascar, where we'd lived and adopted Holly eight years earlier. Our Malagasy teacher-friend Madeleine—Tim's kindergarten teacher and Holly's godmother—had facilitated, staging the reunion in her spacious, poinsettia-rimmed yard.

We took places around the table. Seated between me and her other mother, Holly smiled shyly and clung to me, but soon warmed to the occasion and dropped my hand. We visited quietly. Madeleine translated English to Malagasy and vice versa, our scraps of French on both sides insufficient. Holly's mother, Rindra, spoke to Madeleine. "She says they thought they'd lost their daughter forever. They are very, very happy." Rindra fondled Holly's braids. As Holly leaned toward her, I felt a pang of sympathy. It was my good fortune to be raising this child in place of her birth mother—it wasn't fair. Yet Rindra seemed grateful simply to see her daughter again, loved and thriving.

Holly's square jaw and almond eyes resembled Rindra's, but her birth mother's skin was lighter, and unlike Holly's, her hair was straight. I asked to see the father's hair. He removed his woven-raffia Homburg-style hat, and we all laughed: Pascal was bald—though the short fringe above his ears seemed straight. Madeleine relayed Pascal's words. "All their children have curly hair, like Holly's." There were eight, including Holly.

Madeleine served Malagasy rice with chicken and local greens, and cake for dessert. After lunch she packed leftovers for Rindra and Pascal, and we gave our gifts: a framed school photo of Holly, and the equivalent of two hundred dollars in francs—going on a year's salary in Madagascar at the time. Holly's parents beamed.

We took photos, distant and close-up—of Holly with her birth parents, Holly with all four of her parents, Holly with everybody. She took Russ's and my hands and smiled. "This is fun."

On a little piece of paper, Rindra painstakingly printed her and her husband's names and a list of all of Holly's siblings according to age, with *Iony Misa*, our Holly, near the middle. Then Rindra put a hand on her belly and whispered to Madeleine.

Selling what market goods they could, she and Pascal were barely getting by, Madeleine explained, and they had a ninth child on the way. Madeleine looked at me, her smile gone. "She asks if you could take this baby."

Russ and I had agreed two were enough. I touched Rindra's hand. "*Je suis désolée*"—I'm sorry.

By chance, our visit in 2001 coincided with a total eclipse of the sun, and Madagascar's geographic location made it an excellent place for a view. We were in Nosy Be, the big northern island-off-the-island that we'd visited when we lived in Madagascar. Splayed in beach chairs facing the Indian Ocean, wearing iridescent, foil-looking glasses, we watched the dramatic darkening of the day.

At our hotel Holly bought a *pagne*—a light cotton wrap—with words and flowers in blue and yellow on white, commemorating the eclipse. Back in Arizona she put it on the blue wall in her room and strung it with gold spangles.

Holly also made a scrapbook of the trip, with tickets, bottle caps, postcards, and photos—some of which she'd taken herself with the camera we'd given her. On one page, by a picture of her with her two sets of parents and her brother Tim, she wrote simply, FAMILY.

Two months after Madagascar, on the morning of September 11, 2001, I was driving to my teaching job in Prescott Valley when NPR interrupted its program. Arriving at the middle school I made a beeline to a classroom where horrified teachers watched TV. Before the first bell rang, the principal's voice on the loudspeaker directed us to keep our classes calm and carry on. We could watch unfolding news on TV, or follow our planned lessons.

By then we knew enough: the Twin Towers ablaze and crumbling, a chunk of the Pentagon in burning rubble, all the passengers of a hijacked plane dead in a Pennsylvania farm field. My upstairs classroom's TV reception was faltering and fuzzy. I turned it off and plunged my sixth graders into the dynasties of ancient China.

Staff members were invited to meet after school in a windowless classroom downstairs, where we sat in student desks. Some colleagues called on God and Jesus. "We pray God our nation will prevail," the music teacher said, her voice hushed. Someone said Amen, and someone else, more loudly, "May Muslim evildoers be punished." There were nods of assent.

I took a shaky breath and spoke. "May people of all faiths and cultures come together and find comfort." I soon left the room.

The reactions of my teaching peers to the tragedy of that day brought to the surface my growing discomfort at Glassford Hill Middle School, where weekly Bible classes met in a classroom after school, Jesus was a lunchtime conversation staple, and God and George W. Bush seemed to be regarded as equals. I began secluding myself in my classroom.

Within a few years, circumstances would knock me from my high horse, the Program to help deal with my alcoholic son yielding emotional and spiritual footings I didn't know I lacked. But at Glassford Hill I still clung to my intolerance of crosses, church, and Christ.

♫

I'd been grateful for good discipline, pleasant kids, and freedom to be creative at my middle school job. But after three years, the prison-like building's viewless windows and crowded hallways, in addition to my lack of ease with colleagues, had worn me down. When a teacher-friend at Bradshaw Mountain High School suggested I might transfer across the road to the airy architecture and more open attitudes of her school, I moved.

Our own kids progressed through Prescott's middle and high schools. Though Holly worked hard for her good grades, neither child seemed sparked by academics; both were more eager to get their driver's license. We'd told them if they wanted a car they'd have to pay for half. When they hit sixteen, each soon had a job and a used car.

The first day Tim drove his frog-green Jeep Cherokee to high school, he loaded up some pals at lunchtime, turned dust-raising donuts on the track, jumped the Jeep over a dirt mound, and got caught by the campus police for speeding and reckless driving. His new job bagging groceries at Safeway enabled him to pay the $120 fine and make payments on the Jeep.

Tim looked sharp in his work clothes—button-down white shirt, black pants and shoes. When we shopped at Safeway we made a point to go through his check-out, where we would brag to the clerk that we were his parents. They'd flatter him with kind words about his work, and he'd look sheepish but pleased.

One evening when he'd been on the job a few months, a Safeway manager called. "Tim's been accused of stealing."

Arriving at Safeway, Russ and I hurried up the stairs through a fluorescent-lit hallway and into a plain office. Tim slumped over a desk at one side, his back to us; he didn't look up as we entered. The tall blonde manager rose from behind her desk to meet us. Glancing at a paper, she laid out the facts: "At 5:07, inside the sliding glass front doors, a male customer held Tim by the arm and accused him of being a thief. He told a floor manager he saw Tim take money from a woman's wallet left in an empty cart in the parking lot. When Tim was questioned he admitted to the theft and gave up the money, sixty-five dollars." The manager cast a sympathetic look Tim's way. "I'm sure it was rough for Tim to be accused like that in public. But unfortunately, we have to dismiss him."

Tim swiped a finger below an eye, and my stomach caved. Tears burned as I imagined the scene: this mean, meddling customer purposely shocking and embarrassing Tim in public—and he man-handled my son. Was that even legal? My face flamed. "The guy was white, right? Did he attack like that because of Tim's color?"

The manager wasn't going there. "I'm really sorry. The fact is, Tim took the money. But we won't give him a bad reference."

Russ drove Tim home in his Jeep, and I followed in our car, fighting back tears. At home I closed myself in our bedroom and let Russ deal with Tim upstairs. I knew Russ would talk about right and wrong, honesty and trust—useless platitudes, it seemed just now—but I was off the hook. I lay sobbing in a fetal curl on the bed until the pain of my confused thoughts drained away and no more tears would come. Then, catching sight of Russ out on the porch, I drifted up the stairs and entered my son's room.

He was hunched on his bed thumbing game controls, eyes glued to his TV. As I entered, he set the controls aside but kept a hand on them. I sank down near him on the bed and put an arm around his waist from behind, the other around his shoulders. I held him tight and gasped, "I'm sorry." I cried muffled sobs against him, still holding him, my head next to his. "I'm so sorry."

What I meant was, *I'm so sorry for the way this happened—your accuser being such an asshole. I'm sorry you felt compelled to steal again and don't have that nice job any more; I'm sorry that the way we raised you—or didn't—probably had something to do with this. I'm sorry your birth mom gave you up, and you had to be adopted into this foreign world. I'm sorry your life is such a mess and I can't help you.*

As I loosened my grip, Tim picked up the controls and resumed playing his game.

36

A Double Dose

I WOULD HAVE talked to Mom about Tim's transgressions, but she was in her grave. When I shared instead with Dad, he wrote, "Take him out behind the woodshed."

Dad was joking. His family had been Mennonite, steeped in pacifism; he would never strike anyone. I'd inherited his penchant for nonviolence—and other traits, as I was discovering.

After Mom's death Dad had unwittingly swooped in to fill the gap in my life, like the barn swallows that stuffed nests between boards in our old hayloft on the farm. With Mom gone, my eighty-three-year-old father and I learned to communicate. I got to know him for the first time and was startled to discover how much alike we were.

Dad slept downstairs on the couch the week Mom died, as he had been doing for some time to be near her. When she went to the hospital, he stayed downstairs. Home from India, I slept upstairs in their double bed.

One night around 2:00 I awoke to the sound of Dad croaking out words I couldn't understand. He stood like a thin specter in the dim upstairs doorway, a hand at his neck, straining to clear his throat. "I can't swallow."

I switched on the light, got up and stood next to him, and

patted his back.

Dad had acid reflux. I'd seen him experience minor episodes after meals. "He gets 'bubbly,'" Mom had explained. He would leave the table to clear his pipes and settle himself.

I knew this ailment—*gastro-esophageal reflux disease*, or GERD; I'd developed it myself. It wasn't serious, but it could be damned uncomfortable when compounded by stress. I rubbed Dad's back. "Things are hard right now, Mom in the hospital...."

He forced a cough from deep down. "I think I'm choking." A tear ran down his cheek.

My dad was scared, poor guy. I rubbed his back some more. "It'll probably go away in a minute."

But when it didn't, I drove him to emergency at the nearby hospital, where in another wing Mom lay dying. The on-call family doc checked Dad's throat and took his vitals. Then he laid a hand on Dad's knee. "Dick, I'd say you're suffering from anxiety. Simple as that. Otherwise, you're healthy as an ox."

"The *heck!*" Dad exclaimed, as if he'd seen a magic trick. The doctor's words released the fear from his body like a dove freed from a magician's scarf. Dad's shoulders relaxed, and a sheepish grin stretched his lips.

The doc prescribed low-dose Valium which, as a chaser for the doctor's reassurance, kept Dad calm that week. When he said the pills made him too sleepy I cut them in half, as I had done for myself in Bombay.

Panic had gripped my father that night just as it had me in Bombay when Russ was fired. Witnessing Dad's meltdown, I realized it wasn't only Mom who'd passed me the susceptibility to worry and anxiety. I'd received a double dose.

After Mom died, Dad started writing me in Arizona in artistic cursive. An early letter said he no longer liked the senior living place Mom had helped arrange for him to move to after she was gone. He stayed home and got a cat. He learned to cook and clean and even iron. "She wouldn't want me to give up," he said. I admired his independence.

In July of 2005, at his ninetieth birthday party, Dad raised his glass and said he figured he'd live to be a hundred.

On a chilly Monday in February of 2007, I wore all black to school: black turtleneck, pants and shoes, even a black hair clasp.

After several good years there, teaching at Bradshaw Mountain High School was getting me down. When an English teacher quit before the holidays, my ESL classes had suddenly been combined, and I'd had to take on two junior lit classes to save teacher hours and money. I now had too many preps and several troublesome students. Dragging myself out of bed after the weekend, I decided wearing black would warn no one to cross me on that worse-than-blue Monday.

Dusk was coming on that evening when the phone rang. Doing schoolwork at the kitchen table, I rose to answer. "Dad died," my sister Carol whispered from Colorado.

"*What*—?" I sank into my chair.

"Dad *died*."

She was lying. "He just *wrote* me!"

He had sent a picture from the *News Shield* of the inside of the round barn that had been turned into a house a few miles from our old farm; Russ and I had visited the place with Dad during construction. An upright piano stood against a wall in the picture.

Dad had once made me a tiny baby grand from wood, with little paper keys, inked black and white. It sat on my real piano in the living room—I could almost see it from the kitchen.

His housekeeper had found him on the living room floor in front of his recliner. His cat, out of food, dashed around the house.

Probably a heart attack. Dead maybe three days. Fast, without pain. My father was ninety-one and a half.

I knew Dad didn't leave home much during his final months. He couldn't keep his balance, had to clutch at things. He wet himself, but didn't like wearing "diapers." After some fender benders, he'd gone dutifully from driving his 2000 retro T-Bird to a John Deere Gator. When a sign on his street said No ATV's, he got a three-wheel, motorized bike with a basket for groceries and mail. He didn't want anyone to pick him up for church any more; unable to hear, he didn't like having to sit and watch from the window for their arrival, and he didn't want people making a fuss over him. My sister Chrissie set him up with a mobile phone for emergencies, but it sat on the kitchen counter, its batteries dead.

When I'd hit thirty, still single, Dad had told Mom he thought I'd never marry; I was "too independent." I'd guessed he meant I might do well to be a little *de*-pendent and get a mate. Well now, dammit, he'd been the one—too independent to let people help him stay alive.

Me and Dad

37

The Missing Piece

ONE SUMMER AFTER we'd visited my dad in Wisconsin, I'd taken a separate flight back to Arizona, stopping in Houston for a few days to see my nurse-friend Fran from Bombay whose husband, a geologist, now worked for a Texas oil company. Their daughter Sandra, a favorite Bombay student, was also there.

Fran informed me that Russ's secretary at the American School of Bombay, Gayle Giomatti, lived nearby. On my last night, Gayle came for dinner. Over Fran's curry we reminisced, and after a couple of glasses of wine, Gayle blurted, "What happened to you guys at ASB was so unfair."

I gulped wine. "The worst thing was not knowing why they fired Russ. We never did find out."

"I wanted to say something, but the Board warned office people to keep quiet." Gayle sipped wine from her third glass. "It was Hajib Assad who wanted Russ gone...."

Back home in Arizona when I told Russ Gayle's story, he frowned. "It had to be more than Tareef's suspension."

"Fran and Gayle are sure that's what did it. So am I."

Sixth grade Tareef Assad's father Hajib was a rich non-resident Indian from New Jersey. In Bombay with his family on business, he was rumored among staff to have dominion over millions of dollars toward the new-school project. As a member of our ASB school board, he wielded Napoleonic power. He'd once made the Board and all of us teachers sit through a long flip-chart explanation of some unclear, unwanted curriculum plan. He manipulated others similarly: One day as he delivered his son Tareef's school lunch in its array of round silver tiffin boxes to Nipa, our librarian friend, he commanded, "See that he eats it."

Tareef, already as tall as his dad, was the only kid in my 6th grade class who blurted out at the expense of others during lessons. One day as a South Korean girl defended U.S. action in World War II, he cut her off. "That's stupid! America should never have dropped the bomb."

Tareef was sharp—but he was also the closest thing I had to a discipline problem in that gentle place. I wasn't surprised or sorry when, during the last week of school that spring, our English teacher and friend Laura nabbed him. "Tareef yelled *asshole* in that tiny crowded hallway; I heard him all the way from my desk," she told me later. "When I rushed out there, he looked ready to slam Philip against the lockers. I took him straight to Russ."

My husband, the principal, had called Assad and his wife into his office and explained what happened. "We can't allow students to bully classmates without consequences." With the full understanding and cooperation of the parents, Russ had suspended Tareef for a half-day; they'd shaken hands on it.

In Arizona a handful of years later, hearing of his Bombay secretary's words to me in Houston, Russ shook his head. "I still think there had to be more to it."

"But Gayle was right there in your office when Assad spoke to Borg," I said. "She quoted Assad's exact words: '*Erickson goes, or I pull my money from the new-school project.*'"

I could have lived without knowing. But getting to the bottom of the mystery shrouding our last months in Bombay felt good. I slipped in the missing piece and laid the India puzzle to rest.

38

Best Thing

It's early August, a week before Tim's wedding. Russ and I are on the porch with morning coffee, looking out at our new little front yard. Red, yellow, and pink roses hug the old chain link fence. The birdbath stands beside a stately granite boulder at one side, and birds flit around the feeders. Torch lilies and blanket flowers line the skinny sidewalk to the house. Herbs peek out here and there. All are comfortably nestled into the tan, natural-looking decomposed granite—"DG"—that covers the ground.

I pull my gaze from our perfect front yard and sigh.

Russ takes a slow sip of coffee, then looks at me. "What?"

"The back yard...."

He nods. Unlike the front, our back yard is a sea of pointy gravel which both of us dislike.

Previously laden with old flagstones, crumbling cement and weedy dirt, the back had demanded something new. We'd decided on gravel. "We won't track in so much dirt," Russ said.

I agreed. "Neither will the dog."

From pictures on landscaper Miguel's phone, we chose "calico," a pink and gray mix of sharp, half-inch rocks that would match flagstone paths—but the stuff doesn't go with anything. Though offset by the small roofed patio in the middle, and punctuated by trees, vines, other plants and the flagstone paths, it is an expanse of hard, not-pink-at-all, unnatural-looking ground.

"We made a mistake," Russ says. "We'll get Miguel to take it out and put in DG."

Frugal myself, I've become grateful for Russ's willingness to shell out money. I take a breath and remind him of the guest room carpet. It's the room we stored stuff in during the remodel, the only room we didn't strip down to the old fir floorboards. We want wood there, like in the rest of the house.

"Okay, the carpet first. Then the back yard."

We can't afford either at the moment. Tim's wedding is coming up, then birthdays, and the holidays....

And before long we'll need a new couch.

I stand up on stiff legs to go for coffee refills, and Russ rubs his bursitis-ridden shoulder. Nearing seventy, we're showing more signs of wear and tear. Russ has a knee replacement planned. My dermatologist keeps nipping off bits of what he calls "benign" skin cancer. I've been diagnosed with glaucoma, will be using drops forever.

As I walk to the kitchen, my right knee wobbles. It's been doing that lately, but this comes and goes. Pouring coffee, I flex my leg. Exercise, my Program, and meditation help me deal with these maladies.

I return with coffee and settle back into the porch glider, swinging in time with Russ. "Maybe our guy could start pulling out that carpet the week after Tim's wedding," I say. Russ nods.

Tim's sudden engagement to Renee had stunned me. He wasn't ready for marriage! Sure, he'd matured, and he hadn't had a drink of alcohol in five years—but I still sensed depression and anxiety in him.

The week before his engagement announcement, when he was stressed, scrambling to sell his car for needed cash, I'd had a dream: Tim stood near me sobbing so hard it made my heart cave and I was gasping for air. I held him tight and took deep, calming breaths until I relaxed; then I released him.

I awoke unburdened. When I'd let Tim go in the dream, he was still crying—but I felt better. It took me a moment to understand:

It was *I* who needed relief, and I received it in my dream through showing love the best I could, then letting go. Awake to the truth, I remembered that the best thing I can do for my son is love him.

"He may *never* get over this," I sobbed at a Program meeting soon after the dream—much as I had done over Tim's drunkenness at my first meeting years before. Someone passed the tissue box; I grabbed one, swabbed my eyes, and felt the torrent subside.

Outside in bright sunshine afterwards, a Program friend said, "You never know. Tim may surprise you."

I remembered when my own mother longed for my happiness. If she were alive today, I'd surprise her with it.

I soon realized it was *I* who wasn't ready for Tim's marriage, not he. But I've come 'round and warmed to my role as Mother of the Groom.

Renee's wedding colors, aqua and coral, aren't ones I usually wear, but I discovered the perfect calf-skimming dress in flattering shades; I even happened on short-heeled aqua sandals to match. I modeled for Renee, and she approved.

The wedding is the third Sunday in August. The weather's perfect, fresh and sunny as we drive out of town to the Groom Creek site, among pines and boulders in the national forest. Russ and I and Holly and Rick are the first of thirty guests who settle outside on wooden benches.

At 4:00 Renee's three-year-old step-sister begins the ceremony, toddling between the benches in her long ruffled dress. Guests chuckle when she wanders to one side, shirking her petal-tossing duty; her dad guides her back to the path. Then Tim's three groomsmen in white shirts and gold cotton pants—pantlegs folded up at the bottoms in make-shift cuffs—process solemnly, one after the other. On their arms are three young friends of Renee in a mix of dress styles, but all aqua and coral. Bouquets and boutonnieres are fleshy-leafed synthetic succulents.

Guests rise in silence as the beaming bride appears. She's in long, filmy, sleeveless white, a frothy waterfall of veil flowing down her back, her colorful tattoos visible on her upper arms. Her lithe, mid-fortyish mother walks beside her in a long, slim dress, her arm linked with her daughter's. She will give away the bride; Renee's birth father has not been in her life since her parents' divorce when she was little.

The bride and her mom are halfway up the short path when Renee, eyebrows suddenly frozen in a frown, falters and looks down. But her mom shepherds her along and she regains her poise. Later Renee says her garter sprang and began slipping down her leg.

Beneath a wooden archway strung with big coral and aqua pompoms, tall pines behind, Tim waits, mature and exotic-looking with his summer-bronzed skin and black-rimmed glasses. Near him stands Renee's wiry, white-haired grandpa in bluejeans and a white dress shirt, ready to officiate. When the bride arrives, Grandpa directs the couple to face each other and leads them in speaking the simple vows they found on the internet. Then he tells guests, "Renee and Tim have private vows they want to say to each other. Let's give them a moment." He steps back and looks away. Touching foreheads, bride and groom take turns reading quietly, becoming teary as they listen to each other. I wipe a tear and clutch Russ's hand.

♫

Back in Prescott for the reception, we take a tiny elevator to the third floor of the 'Tis Art Gallery and enter a tall, narrow room with wood floors, and brick walls above wainscoting. Guests sit at white-covered, flower-decked tables down the center of the room. The newlyweds have their own table next to the cake. A Mexican buffet from Panchito's waits near the entrance. Before settling in we walk around sipping punch, visiting, and viewing childhood photos of the bride and groom. Meeting Renee's mom and grandmother for the first time, I hug them. Each of us expresses gratitude for the other's support; we know both sides of the family have forgiven our kids' debts.

At first, Russ and I weren't of the same mind about the wedding gift. We'd asked Tim, and he said they'd appreciate help paying for the five-day honeymoon at Joshua Tree National Park in California; it would cost $500. We told him we would do that. But a few days later I awoke with the magnanimous notion to erase Tim's $1500 debt as well. Over coffee I said, "It would give them a fresh start."

Russ said, "Wouldn't that destroy the lesson he needs?"

"I don't know. This just feels different. Some people give their kids cars and houses when they get married. This isn't that grand, just something extra we could do, and we can afford it." We'd negotiated loans with Tim for years, debating how much would be enabling, how much supporting. I'd love to forget all that and go with my heart for once.

We let it rest, and when I brought it up a few days later, Russ was with me. "I can see how it would be nice. A load off for him and us both, really."

I typed an official-looking certificate in a floral font on grey-flecked stationery. Russ and I signed it in pen; then I folded it carefully, slipped it into a matching business envelope and tied it with an aqua ribbon.

♫

The wedding guests are seated with full plates as the toasts begin. After the maid of honor and best man have spoken, Holly, in her swingy sleeveless turquoise dress and black heels, walks confidently to the microphone. "I'm very proud of my brother Tim today. Yeah, he teased and harassed me when we were kids." Tim looks sheepish. "But he was my big brother, and I always admired and wanted to be like him. When he decided to be a marine biologist, I did too.... I love him and I'm happy for him."

My twenty-four-year-old daughter is a poised and stunning grown-up. Watching them on this day, it's hard to believe I've had any part in either of my kids' becoming the young adults they are.

Another bridesmaid and a groomsman take the mic to extol and joke with the couple; Renee's family members express warm thoughts; Russ offers congratulatory words.

My shoes pinch, and I think I may not speak at all—but then Tim's friend Pierson goes up and talks about how close he and

Tim have been for years, ending with "I love you, bro." It moves me to brave my sore feet and walk to the front, where I blurt out thoughts about Tim's arrival from India as a sick baby; his Alaska hardship trek at age nineteen; his "journey through tough times a few years back"—I do not say the words *addiction* or *alcoholism*, though everyone knows. "He's always been a survivor. I'm so proud of him." I take a quavering breath and face the couple. "Tim, I'm so glad you have Renee to share your life with now. I know you will survive and thrive. I love you both." Trying not to limp, I walk over to hug Tim first and then Renee. Then I hobble back and sink into my chair next to Russ, who pats my knee.

Cake follows the toasts. Posed on its own table, the three-tiered confection is adorned with succulent-plant blooms of coral sugar and green frosting leaves, my clever new daughter-in-law's idea. I take photos as the couple cuts and feeds each other a piece, Renee giggling as she brushes crumbs from her face and dress.

Then comes dancing, bride and groom first. After they've danced to their song, John Mayer's "XO," Tim takes my arm; I cling to his slim frame as Renee dances with her step-dad. I'm dancing with Russ for the next song, and soon the floor is full of people. I catch sight of Holly's skirt swinging as she twirls beneath the arc of Rick's raised arm. My feet hurt, but I don't care. I hold Russ closer.

After two hours the party is winding down. Everyone helps with clean up. As Renee's grandma and I clear tables, she insists I set aside bunches of flowers to take home. By 8:00, no evidence of the reception remains.

On the sidewalk below we send the smiling newlyweds off in an old white Lexus, its windows sporting JUST MARRIED signs and *#love*.

Back at our house, Holly and Rick are spending the night before heading home to Tucson. As we sit at the dining room table talking, Holly turns to her mate. "Shall we tell them?"

Russ and I glance at each other.

Holding Rick's hand, Holly says, "We're planning to find a place together."

"Don't rush into anything," Russ says. These kids have been

a solid couple for what—three years?

By 10:00 we're all tired. Holly and Rick disappear into the guest room.

I stand barefoot at the kitchen sink to arrange the wedding wildflowers; then I set vases of the multicolored blooms around the house against our walls' vibrant colors: "Tomato Bisque," "Sprig of Ivy," "Feelin' Blue."

In the bathroom, I pull on a headband to wash my face. I check myself in the silver filigree-framed mirror, then touch the brushed-nickel faucet. Coming in, Russ stands at his sink beside mine, and I say, "I love this house." Hair back from my face, I curl my top lip under and mug a goofy grin at him. "We did such a good job on it." We've done this before—gloated shamelessly over some bit of shared good fortune.

"Really." Russ squeezes toothpaste and holds his loaded brush in mid-air. "We didn't do so bad on our kids, either."

"We co-created a couple of colorful characters." I flash another foolish grin.

But I don't take this blessed Sunday lightly. It's filled me to the brim with gratitude—for my son's triumphs over adversity; for his maturing into what he is, suddenly, today: a happily married man. For my unflappable daughter's independence, for her still-measured but deeper easing into her comfortable relationship. For Russ and me, thirty years going and still growing. He's shed some pounds; I'm less critical—and Best Thing: we're both more grateful and accepting.

In our cozy bathroom we spit, rinse, and rattle pills from bottles. We brush, wash, and flush. We run more water, blot with towels.

Then we crawl between the sheets. As usual, little log-dog Iris is curled near the pillows, and we coax her to her rightful spot at our feet. Russ strokes my arm and says, "See you Monday."

I squeeze his hand. "Yep, Monday." I arrange my pillow and snuggle down beside him.

Our house on Garden Street

Prescott, AZ

Postlude

This morning Tim called, and we had him over for breakfast. Then, while he was at work, I delivered a care package to his house: two dozen eggs, frozen chicken, a bag of meatballs, Bagel Bites, peanut butter and a loaf of homemade bread. He's short of cash again, and though he gets paid tomorrow, he says he won't have enough to cover monthly bills—so he doesn't buy food, and doesn't want to rely on friends who've invited him for meals. He ate only a can of corn last night.

"I'm really sick of being so sad all the time," Tim wrote on Facebook this week. He and Renee have recently split. "Wish I could drink," he told me.

I felt helpless. Though we give our thirty-year-old son loans, we can't cure his financial ailments. But I will not see him starve. He's working two jobs, a new one at the Barley Hound, where the boss is relaxed—like his long-time boss at Panchito's, he says, but more caring. He walks many blocks to work, but will ride Russ's unused bike as soon as it's fixed up. He's taking care of his three cats, and now the Papillon he'd shared with Renee. Best thing is, he glimpses light at the end of the tunnel— has hope for the "end of the struggle," he says—and I have faith he'll come through.

Meanwhile, I'm emerging from my own tunnel of gloom and doom following a major medical procedure I hadn't seen coming.

Three summers ago, Russ and I traveled to five European

countries in four weeks, taking Aleve to keep our aging bodies pain-free while clambering on and off trains, driving rental cars, and tramping miles on foot. Home again, I went back to zumba and hiking the butte. Russ had his left knee replaced as planned; I nursed him mostly patiently, and within two months he was walking better than he had in years—no drugs, no pain.

Then *I* began limping. The doctor's diagnosis: bone on bone in my right knee, time for a new one. I resisted—but when shots and braces didn't fix it, upon urging from friends, I gave in.

I vomited for three days in the hospital post-surgery, then found myself on a merry-go-round of self-pity, a victim of pain and immobility and lack of progress. For weeks I slept under ice more hours a day than I was up. Russ nursed me with patience and tolerance; I was soon able to walk without a walker or cane; physical therapists helped me exercise. But I *hurt*; I was a *wuss.* After weeks, when I still could neither bend nor straighten my leg the number of recommended degrees, my therapist said, "Sometimes people need a second surgery to 'manipulate' the joint." *No way!* I did all his assigned exercises and more, pushing through the pain with not enough help from Percocet—nor from the Universe, my faith in that entity having slipped.

After three months of little improvement, I asked the ortho-doctor if I'd ever be normal again. "You're doing very well," he pronounced. "You have a nice-looking scar and little swelling." He patted the new knee he'd installed. "This was brutal surgery, and you're not twenty-five any more—you're just beginning recovery. It'll take a year, and even then, it won't be the knee God gave you...."

I was devastated, and relieved—still on the merry-go-round, but the doc had slowed it down, brought back hope. After all, I *had* been getting better, acting normal for some time—driving, playing piano, walking the dog. I eased up on myself, let some gratitude replace impatience. The serenity that had been trickling in became a steady stream.

Tonight I arrived five minutes late to see a UU-sponsored film, and I found myself running through the fellowship hall to get to the show. *Running!*—without realizing it, until I'd slid into a chair.

I also spent time sitting today—meditating silently with Russ, outside, on chairs among the fallen golden elm and cottonwood leaves. We sat quiet for fifteen minutes; I'd set the timer. Afterwards we gazed at the side yard. "We could put that thrift-store mirror right there," I said, pointing at the neighbors' garage wall facing us. "It would reflect the vines on the house."

We talked about our upcoming Thanksgiving trip to my sister Chrissie's in Wisconsin. We're flying Tim and Holly and Rick with us, all staying in a hotel. It was my sister Carol's idea to bring the kids; she's bringing hers. "There'll be thirty-nine people for turkey this year," I told Russ.

"Didn't I hear we'll be eating in the workshop?"

"Yep. I told Chrissie she could leave the sawdust on the floor for ambience."

We sat outside for a while longer, savoring the autumn day.

A crisp cottonwood leaf skittered across the path and landed at our feet. "Does this mean it's time to *leaf*?" Russ said.

I chuckled. "Probably." I rose on my two good legs and preceded him down the flagstone path to the back door.

Made in the USA
San Bernardino, CA
14 May 2018